THOMAS COLE'S
REFRAIN

THOMAS COLE'S REFRAIN

THE PAINTINGS OF CATSKILL CREEK

H. DANIEL PECK

Published in association with the
THOMAS COLE NATIONAL HISTORIC SITE

and with the support of the
HUDSON RIVER MUSEUM

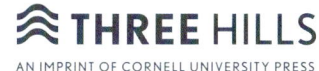

AN IMPRINT OF CORNELL UNIVERSITY PRESS

Thomas Cole's Refrain: The Paintings of Catskill Creek is published on the occasion of the exhibition at the Thomas Cole National Historic Site, Catskill, New York, May 4–November 3, 2019 and at the Hudson River Museum, Yonkers, New York, November 21, 2019–February 28, 2020.

Supported by the National Endowment for the Arts, Wyeth Foundation for American Art, Marshall Field V, New York State Council on the Arts with the support of Governor Andrew M. Cuomo and the New York State Legislature, Empire State Development's I LOVE NEW YORK program under the Market NY initiative, The Bay & Paul Foundations, The Enoch Foundation, The Educational Foundation of America, Joan K. Davidson (The J. M. Kaplan Fund), and the Kindred Spirits Society of the Thomas Cole National Historic Site.

Published in association with the Thomas Cole National Historic Site, 218 Spring Street, Catskill, New York 12414 and with the support of the Hudson River Museum, 511 Warburton Avenue, Yonkers, NY 10701.

First published 2019 by Cornell University Press
Printed in Canada

Library of Congress Cataloging-in-Publication Data
Names: Peck, H. Daniel, author.
Title: Thomas Cole's refrain : the paintings of Catskill Creek / H. Daniel Peck.
Description: Ithaca : Three Hills, an imprint of Cornell University Press, 2019. | Includes bibliographical references and index.
Identifiers: LCCN 2018033688 | ISBN 9781501733079 (pbk. ; alk. paper)
Subjects: LCSH: Cole, Thomas, 1801–1848—Criticism and interpretation. | Cole, Thomas, 1801–1848—Homes and haunts—New York (State)—Catskill Mountains Region. | Catskill Mountains Region (N.Y.)—In art. | Hudson River school of landscape painting.
Classification: LCC ND237.C6 P43 2019 | DDC 758/.1747—dc23
LC record available at https://lccn.loc.gov/2018033688

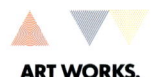 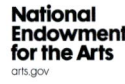 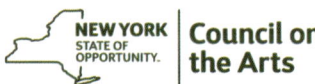 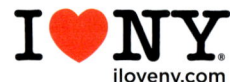

For Emilia and Hudson

CONTENTS

Foreword

Elizabeth B. Jacks
Executive Director, Thomas Cole
National Historic Site

Certain places are inviolable. We have all experienced the power of place at one time or another in our lives—a beloved landscape that feels too important to lose, a place that evokes peacefulness or awe, where, as Thomas Cole put it, "the mind is cast into the contemplation of eternal things."

For me, one such place is a large sun-warmed rock at the edge of a slow slip of water where I liked to sit as a child. It is a place that has steadfastly refused to change across nine different presidential administrations, and its constancy has an outsized importance in my mind. If I were to discover one calamitous day that "my" rock (I do not own it) and the rest of that timeless scene had been thrown aside by a bulldozer, I would be bereft. How much more deeply must the dramatic developments along Catskill Creek in the nineteenth century have affected Thomas Cole, for whom landscape was not only the central focus of his career but also a matter of religion. When Cole considers his most revered landscapes, "the consequent associations are of God the creator.

Among all of Cole's beloved locations for walking, sketching, and contemplating divine forces, Catskill Creek must rank at the very top. He painted its course and its surroundings more often than any other subject. Moreover, he kept returning to that place and subject again and again for nearly two decades, as to the refrain of a favorite song.

Given that interest and attachment, it is understandable that Cole would have seen the construction of a railroad line along the banks of this creek as an act of unfathomable barbarism. The "wantonness" (as Cole referred to it) of this act of destruction at Catskill Creek became for him a symbol of what was increasingly wrong with America and, furthermore, with human nature itself. Today it is obvious that his concern for the future of our landscapes was more than warranted—so much so that the arrival of a mere railroad line seems quaint to us now, when considered in the context of the massive transformation that has taken place in landscapes all across America since the 1830s. But there is a lot of good news too. Many of the views in Cole's paintings have been preserved by forward-thinking nonprofit organizations. Cole's "favourite haunt," a meandering stretch of Catskill Creek, has been purchased by the seminal environmental organization Scenic Hudson and is now managed by the Greene Land Trust. The nineteenth-century railroad line that once cut through the grove of trees along the creek's edge is now barely perceptible and has been swallowed up by the surrounding woods. You can visit this beautiful place today. I encourage you to do so. To quote Thomas Cole, "May we at times turn from the ordinary pursuits of life to the pure enjoyment of rural nature; which is in the soul like a fountain of cool waters to the way-worn traveler."

The insistent narrative that has been hidden in Cole's Catskill Creek paintings has now been revealed by the remarkable scholar H. Daniel Peck, with whom we have been most fortunate to collaborate on this project. I'd like to express my profound thanks to him for bringing his intensely researched manuscript to us. Working closely with Dan has been our brilliant curator, Kate Menconeri, whom we are so fortunate to have on our team. I also thank the independent scholar and author Annette Blaugrund for advising us on this project, the Hudson River Museum for their partnership, and the museums and private collectors who have so generously lent their most prized artworks for the exhibition.

FOREWORD

MASHA TURCHINSKY
Director, Hudson River Museum

How I have walked . . . day after day, and all alone, to see if there was
not something among the old things which was new!
—Thomas Cole

Long before Yonkers' strategic location along the Hudson River fostered its development into a major trading center and eventually one of the largest cities in New York,
Thomas Cole traveled up the Hudson River in the summer of 1825. On his journey to
the eastern Catskill Mountains, he passed the majestic Palisades and the shores of the
town of Yonkers, then a small patchwork of farms, grist mills, and open countryside
where the Hudson River Museum would one day stand.

Catskill Mountain tourism developed in the second decade of the nineteenth century, largely inspired by the works of writers such as Washington Irving, James Fenimore Cooper, and the painters led by Thomas Cole. Cole, after years of traveling to the
mountains in the summer, was not content to remain a tourist and settled permanently
near Catskill Creek, surrounded by the landscape he loved to paint. As this exhibition
and catalog beautifully illustrate, the location was one of the only subjects he painted
repeatedly. Cole depicted the creek as he wished it might look; his pastoral scenes were
aesthetic responses to a mythic past, one that stood in contrast to the Catskill Creek of
the 1830s, which had become the focus of intense industrialization.

From our riparian perch, we have a rich and long-standing record of presenting
and interpreting the works of the Hudson River School. The feeling that Thomas
Cole had about nature is similar to the sentiment that has driven our work in exhibiting, teaching about, and preserving scenic views along the southern portion of the

Hudson through scholarship, programming, and partnerships. As early as 1954, the Hudson River Museum featured Hudson River School paintings at a time when the works by this alliance of landscape artists were just achieving new appreciation. In 1982, the museum achieved national recognition for a series of scholarly drawing exhibitions including *To Walk with Nature: The Drawings of Thomas Cole*, followed by a major interdisciplinary exhibition, *The Catskills: Painters, Writers, and Tourists in the Mountains,* in 1988. In the spirit of Cole, and during the Hudson River Museum's centennial year, we delight in making a return visit to offer fresh perspectives on his work and the storied Hudson Valley.

It is most fitting that we have the opportunity to partner with the Thomas Cole National Historic Site to bring this show to light. We respect and share our esteemed colleagues' profound commitment to exploring Cole's work and to preserving the beauty of the Hudson Valley and its environs. Just as Thomas Cole identified with Catskill Creek and the mountain scenery around his home, so too do we feel re-energized in our landscape. Thomas Cole's revolutionary creativity and his perceptions of the wildness inherent in American scenery not only continue to reward our close looking but inspire our tireless advocacy. We invite you to walk alongside us and to discover something new each time.

Thomas Cole's
Refrain

Catskill Creek and a Sense of Place

On August 1, 1836, Thomas Cole recorded in his journal an entry about Catskill Creek, a tributary of the Hudson entering the larger river from the west at Catskill, New York. "Last evening," he wrote, "I took a walk up the Catskill above Austin's Mill where the Rail Road is now making. This was once a favorite walk but the charm of quietness & solitude is gone." The closing word, "gone," expresses an intensely felt sense of loss on Cole's part. About two decades later Henry David Thoreau would use this same word, in a remarkably similar context, in *Walden* (1854): "Now the trunks of trees on the bottom, and the old log canoe, and the dark surrounding woods, are gone." "That devilish Iron Horse, whose ear-rending neigh is heard throughout the town," he continued, "has browsed off all the woods on Walden shore."[1]

Cole and Thoreau were both addressing one of the deepest issues of nineteenth-century America, the intrusion of industrialism into agrarian and pastoral landscapes, and both were expressing their sorrow about the resulting destruction. In the rest of Cole's journal entry he allowed himself some compensation but at the same time showed how angry he was. His cherished walk along Catskill Creek, he said, was "still lovely; man cannot remove the mountains & he has not yet felled *all* the woods & the stream will have its course." "If men were not insensible to the beauty of nature," he wrote, "the great works necessary for the purposes of commerce might be carried on

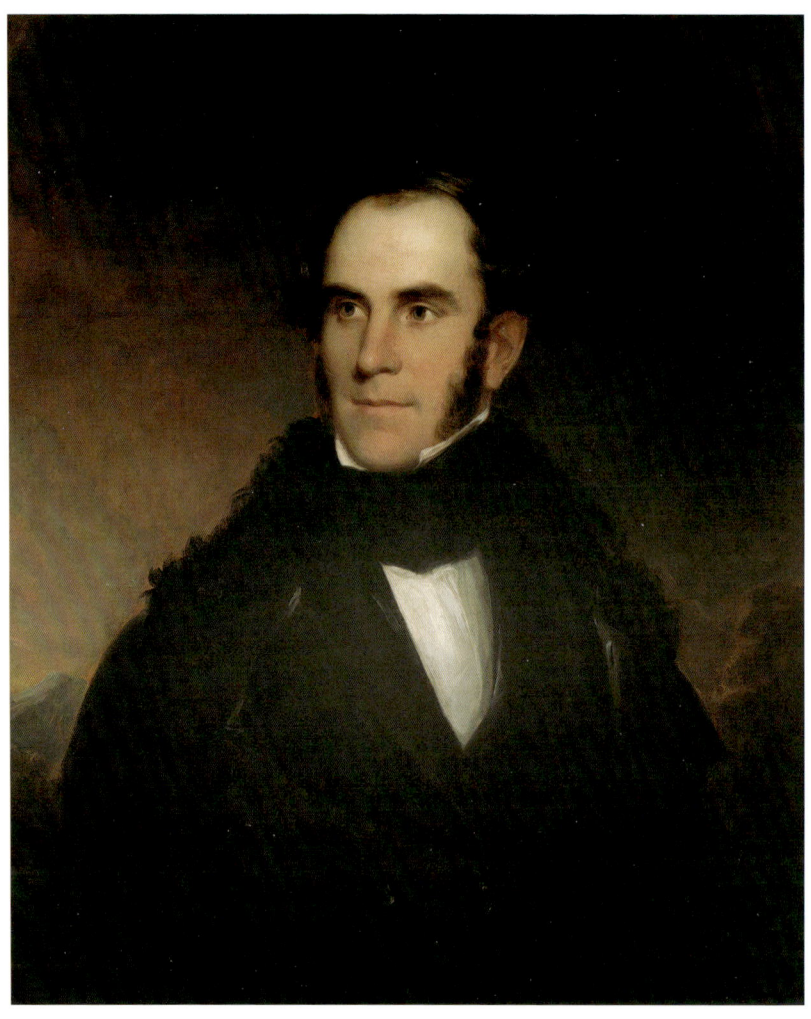

P.1 Asher B. Durand, *Portrait of Thomas Cole*, 1838.
Oil on canvas, 29½ x 24½ in. (74.93 x 62.23 cm).
Courtesy of the Berkshire Museum, Pittsfield, MA,
gift of Zenas Crane (1917.13).

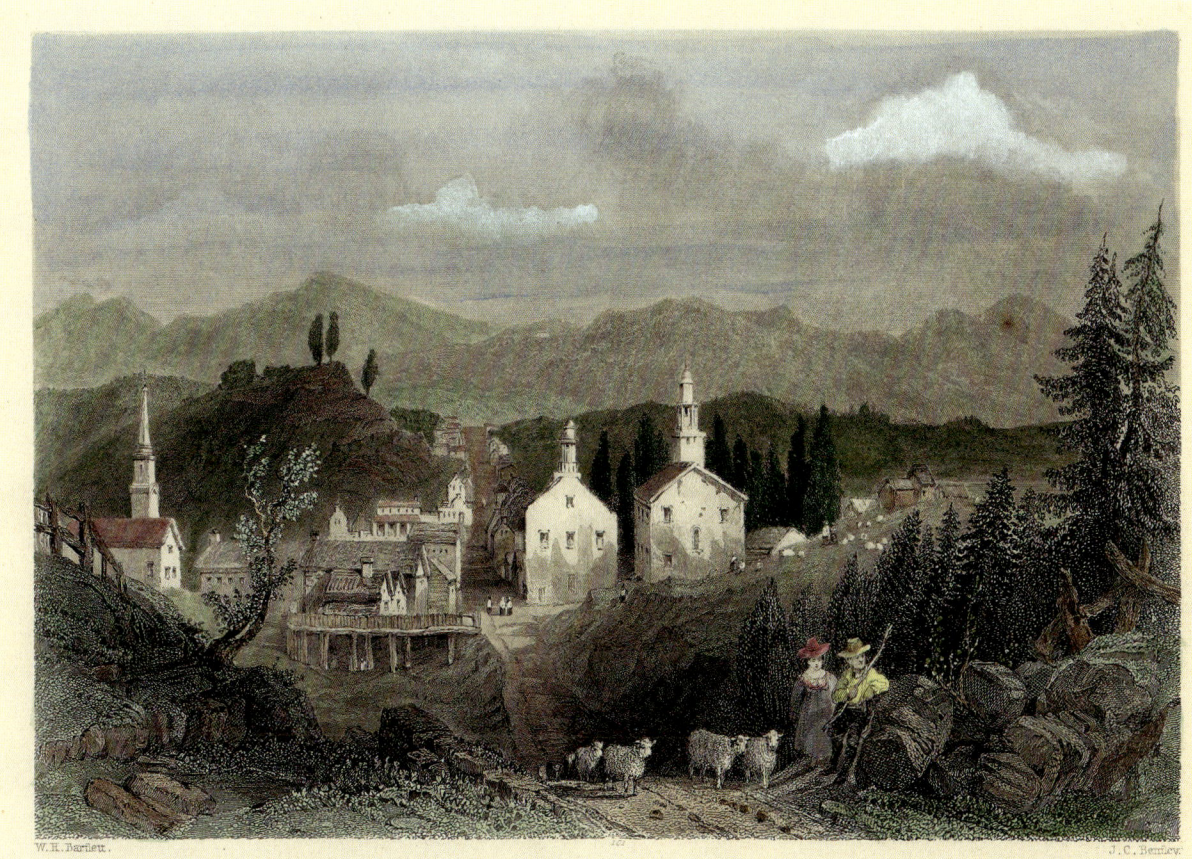

VILLAGE OF CATSKILL.

P.2 William H. Bartlett, *Colorized View of Catskill.*
Plate 40 in Nathaniel P. Willis, *American Scenery; or
Land, Lake, and River: Illustrations of Transatlantic
Nature* (London: J. S. Virtue, 1840). Collection of the
Vedder Research Library.

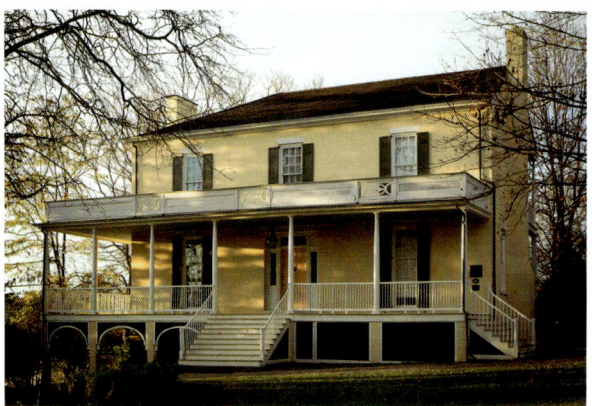

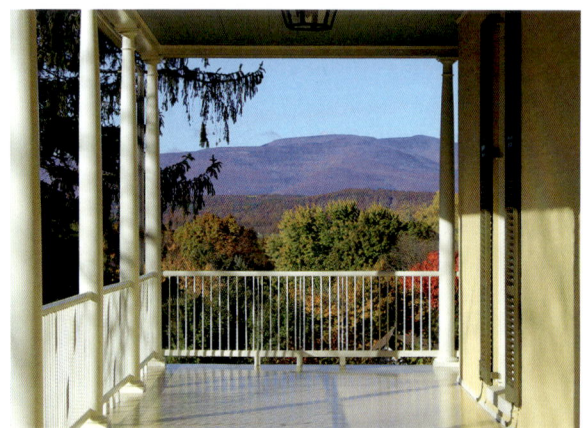

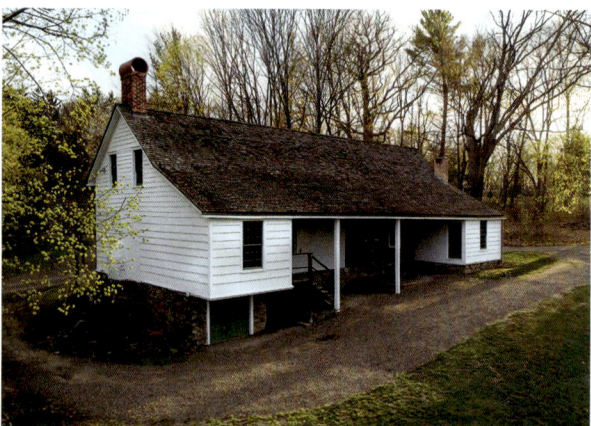

P.3 The main house at Cedar Grove, Thomas Cole National Historic Site

P.4 View from the Cedar Grove main house porch, Thomas Cole National Historic Site

P.5 Cedar Grove studio used by the artist from 1839 to 1846, Thomas Cole National Historic Site. Photo by Devin Pickering.

without destroying it, . . . but it is not so. They desecrate whatever they touch. They cut down the forests with a wantonness for which there is no excuse, even gain, & leave the herbless rocks to glimmer in the burning sun."

Earlier in 1836 Cole had made some of these same points in a public setting, where he expressed them more moderately. His "Essay on American Scenery" had been published in January, and it was based on a lecture he had given at the New York Lyceum the previous year. Cole's overt purpose in this essay was to celebrate the beauty and wildness of American nature. Yet near the end he issued a sharp warning: "The ravages of the axe are daily increasing—the most noble scenes are made destitute, and oftentimes with a wantonness and barbarism scarcely credible in a civilized nation." The larger purpose of Cole's essay and its rhetorical structure, however, required that he quickly silence his anger, and, turning philosophical, he did: "This is a regret rather than a complaint; such is the road society has to travel."[2]

By the time Cole wrote his sad and angry journal entry in the summer of 1836 he had been visiting Catskill Village, about two-thirds of the way between New York and Albany, for more than a decade, and he knew it well. He had discovered Catskill and its surrounding landscape in the summer of 1825, during his first sketching expedition into the Hudson Valley. Subsequently, Cole spent several summers in Catskill, and he established a studio there in 1834. In 1836 he married a local woman, Maria Bartow, and they took up residence together in her family's elegant Federal home on a property called Cedar Grove, at the eastern edge of the village and near the Hudson River.

Cedar Grove then as now (it has been beautifully restored over the last few decades) looked westward out toward the dramatic mountain profiles of the Catskill high peaks, which lie only about eleven miles away. In the mid-1820s Cole had painted scenes in these mountains, including several works depicting Kaaterskill Falls, to great acclaim.

The Catskill Creek Paintings

In the same period that the artist was sketching scenes in the rugged mountains he began to draw a distant view of the Catskills from points along Catskill Creek, near a broad meander just to the west of the village. His evening walk of late July 1836 would have taken him along the northern shore of this meander.

By the time Cole moved to Catskill late in 1836 he had completed four paintings of this view, and during the dozen years remaining in his relatively short life he would

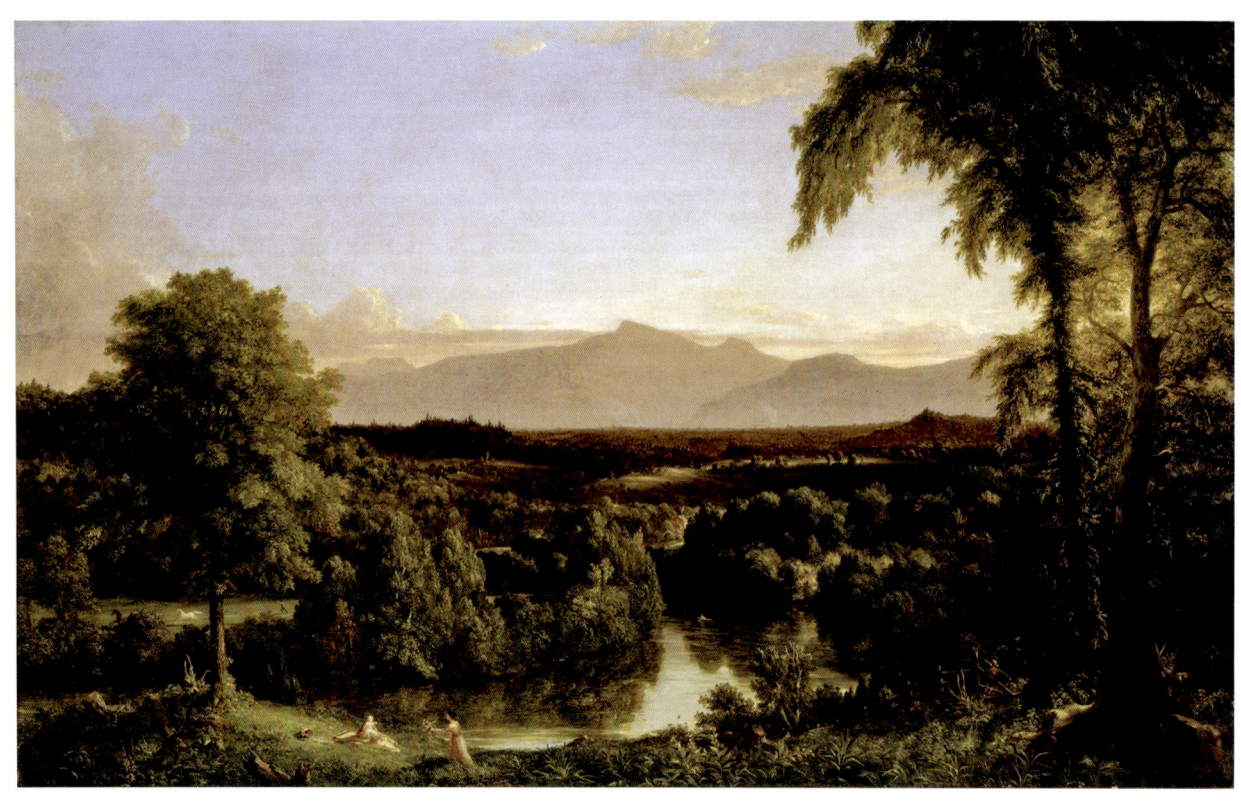

P.6 Thomas Cole, *View on the Catskill—Early Autumn*, 1836–37. Oil on canvas, 39 x 63 in. (99.1 cm x 160 cm). Metropolitan Museum of Art, gift in memory of Jonathan Sturges by his children, 1895 (95.13.3).

complete at least six more. In other words, over the course of eighteen years he would create ten such paintings. Here was a scene Cole kept returning to, and it clearly had great power over him. The Catskill Creek paintings, as I am calling them, reveal an intimate sense of place in Cole's work that viewers generally do not associate with him.

After all, some of the artist's most ambitious and well-known paintings are, in a certain way, placeless. Eighteen thirty-six was also the year that Cole completed his epic series *The Course of Empire* (1833–36) (figs. 1.2–1.6), where in five large canvases he created a deliberately universalized landscape. Here a Roman-like city's creation and destruction represent the largest cycles of history and—except by inference—belong to no particular time and place. In one of Cole's later series, *The Voyage of Life* (1839–40) (figs. 2.1–2.4), a solitary figure in a boat is transported along an imaginary river through an entirely symbolic landscape. These are the kinds of paintings on which Cole staked his reputation, and the ideas that stand behind them inform many of his other works as well.

"Essay on American Scenery"

Where might we look to understand the relationship between these two sides of Cole's work, one speaking to universal concerns and the other grounded in a highly specific local environment? His "Essay on American Scenery," because of its broad and programmatic agenda, would seem an unlikely place. In this essay his goal—shared by others in his circle of New York artists and writers—was to anchor American cultural identity in what he regarded as the country's unique relationship to nature. He does so by distinguishing particular landscape features in the United States from comparable ones in Europe, taking up in order mountains, lakes, waterfalls, rivers, forests, and the sky.

Despite the essay's methodical examination of these elements of scenery, however, it indirectly expresses a powerful sense of place. One thing that becomes clear as Cole reviews American scenery is the degree to which he represents a national landscape with features and forms that for him were regional and even local. Sometimes the artist refers to faraway places he had never seen, such as "the central wilds of this vast continent," but for the most part he draws his imagery from landscapes he knew firsthand. For example, the first mountains Cole describes are the "heavy in form" Alleghenies. In his youth, not long after he and his family had emigrated to the United States from England in 1818, he twice traversed this difficult range. The White Mountains of New

Hampshire (which, he says, present a "union of the picturesque, the sublime, and the magnificent") were also home ground for him; he began traveling to and painting them in the 1820s.[3]

But the mountains to which Cole gives the most attention are those, the Catskills, that by 1836 had become a landscape of home for him. They do not have the great altitude of the "snow-crowned Alps," he says, and they are "not broken into abrupt angles like the most picturesque mountains of Italy." But they do "have varied, undulating, and exceedingly beautiful outlines—they heave from the valley of the Hudson like the subsiding billows of the ocean after a storm."[4] Looking at any of Cole's Catskill Creek paintings will bring this description vividly to mind.

By the time Cole published "Essay on American Scenery" in 1836 he had mastered the Catskills' "beautiful outlines" and inscribed them into several of these paintings. Consequently, the essay is both a theoretical work distinguishing American from European landforms and a record of his own experience. The essay reflects the process through which Cole—in creating his early paintings of the Hudson River Valley—learned about American scenery, about his own distinctive vision of it, and indeed about his deepening attachment to the region.

In his developing inventory, Cole moves from mountains to lakes, which he finds one of the most distinctive of American landscape features. "In this great element of scenery," he asks, "what land is so rich?" Quickly setting aside the Great Lakes as "inland seas," he turns to "smaller lakes, such as Lake George, Champlain, Winnipisiogee, Otsego, Seneca, and a hundred others, that stud like gems the bosom of this country."[5] The final phrase characteristically establishes a national context for considering these lakes, yet four of the five he names are in eastern and central New York State and the other one is a New England lake that Cole had visited and painted early in his career.

One of the lakes on his list is Otsego, which would later be transformed by James Fenimore Cooper, a member of Cole's New York circle of writers and artists, into the magical "Lake Glimmerglass" in his novel *The Deerslayer* (1841). The artist, in fact, may have learned about Lake Otsego from one of Cooper's earliest novels, *The Pioneers* (1823), which has the same setting, Otsego, as does *The Deerslayer.* In *The Pioneers* Cooper expressed his own fears about the "ravages of the axe" and in terms that clearly anticipate Cole's "Essay on American Scenery." Such was the rich exchange between artists and writers in the early Republic.

Cole's special attraction to American lakes is reflected in his earliest paintings of the Catskill Creek landscape. In these works, which date to the 1820s, the part of the

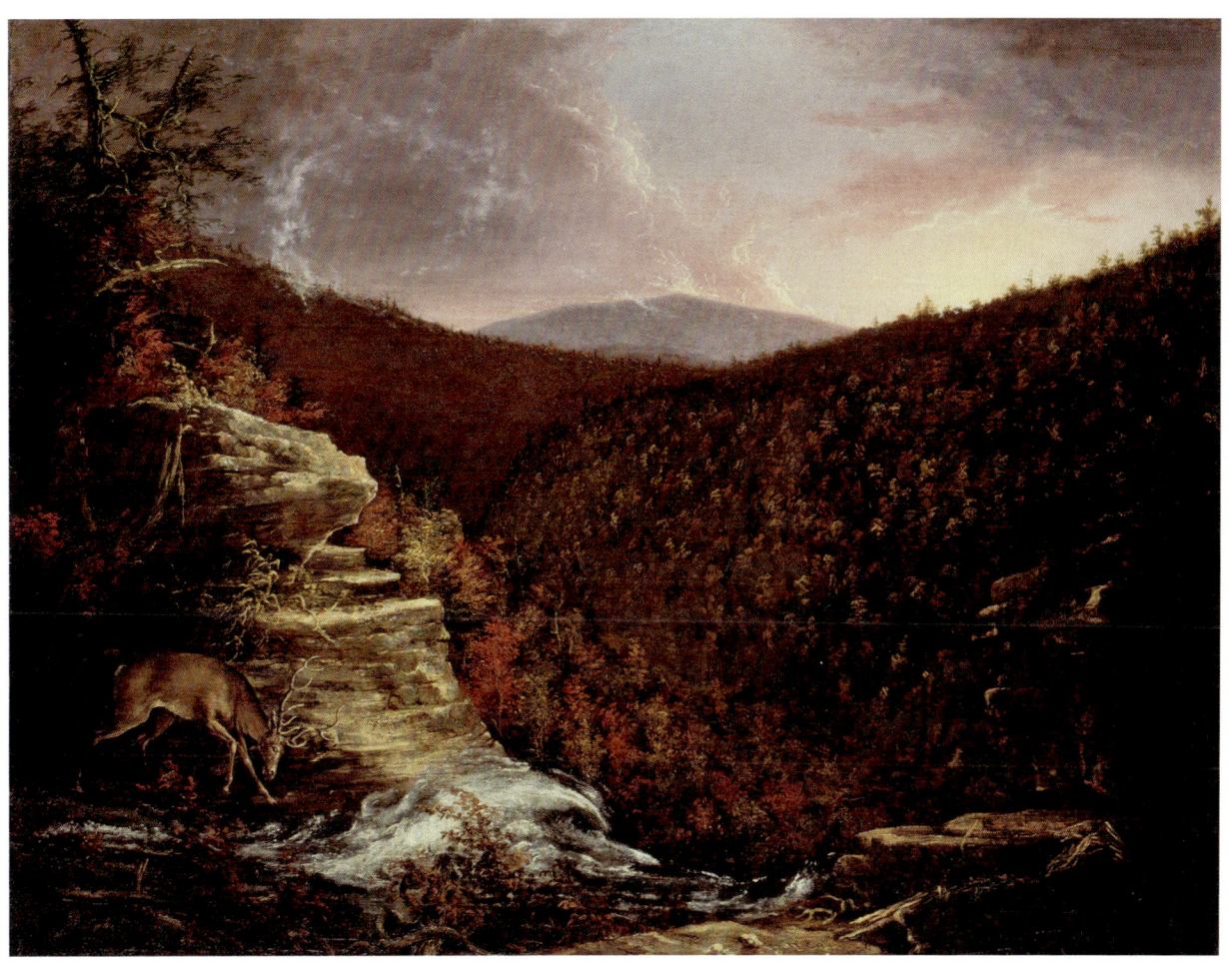

P.7 Thomas Cole, *From the Top of Kaaterskill Falls,*
1826. Oil on canvas, 31⅛ x 41⅛ in. (79.1 x 104.5 cm).
Detroit Institute of the Arts. Founders Society
Purchase, Dexter M. Ferry, Jr. Fund (46.134).

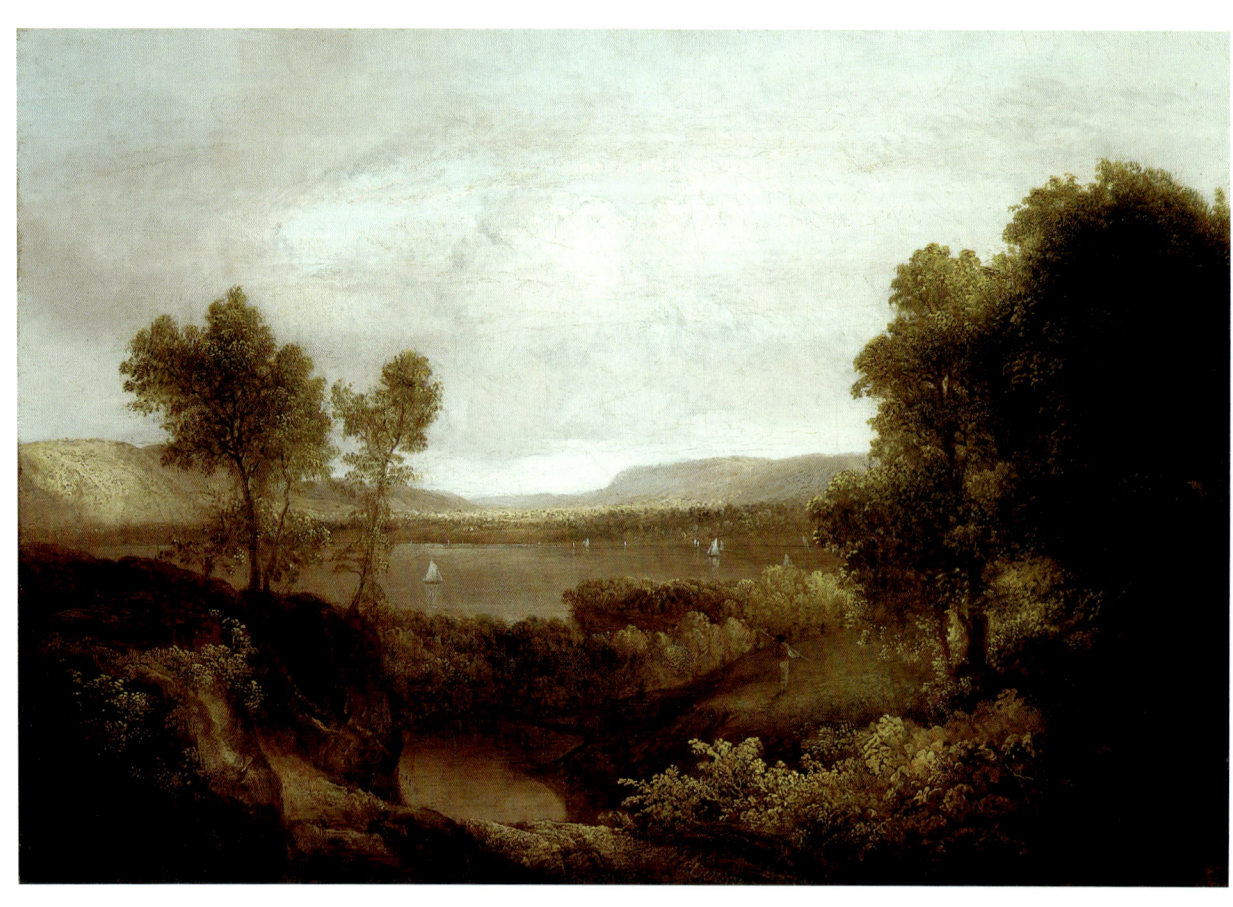

P.8 Thomas Doughty, *On the Hudson*, 1830–35.
Oil on canvas, 14¾ x 21½ in. (37.5 x 54.6 cm).
Metropolitan Museum of Art, gift of Samuel P.
Avery, 1891 (91.27.1).

river he focused on was not its course flowing out of the mountains but a bay-like oval portion in the middle distance (figs. 3.3 and 3.10). In other words, he painted Catskill Creek as if it were a lake rather than as the middle-sized river that it actually is. Only later, following Cole's first European tour (1829–32), would he shape this body of water like a river; even then the aesthetic values he associated with lakes—tranquility and reflectivity—remained an essential part of his vision in almost all the Catskill Creek paintings. Their "reflections of surrounding objects, trees, mountains [and] sky," to quote from Cole's "Essay on American Scenery," are key to the complex beauty of their landscapes.[6]

When Cole moves on to waterfalls, this is what he has to say. The United States is a country "abounding" in them, and the most sublime is of course Niagara, "that wonder of the world." But the artist's more intimate connection was with Kaaterskill Falls in the mountains above the Village of Catskill, a much smaller though spectacular waterfall. It is formed, he says, by a "diminutive" stream "throwing itself headlong over a fearful precipice into a deep gorge of the densely wooded [Catskill] mountains."[7]

In Cole's first excursion into the Hudson River Valley, he sketched Kaaterskill Falls from below, from above, and from under a central projecting rock—taking account of it from these various perspectives. Here too he was learning a landscape through his direct experience of apprehending it and making it into art. He soon thereafter translated these sketches into several remarkable paintings. Even as Kaaterskill Falls was for Cole a symbol of what he called American "wildness," it was at the same time part of a regional and even local landscape. Waterfalls even closer to home—that is, literally close to Cedar Grove—were the Catskill Creek rapids. They appear in more than one of the Catskill Creek paintings, and while we get only glimpses of them, they have an important presence in these works.

Regarding America's major rivers, Cole focuses exclusively on the Hudson. He compares it to the Rhine, and while acknowledging that its shores "are not besprinkled with [the Rhine's] venerated ruins," he celebrates the "natural magnificence" of this "deep-flowing river." And in making a response to European perceptions that American scenery lacked "associations," he takes note of a "legend" of the lower reaches of the Hudson (the reference is to Washington Irving's Sleepy Hollow), a legend "which has been so sweetly and admirably told that it shall not perish but with the language of the land."[8]

While Cole understood the Hudson River as the defining, literally shaping, feature of the region he lived in, he seldom painted it. After he moved permanently to Catskill in 1836, he lived almost within sight of this river of "natural majesty," as he describes it in "Essay in American Scenery." But the nearby waterway that most deeply engaged him was the Hudson's tributary, Catskill Creek—so modest and merely local a stream that it finds no place in Cole's review of national scenery. But we may catch a glimpse of it in this description, late in his essay, of an unnamed river: "A silver stream winds lingeringly along—here, seeking the green shade of trees—there, glancing in the sunshine."[9]

Cole says that American forest scenery "differs widely from the European" and not only in its far greater extent. "For variety," he writes, "the American forest is unrivalled; in some districts are found oaks, elms, birches, beeches, planes, pines, hemlocks, and many other kinds of trees, commingled—clothing the hills with every tint of green, and every variety of light and shade." Cole captured this variety in a number of his early works that depict forests in the Catskills—*The Clove, Catskills* (1827) is a good example—and in the White Mountains of New England. Landscapes like this represented what in his essay he calls "wild and uncultivated scenery."[10]

But, the artist was careful to add, "the cultivated must not be forgotten."[11] Here Cole was referring to the American rural or domesticated landscape—the Catskill Creek paintings are his most sustained portrayal of it—and trees were no less important to his representations of this landscape than to his "wild and uncultivated" scenes. In fact, the Catskill Creek paintings, with their pastoral and agricultural settings, opened the opportunity for Cole to highlight particular species of trees, such as a beautifully rounded maple or oak standing alone in a meadow or an elegant willow bordering a river. These paintings show how much Cole knew about trees in their particular aspects and environments, and his particularity of description in the Catskill Creek paintings is a measure of his developing sense of place.

Finally Cole comes to the sky. He calls it the "soul of all scenery" and says that "in it are the fountains of light, and shade, and color." "Whatever expression the sky takes," he continues, "the features of the landscape are affected in unison." When Cole wrote these words, his first European tour (1829–32) was not far behind him, and his memories of Italian sunsets were vivid. He takes note of them here, asking, "Who will deny their wonderful beauty? At sunset the serene arch is filled with alchemy that transmutes mountains, and streams, and temples, into living gold."[12] The Catskill Creek paintings are unified, in part, by the sunsets that many of them portray, and Cole's response to the sunsets he saw in Italy undoubtedly informs some of them.

But Cole's celebration of American skies, when he compares them with Europe's, is unrestrained. He departs from his generalities ("the blue unsearchable depths of the northern sky") and brings his focus to a single region, the one he knew best: "If he who has travelled and observed the skies of other climes will spend a few months on the banks of the Hudson, he must be constrained to acknowledge that for variety and magnificence American skies are unsurpassed."[13] As we consider this passage in Cole's final category of scenery, we see again how often he has called upon a regional landscape to characterize American scenery at large.

One obvious reason is that this was a landscape that Cole knew and that he could confidently describe in detail, rather than depending on the descriptions of others. And it's also true, of course, that in 1836 the landscape of what we would now call the Far West would have been known to most people only through explorers' accounts and maps. The American national landscape—a cultural construction as opposed to the territorial holdings of the United States—included only a small area of the country.

Even so, a close reading of "Essay on American Scenery" shows how much Cole has depended on regional and local landscapes in his portrayal of "American scenery." Another way to say this is that the particular imagery of the essay and the rhetorical purposes that Cole had for it are somewhat at variance. Because "Essay on American Scenery" is designed to describe a national landscape, the imperative to generalize from the particular is everywhere present. For this reason, Cole is careful to avoid stating openly any regional or local attachment of his own—that is, a personal and deeply felt sense of place—and one reason may be the large ambitions he had for his art. He wanted to play out his career on a national and, indeed, international stage. "Essay on American Scenery" is in part an expression of that ambition, for himself and for his adopted country. That his "Essay" first took form as a public lecture he gave to an important American cultural institution suggests this ambition.

Recognizing the centrality of regional and local landscape elements in Cole's "Essay on American Scenery" should focus our attention on the *process* through which he turned to his own visual experience in marshaling his case for a national landscape. What stood behind his descriptions of scenes in the Hudson River Valley, the Catskills, and New England was a series of profound perceptual encounters in these very landscapes. To some extent the essay's rhetoric hides the experience that produced its images; but in the aggregate these images tell us something important about his actual experience of American scenery. One of those encounters was with the Village of Catskill and its surroundings. As we will see, the very first Catskill Creek painting, *View Near the Village of Catskill* (1827) (fig. 3.3), is charged with a sense of fresh discovery. In Cole's continuing representations of the Catskill Creek scene, over many years, appear different aspects of his developing attachment to it.

Ultimately, however, these representations come to express a sense of loss, and we have examined in Cole's journal entry of August 1, 1836, an important instance of that loss. His fears about the destruction of American scenery through the "ravages of the axe" had their origins in a very real threat to his own local landscape, a railroad-building project that destroyed many trees and sullied the river. The Catskill Creek paintings are the best source for understanding the emotional toll for Cole in witnessing this destruction. These paintings remind us of how, in many works of art and literature, a deep sense of place carries with it feelings of loss, or the possibility of loss. "Essay on American Scenery" was, on the one hand, a way for Cole to distinguish and celebrate American landscapes. But, to quote from the closing of his essay, it was also a way for him to express his "sorrow that the beauty of such landscapes is quickly passing away."[14]

CHAPTER ONE

THE DISCOVERY OF THOMAS COLE

"His fame spread like fire." So Thomas Cole's discovery by the New York art world was described by his friend and fellow artist Asher B. Durand.[1] The dramatic story of this discovery, told many times, has become central to the larger story of American art in the nineteenth century. In April of 1825 the unknown twenty-four-year-old Cole moved from Philadelphia to New York, joining his parents and sisters, who had arrived there a few months earlier. In the summer he departed on a sketching expedition into the Hudson River Valley sponsored by a New York merchant, George W. Bruen.

We know at least a part of Cole's itinerary because he kept a list of scenes he sketched, and while the entries on the list are undated, they are organized chronologically. The sequential nature of the list tells us the order in which the artist visited the various places where he sketched, and map 1.1 shows their locations. On his three-page list, Cole made twenty-two entries describing briefly the scenes he was drawing, and on the actual sketches he wrote titles that corresponded to his descriptions.[2]

Cole's list shows us that his trip took him from New York northward into the Hudson Highlands, where he sketched at West Point, Buttermilk Falls (now called Highland Falls), and Cold Spring. Then he continued his journey upriver beyond Albany,

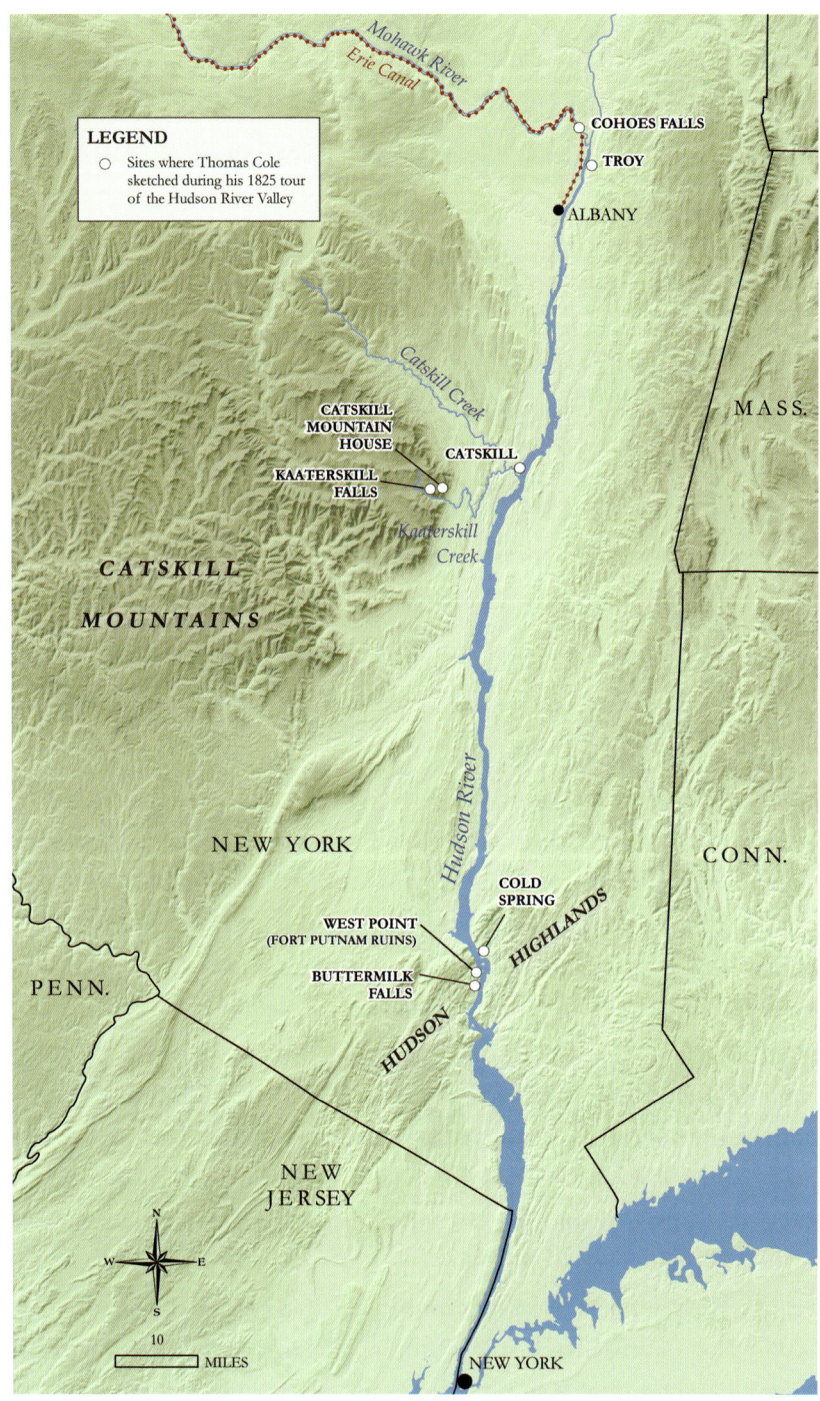

Map 1.1 The Hudson River Valley, with sites where Thomas Cole is known to have made drawings during his first tour of the region in the summer of 1825. Map by Neil Curri.

where he sketched a view of the Hudson River near Troy, and still farther northward he made several drawings of scenes at Cohoes Falls on the Mohawk River, a mile or so west of its confluence with the Hudson.

On his return to New York City Cole stopped at Catskill Village. He spent several days sketching scenes in the area, and it was this part of his expedition that came to mean the most to him. The paintings inspired by his visit to Catskill are the ones that led most directly to his discovery by the New York art world, and Catskill was a discovery for Cole himself. It would become over time the center of his imaginative life, and indeed the place that he would eventually make his home. What began as a summer's exploration of a region, the Hudson River Valley, became a lifelong exploration of a particular place, charted by the Catskill Creek paintings that are the subject of this book.

When Cole returned to New York, he painted a number of pictures from sketches he'd made on his expedition and showed several of these in William A. Colman's picture gallery and bookstore. There John Trumbull, president of the American Academy of the Fine Arts and a revered figure, happened upon them. He bought one of the works and described them to writer and artist William Dunlap, who bought another. Durand, a noted engraver at the time, purchased the third, and soon the three paintings were exhibited together at the American Academy. Dunlap later that year told the story in the *New-York Evening Post*, quoting Trumbull's response to Cole's paintings in this way: "This youth has done at once, and without instruction, what I cannot do after 50 years' practice."[3]

Opening of the Erie Canal

Cole's sudden appearance on the stage of the New York art world coincided almost exactly with another dramatic event: the opening in October of 1825 of the Erie Canal— an engineering achievement of enormous consequence. The canal ran from Albany to Lake Erie and thereby connected New York City, via the Hudson River, with the Great Lakes and western markets. It opened areas of the Midwest to further settlement and brought the cost of shipping down tenfold. In short, the Erie Canal made New York, which was already competing with Philadelphia as the United States' chief commercial center, the major port of the United States and the engine of a new market economy. At the same moment that Cole's career took off in New York the city itself entered a new stage of development, one friendly to a successful young artist—in part

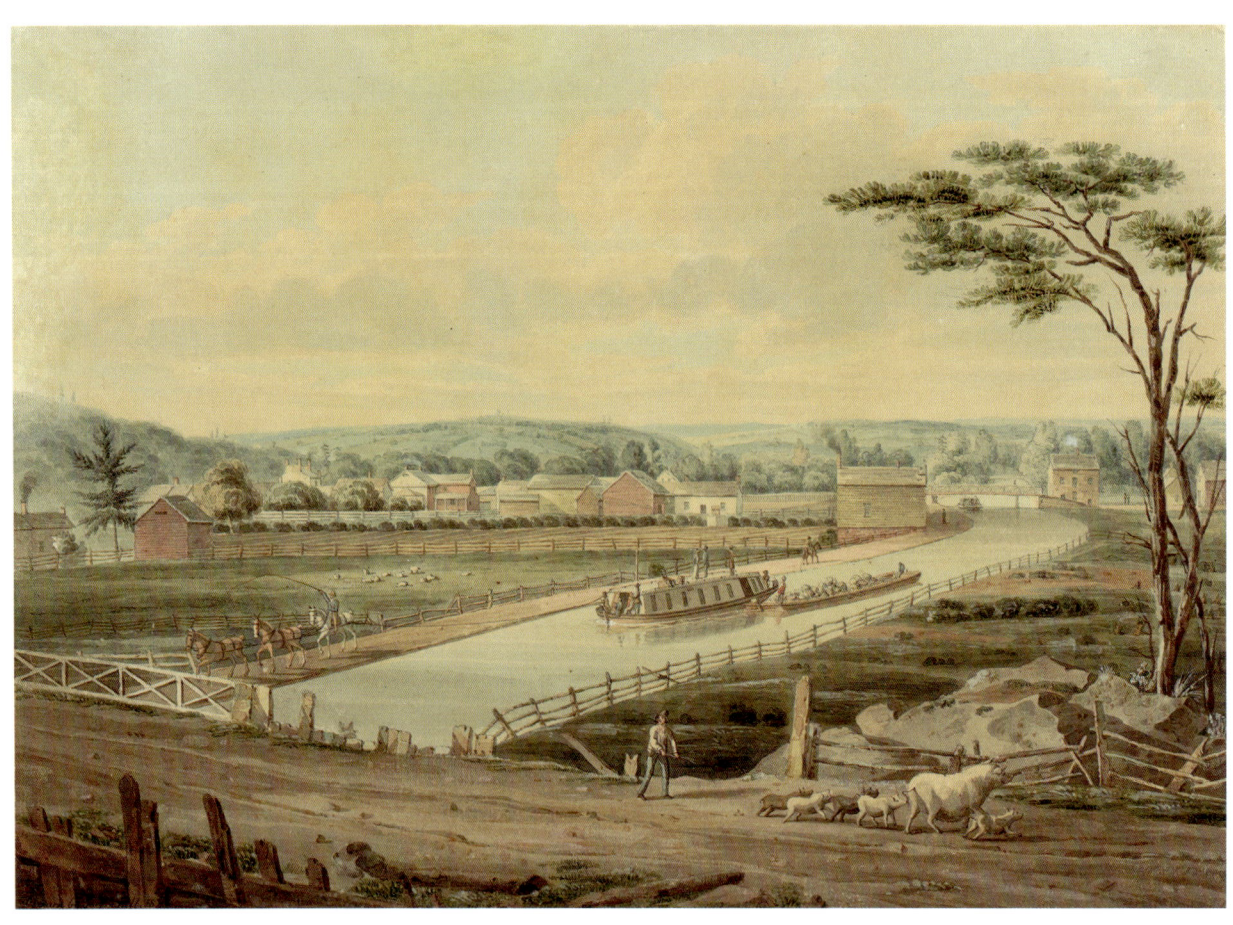

1.1 John William Hill, *View on the Erie Canal*, 1829.
Watercolor, 9¾ x 13¾ in. (24.8 x 35 cm). The New
York Public Library, Astor, Lenox, and Tilden
Foundations, Miriam and Ira D. Wallach Division
of Art, Prints and Photographs, The Phelps Stokes
Collection, Print Collection 1830-32E-29.

because of the emergence of a new merchant class, some of whose members would later become his patrons.[4]

The new market economy spurred by the Erie Canal immediately increased trade between the United States and other countries and encouraged an economic nationalism that had its counterpart in a developing cultural nationalism. Even though Americans had achieved political independence in the Revolution, it wasn't until at least the War of 1812 that they began to widely identify themselves with the nation more than with the particular region they lived in. As many historians have written, the decade of the 1820s was the one in which cultural nationalism fully took hold, especially in the Northeast.

American writers and painters played an important role in this development, as they vied for artistic parity with their European counterparts. Cooper, early in his career, became known as the American Walter Scott, and his Leatherstocking tales were compared to the English writer's Waverly novels. The poet William Cullen Bryant, in turn, was called "the American Wordsworth." Cole's discovery in 1825 went hand in hand with these developments, and his rapidly spreading fame in this period was not unrelated to cultural readiness on the part of Americans to claim their own artistic and literary achievements, as against those of Europe's older cultures.

While Cole's early landscape paintings of the Catskills and New England were appreciated by American viewers for their depictions of regional scenes (for him too, as we have seen, they had regional significance), they were also understood as celebrations of American scenery. For all the diversity of these scenes, they were understood as part of a unitary national landscape, and certainly the overt agenda of Cole's "Essay on American Scenery" was to conceive them this way. Just as the Erie Canal had joined regions of the United States commercially and furthered economic nationalism, Cole's landscape art—along with the work of contemporary writers—was inescapably linked to cultural nationalism.

The discovery of Cole and the completion of the Erie Canal are usually described in this way, as mutually auspicious and complementary events, both of them announcing a moment of national significance. And there is no doubt about the positive effects of this coincidence on his career. However, the pairing of Cole's emergence as an important artist with the inauguration of an industrial waterway might have made him uneasy. He grew up in Lancashire, England, during the height of the Industrial Revolution, and spent the first seventeen years of his life there before emigrating to the United States with his family in 1818.

To understand Cole's complex relationship to American culture, it is necessary to briefly take account of his youth in England. Most important, he would have known

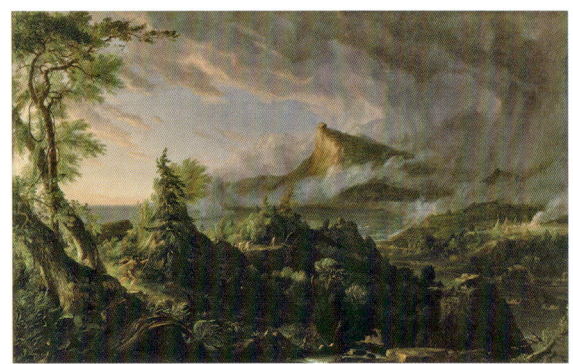

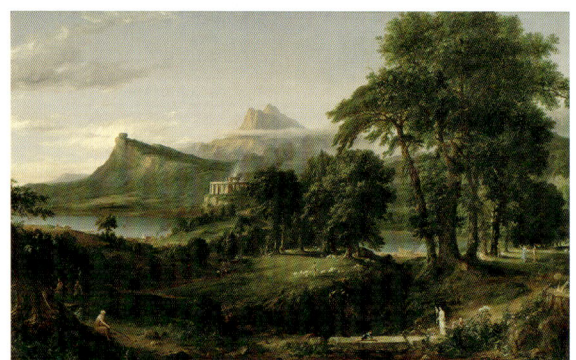

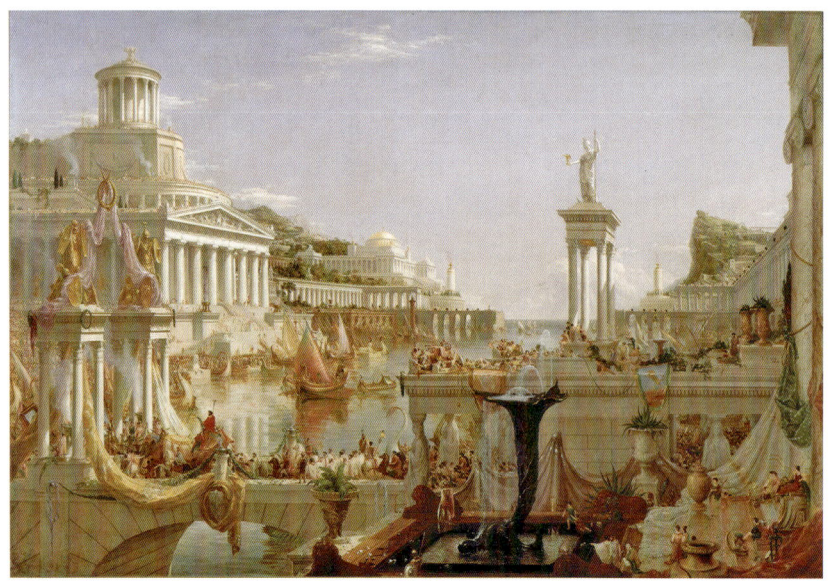

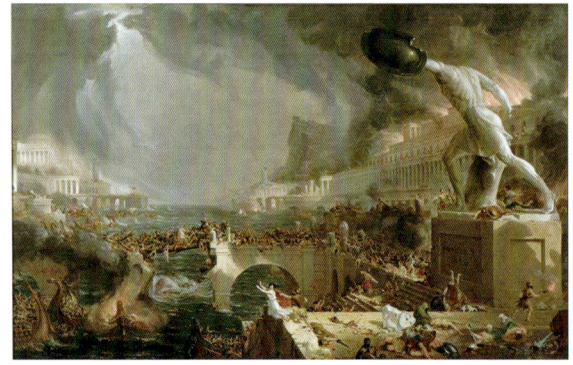

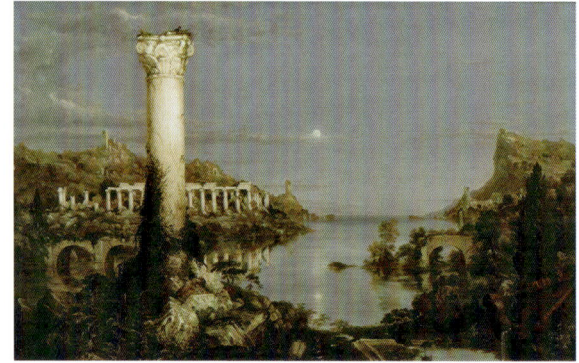

firsthand a landscape severely damaged by industry. The Lancashire town Bolton-le-Moors, where he was born in 1801 and spent most of his childhood, was a center of the textile industry.[5] In Bolton-le-Moors, the socially destabilizing and destructive environmental effects of early nineteenth-century industrialism would have been everywhere evident. Steam-powered textile mills were a dominant feature of the city's skyline, and they caused intense air pollution. A part of this noxious industrial landscape, as Tim Barringer explains, was the Manchester, Bolton, and Bury Canal, which, he writes, "created a vast geometric gash across the rural landscape." This large-scale canal system, whose construction began in 1791, "provided a route for raw materials, such as coal and iron-ore, from their origins to the factories, and carried finished goods, especially textiles, from Lancashire to markets across the country and, via the Liverpool docks, to markets in the British Empire and across the world."[6]

Although cargo on the Erie Canal, which included farm produce, was somewhat different from that of the Manchester, Bolton, and Bury in England, America's cross-regional canal was no less ambitious and far-reaching a project. Its completion signified that the United States was entering a new phase of commercial development that, in turn, would lead to modern industrialization. Cole's childhood and adolescence in industrial northern England would have been a window—indeed, a dark window—into America's potential future.

There are signs throughout Cole's career that he was deeply concerned about that future. His allegorical series *The Course of Empire* (figs. 1.2–1.6) was understood by

1.2 Thomas Cole, *The Course of Empire*: *The Savage State*, 1834. Oil on canvas, 39¼ x 63¼ in. (99.7 x 160.6 cm). New-York Historical Society, gift of the New York Gallery of the Fine Arts. Digital image created by Oppenheimer Editions (1858.1).

1.3 Thomas Cole, *The Course of Empire: The Arcadian or Pastoral State,*1834. Oil on canvas, 39¼ x 63¼ in. (99.7 x 160.7 cm). New-York Historical Society, gift of the New York Gallery of the Fine Arts. Digital image created by Oppenheimer Editions (1858.2).

1.4 Thomas Cole, *The Course of Empire: The Consummation of Empire,* 1835–36. Oil on canvas, 51¼ x 76 in. (130.2 x 193 cm). New-York Historical Society, gift of the New York Gallery of the Fine Arts. Digital image created by Oppenheimer Editions (1858.3).

1.5 Thomas Cole, *The Course of Empire: Destruction,* 1836. Oil on canvas, 33¼ x 63¼ in. (84.5 x 160.6 cm). New-York Historical Society, gift of the New York Gallery of the Fine Arts. Digital image created by Oppenheimer Editions (1858.4).

1.6 Thomas Cole, *The Course of Empire: Desolation,* 1836. Oil on canvas, 39¼ x 63 in. (99.7 x 160 cm). New-York Historical Society, gift of the New York Gallery of the Fine Arts. Digital image created by Oppenheimer Editions (1858.5).

viewers in his time as a lesson in American exceptionalism—the idea that the United States was exempt from the cyclical turns that brought down civilizations like Rome. For scholars in our time who have studied Cole's writings, this series has been understood instead as his warning to Americans that they might repeat the tragic histories of Europe.[7]

Cole's list of sketches of scenes in the Hudson River Valley makes no mention of the Erie Canal—nor do any of the surviving actual sketches show it—even though he was never very far away from the canal during the last part of his northward journey up the Hudson. When Cole made this journey, it was already in service; the segment beginning in Albany had been opened in 1823, to great fanfare, two years prior to his first excursion into the Hudson River Valley. Well before the canal's grand opening in the fall of 1825 it was already being heralded, in the words of one chronicler, as "the masterwork of the age," a view widely shared by Americans.[8]

Map 1.1 shows that the canal from Albany ran directly northward along the west bank of the Hudson River for several miles before joining the Mohawk River and heading westward toward central New York State.[9] The canal paralleled the final leg of Cole's outbound journey from New York. If he took a steamboat from the Hudson Highlands to the Albany-Troy area, he might not have been able to see the canal (though he surely would have heard about it), which was set back somewhat from the Hudson River shoreline.

But at the next significant stop on his journey he could not have missed it. Cole's most northward destination, before heading south again and stopping in Catskill, was Cohoes Falls, a major waterfall on the Mohawk River and already in 1825 a tourist destination. Near the falls Cole drew several sketches, one that shows a mill, another that includes a bridge, and still another that he drew from a bridge. As for another human structure in the neighborhood, the Erie Canal, it is nowhere to be seen.

This omission is all the more remarkable because Cole was so close to the canal. In the only one of his four Cohoes Falls sketches that takes in the whole of the waterfall (fig. 1.7) he described very specifically his vantage point: "This view of the Cohoes Falls is taken from the cliff on the west bank of the Mohawk. The light from the left; that part on the right of the large rock in shade." From his description we can locate Cole's position when he made this sketch, and from period maps we know exactly where the

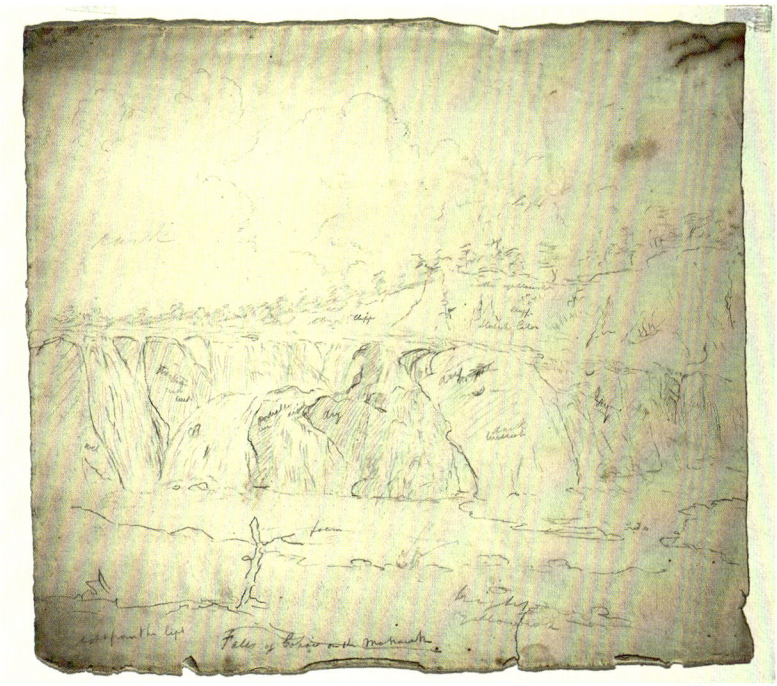

1.7 Thomas Cole, *Falls of Cohoes on the Mohawk*, c. 1825. Graphite pencil on paper, sheet (irreg.): 10⅜ x 12 in. (26.4 x 30.5 cm). Detroit Institute of Arts, Founders Society Purchase, William H. Murphy Fund (39.223.A).

canal was in relation to this position—directly below him, at the base of the cliff where he was standing. He was literally on top of it.

What Cole also had to have seen during his time near Cohoes Falls was an elaborate series of locks (they were known as "the terrible sixteens") that made possible the canal's ascent over a steep escarpment. As the canal ran along the southwest side of the Mohawk River at this point, these locks brought the canal up and around the falls. At no other place along the entire 360-mile length of the Erie Canal would the machinery of its operations have been more in evidence.

It may not be surprising, given Cole's youth in industrial northern England, that he ignored the masterwork of the age. If we understand the Erie Canal's absence from his sketches as a kind of erasure, then such a judgment has larger implications for the development of his career. Cole's first tour of the Hudson River Valley is often regarded as a transforming experience, in which his genius emerged spontaneously through his interaction with the American landscape. But he may have brought to this landscape a strong preconception that led him to exclude forms reminding him of the large-scale industry he had witnessed during his youth in northern England.

Such a response would be consistent with artistic strategies expressed in some of Cole's later works. As we will see, in one of his Catskill Creek paintings he erased an existing railroad—at least the bridge that carried it—and in another, as one scholar has persuasively argued, found a way to include the railroad while also expressing his rage against it.[10] It's possible that from the very beginning of Cole's career as an American landscape painter he had determined to keep the machine out of the garden, to rephrase a well-known formulation.[11]

Cole's Landscape Artistry

Cole may not have found the Erie Canal a subject worthy of his artistry, and artistry was the whole point of his first expedition into the Hudson River Valley.[12] The terms and emphases of his list of twenty-two sketches communicate a singularly aesthetic vision, showing, for one thing, how thoroughly the artist was breaking from contemporaneous topographic renderings of the Hudson Valley, such as those by William Guy Wall in *The Hudson River Portfolio* (first ed., 1821–25).[13]

A central component of Cole's aesthetic was the effect of light at different times of day and in different atmospheric conditions. Of a mist-covered mountaintop (probably Storm King Mountain) near West Point, he says it is "sublime particularly when there is a Thunder storm coming down the river when the distant hills are obscured by the rain." Cole's use of the term "sublime" in this entry reminds us that, like other artists of his time, he was deeply influenced by theories of the beautiful and the sublime that had come down to him, through European Romanticism, from eighteenth-century thinkers such as Edmund Burke.[14]

The sublime was characterized by powerful, even violent, natural phenomena such as waterfalls; mountains like Storm King, and of course the Catskills, belonged to the sublime too. In turn, the beautiful was the opposite of the sublime; it applied to scenes of visual order and harmony (including pastoral and agricultural settings) and to "softer" landscape elements such as lakes and ponds. Part of the power of Cole's American landscapes lies in the sheer energy that he imparted to the contrast between the beautiful and the sublime. His imagination was given to contrasts, as one of the entries in his 1825 list of drawings suggests. Regarding "A View on the North [Hudson]

River near Troy," he wrote, "The scenery viewed about here is singularly beautiful but it is not so grand as that in the Highlands of Hudson." A decade later Cole produced the most impressive of his landscapes contrasting the sublime and the beautiful, *The Oxbow* (fig. 1.8), where a stormy wilderness on the left confronts a pastoral, agricultural scene on the right.

For the most part Cole sketched natural forms during his 1825 expedition: mountains near West Point and in the Catskills, the Hudson and Mohawk Rivers, and waterfalls, most notably the broad Niagara-shaped Cohoes Falls and the narrow, steeply vertical Kaaterskill Falls in the Catskill Mountains. But he drew human structures, too, among them a "cottage in shadow" near West Point. It was an image that Cole may have been attracted to by reading the works of the English author William Gilpin (1724–1804), an advocate of an aesthetic category called the picturesque. Gilpin had recommended to artists that they include in their landscapes elements like rustic cottages for pastoral effect. He also encouraged including mills, that is, small-scale mills such as those Cole found along the Hudson and Mohawk Rivers (not the huge textile mills of England), and bridges as well. Mills are represented in drawings Cole made at Buttermilk Falls and Cohoes Falls, and at the latter site he sketched a bridge.[15]

Cole also sketched another kind of human structure on his tour. His two drawings of the ruins of Fort Putnam at West Point, an important Revolutionary War site, anticipate his lifelong interest in ruins and, more generally, historical associations. As he later wrote in his "Essay on American Scenery," "American scenes are not destitute of historical and legendary associations—the great struggle for freedom has sanctified many a spot, and many a mountain, stream, and rock, has its legend, worthy of poet's pen or the painter's pencil."[16] Cole's drawings of the ruins at West Point would lead soon to his painting *View of Fort Putnam* (fig. 1.9), which is the very work that Durand purchased in Colman's bookstore.

The Fort Putnam ruins had for Cole the aura of historical association, but while he was sketching them his primary interest in them was aesthetic. In the first of his two drawings of these ruins he observed "a very fine effect . . . produced by shadowing the mountain by a cloud," and in the second he took note of the "eastern light." To say that Cole's focus during his 1825 expedition into the Hudson River Valley was primarily aesthetic is also to say that he was engaged in an experimental process, a process in which he applied to a landscape he had never seen before artistic conceptions that had influenced him. In this way, Cole was *creating* an aesthetic—for himself and for American art.

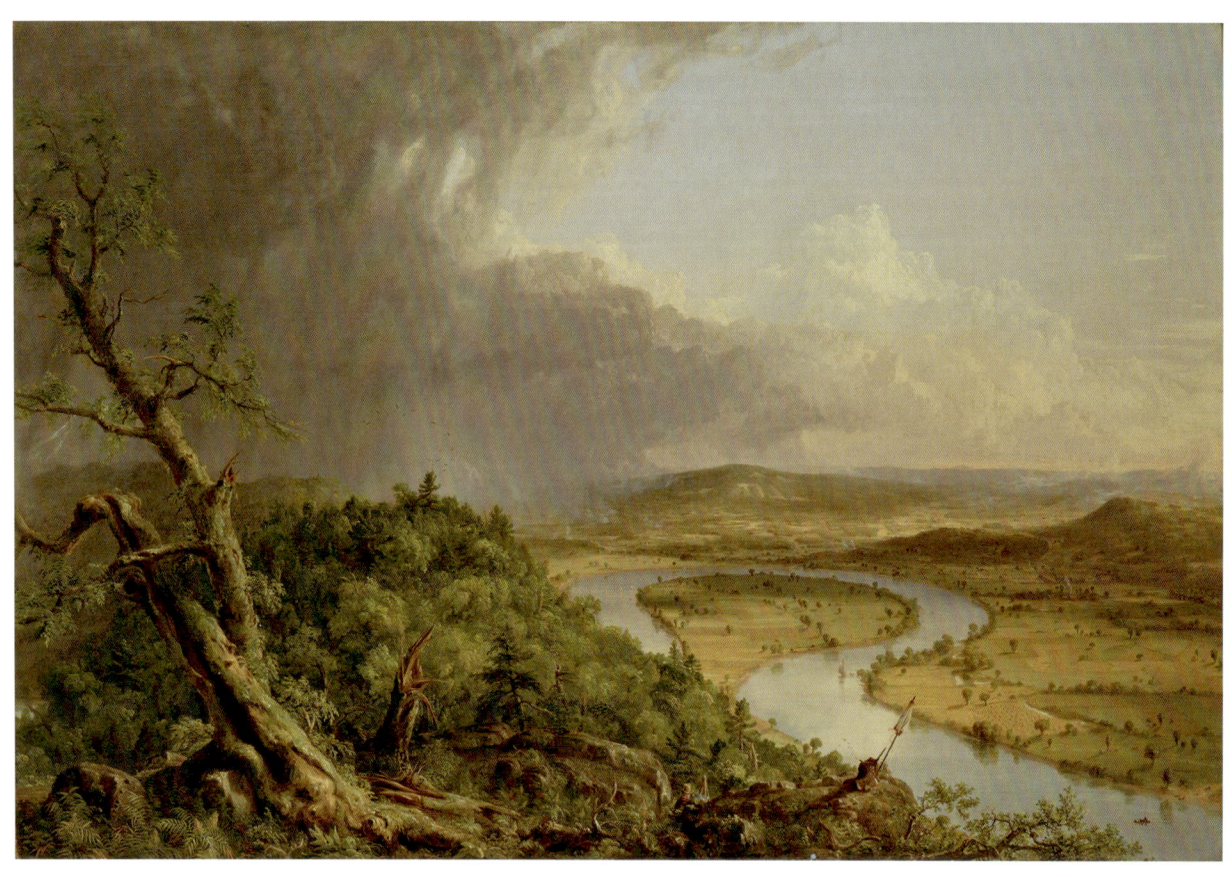

1.8 Thomas Cole, *View from Mount Holyoke,
Northampton, Massachusetts, After a Thunderstorm
(The Oxbow)*, 1836. Oil on canvas, 51½ x 76 in.
(130.8 x 193 cm). Metropolitan Museum of Art,
gift of Mrs. Russell Sage, 1908 (08.228).

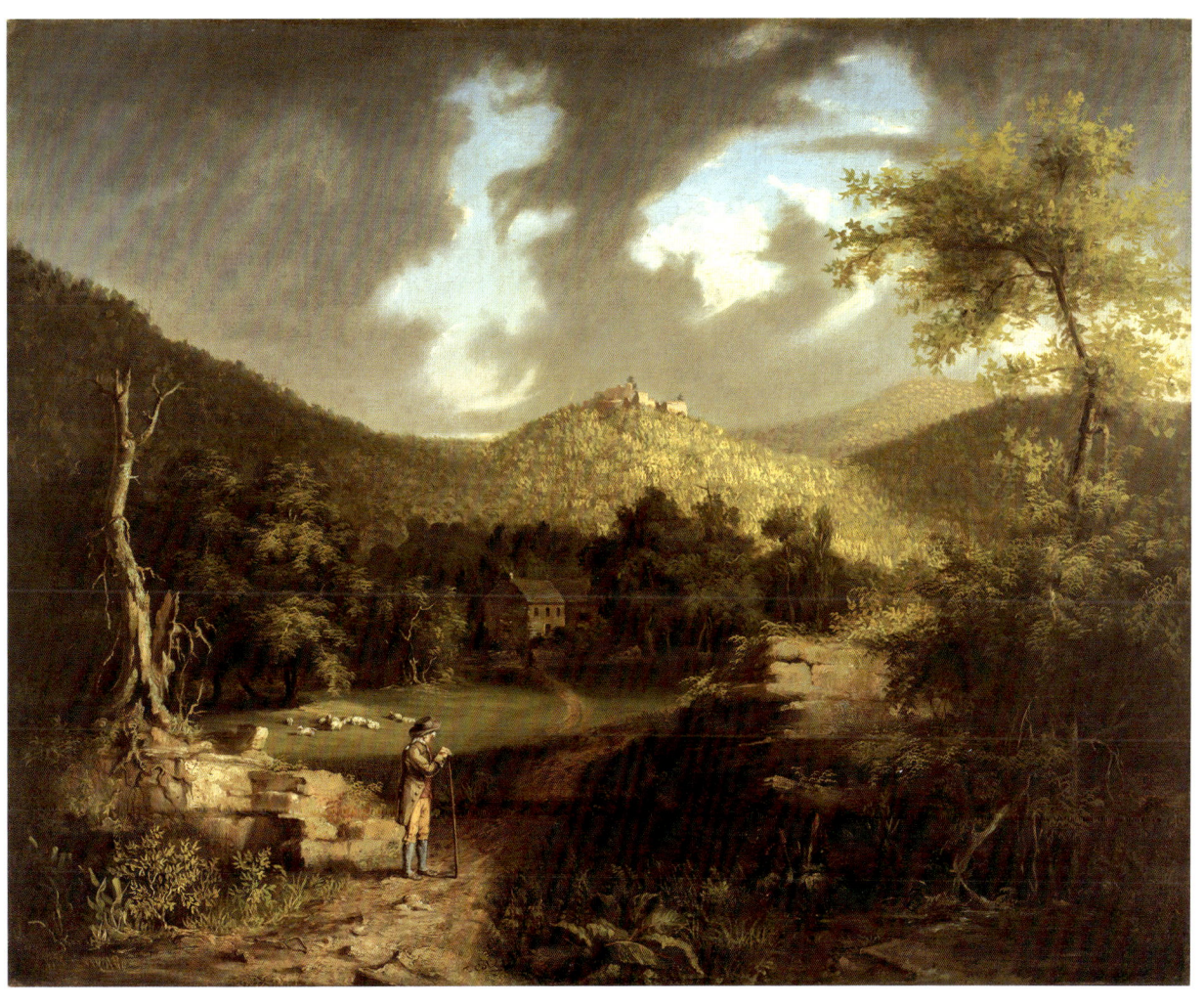

1.9 Thomas Cole, *View of Fort Putnam*, 1825. Oil on canvas, 27¼ x 34 in. (69.2 x 86.4 cm). Philadelphia Museum of Art, 125th Anniversary Acquisition, promised gift of Charlene Sussel (429-1994-1).

Nowhere along Cole's journey into the Hudson River Valley in the summer of 1825 was his experimental process more intensely at work than in the area near Catskill Village. We don't know how he got from Cohoes Falls to Catskill, or how long it took him. But his sheer productivity once he arrived there suggests that the environment was both pleasing and exciting to him. The eight sketches of Catskill scenery referenced by Cole's list far outnumber those he drew at any other specific location along his journey. In the mountains above Catskill Village he made drawings at the site of the Catskill Mountain House, America's first great tourist hotel, including one that showed the hotel "from the Road Below." The Mountain House had opened in 1824, the year before Cole's visit.[17] He made a sketch of a lake scene in the same area, and it became the basis of his early landscape *Lake with Dead Trees (Catskill)* (fig. 1.10); this is the work that was purchased by Dunlap in Colman's bookstore the following fall.

But most of Cole's attention in the Catskill region was focused on Kaaterskill Falls, a spectacular double waterfall that by 1825 had become a popular tourist destination. Four of the eight Catskill sketches on his list depict the falls. One of them described the waterfall from below, two from "under the projecting rock," and still another "from above." Paintings he would soon complete capture all three of these views. One of them, *Catterskill Upper Fall, Catskill Mountain* (1825; unlocated but known from a replica), is the painting that essentially launched Cole's career.

On that fateful day when Trumbull happened by Colman's bookstore and soon thereafter advised Dunlap and Durand about what he had found there, this is the work that Trumbull himself purchased. Still another Cole painting inspired by Kaaterskill Falls, this one based on his view of it from below, expresses vividly the distinctive exchange between sublimity and beauty in his early American landscapes and dramatizes the transformative power of his imagination. In *Kaaterskill Falls* (fig. 1.11), completed in 1826, he removed tourist structures—including a refreshment stand and an observation platform that appear in his sketches—and returned the scene to an imagined primeval wilderness.

In his "Essay on American Scenery" Cole would later write, "The most distinctive, and perhaps the most impressive, characteristic of American scenery is its wildness."[18] By American "wildness" Cole seemed in his essay to be looking westward toward "the central wilds of this vast continent" and even farther west to "distant Oregon"—regions that he never saw.[19] But as *Kaaterskill Falls* and others of his early works illustrate, for him wildness was as much a vision as a reality, and he didn't need distant Oregon to support it. His was a vision that would transform American landscape painting.

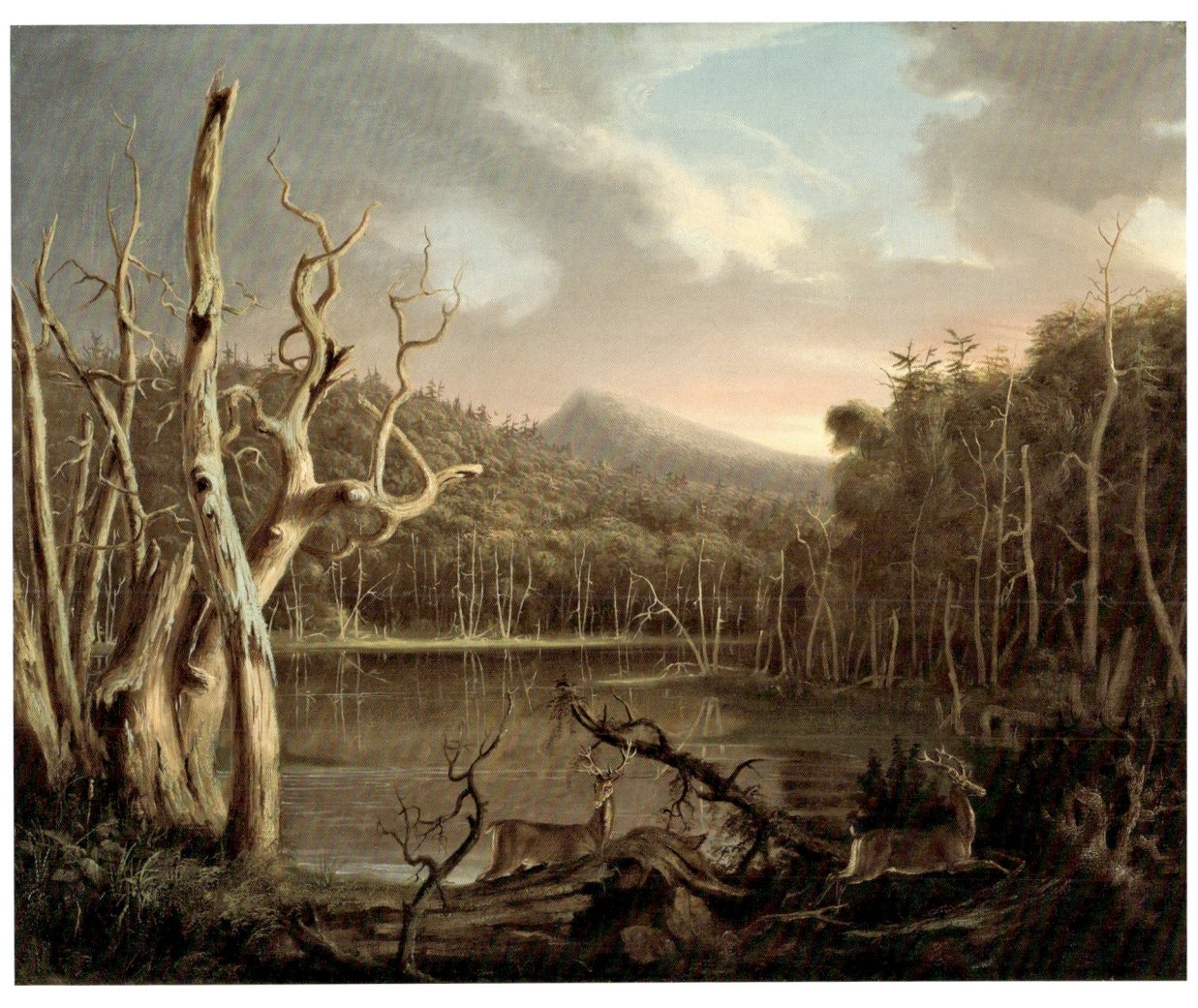

1.10 Thomas Cole, *Lake with Dead Trees (Catskill)*,
1825. Oil on canvas, 27 x 33¾ in. (68.6 x 85.7 cm).
Allen Memorial Art Museum, Oberlin College, Ohio,
gift of Charles F. Olney (1904.1183).

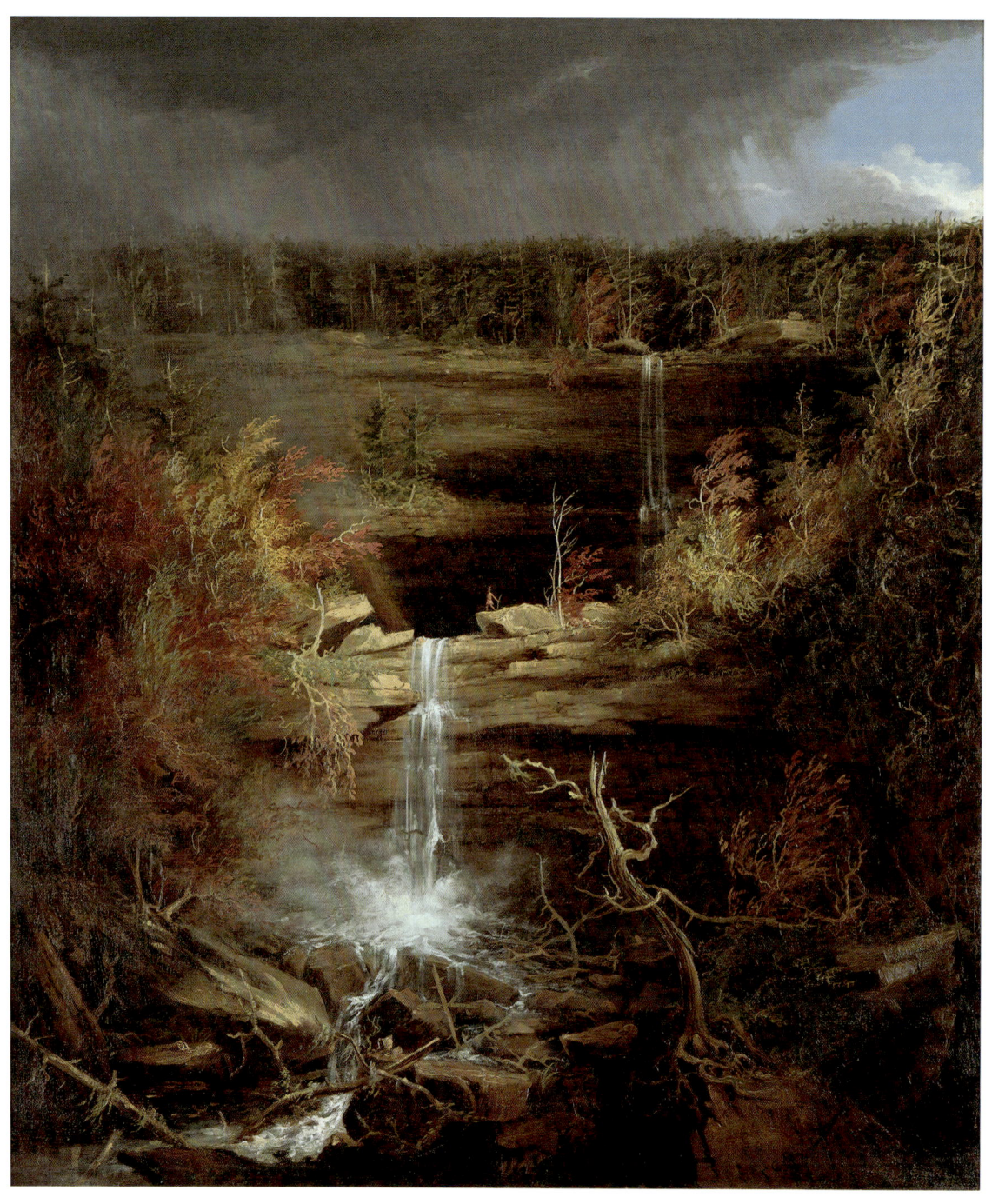

1.11 Thomas Cole, *Kaaterskill Falls*, 1826. Oil on canvas, 43 x 36 in. (109 x 91.4 cm), Private collection / Bridgeman Images.

CHAPTER TWO

A DIFFERENT KIND OF SERIES

Thomas Cole didn't like to repeat himself. Early in his career one of his patrons, Daniel Wadsworth, wanted from him a picture of Kaaterskill Falls closely resembling the one the artist had earlier painted for Trumbull. On November 20, 1826, Cole wrote the following account to Wadsworth: "I have laboured twice as much upon this picture as I did upon the one you saw [Trumbull's]: but not with the same feeling. I cannot paint a view twice and do justice to it."

A reverse situation involving Wadsworth developed the following year. Cole appears to have promised a scene from Cooper's novel *The Last of the Mohicans* (1826) to both Wadsworth and Robert Gilmor Jr. Wadsworth's painting was created first, and on November 26, 1827, Cole wrote to him about the difficulties he had experienced in making a copy for his other patron: "Since I wrote the foregoing I have finished the picture for Mr. Gilmor, it is not an exact copy, and I think it is better than yours—after you left here I commenced a copy immediately, but found after working at it four days I could not paint it, it was drudgery. I then took a fresh canvass and began another picture *varying* the composition from yours. I went on with feeling and have now finished it."[1]

Cole's aversion to repetition reflects his quest for originality, energized in part by Romantic literature of his time. He was especially engaged by the works of Lord Byron and by the intensity with which Bryon's protagonists, such as the hero of *Childe Harold's*

Pilgrimage (1812–18), pursued their quests for fulfillment. But Cole's frustration with repetition is also an expression of his own deeply restless nature. A storm he described in an early prose sketch could be a figure for his imagination: "There was no rest, no fixedness; all things were left unfinished."[2] The interaction between the artist's temperament and his cultural inheritance from Romanticism led him into a career marked by experimentation and change.

Motivated strongly by ideas and broadly informed by his reading, Cole was exceedingly ambitious for his art. Not wanting to be "a mere leaf painter," he aimed to raise landscape to "a higher style," by which he meant, in part, charging it with moral intensity and complex meaning.[3] Toward this end, Cole drew upon his deeply literary imagination to give his works powerful, almost cinematic, narrative movement. He was impatient with what he regarded as the static format of landscape painting, and some have speculated that he took up serial works like *The Course of Empire* as a way of breaking free from the confines of a single image.[4]

Such works invited Cole toward the kind of repetition he *did* like, one that pictured the same landscape or human subject in successive representations but in a way that dramatized transformative change. His two major, completed serial works, *The Course of Empire* and *The Voyage of Life*, are all about transformation; they show how *much* change can occur—through cycles of rise and fall, growth and decline—within the life of a civilization or an individual human being. A viewer of such a series is positioned to fast-forward the developments of a culture's or a person's entire life span—its fateful course or voyage—and in doing so perceive the essential instability of any given stage depicted in the series.

Instability was central to Cole's worldview, as the images of chasms and collapse appearing often in his writings make clear. Describing a frozen Kaaterskill Falls in an 1843 journal entry, he observed, "The royal architect builds but unstable structures, which, like worldly virtues, quickly vanish in the full light, and fiery trial." The "deep black pools" and "furious cataracts" in his poem "The Vision of Life" (1825) clearly represent his *own* vision. And in an early prose sketch, "The Bewilderment," the narrator describes his "descending into a deep valley" where suddenly "the earth beneath my feet broke away & I was precipitated down a shelving steep."[5]

Cole's vision of instability derived from both religious and personal sources and, as scholars have shown, was intensified by the turbulent social, economic, and political changes he lived through.[6] In terms of the aesthetic categories that ruled landscape art in his era, instability was an aspect of the sublime, just as its polar category, the beautiful, was characterized by stability and order.[7] Cole can be distinguished from American contemporaries such as Durand and Thomas Doughty by his dynamic juxtaposition of these categories—revealing the fragility of the beautiful by showing how alarmingly proximate was the chaos of the sublime, and how vulnerable to temporal disruption was its apparently timeless realm.

Several of Cole's works contrast the sublime and the beautiful within a single landscape; the *Oxbow*, as we have seen, depicts a stormy wilderness on the left and a scene of agrarian harmony on the right. His narrative series, on the other hand, dramatize their contrasts sequentially. In *The Course of Empire* (figs. 1.2–1.6) the primeval wilderness of the series' first painting, *The Savage State*, is followed in the second by an epoch Cole calls the *Arcadian or Pastoral State*; and in *The Voyage of Life* (figs. 2.1–2.4) the dreamlike landscape of *Youth* gives way, in the next picture, to the raging rapids of *Manhood*.[8]

Representations of radically different stages of history and states of being can be perceived, in these series, only through the literal, bodily repositioning of the viewer and the viewer's almost visceral participation in the process being represented. Like the panoramas becoming popular in Cole's time—paintings viewed from a tower in a rotunda—and that may have influenced him, these works unroll history and destiny.[9] They move.

In another sense, however, Cole's narrative series are immobile. Dynamic as they are in their shifts of scene from one stage to another, and inventive as they are in their imagery and manipulations of vantage point, they are closed systems ordered by an eschatological narrative, that is, a narrative of preordained final events. Essentially allegories, they take their inspiration from a broad range of literary sources including the Bible, *Paradise Lost* (the British painter John Martin's illustrations of Milton's epic heavily influenced him), Romantic poetic narratives such as *Childe Harold's Pilgrimage*, and especially Bunyan's Puritan allegory *The Pilgrim's Progress*. The artist's final, uncompleted five-part series *The Cross and the World*—with its two pilgrims walking toward their polar destinies—makes Bunyan's influence explicit.[10]

In Cole's narrative series, as one scholar has said about *The Pilgrim's Progress*, "repetition proclaims the cyclical and identical patterns of history."[11] Their endings are predetermined, both in a religious, specifically Protestant sense and in terms of the artist's intentions.[12] He planned these series in full before painting them, and from what we know of his practices, he characteristically executed the works in the general order of their place in the series; their conception was intact before brush touched canvas.[13]

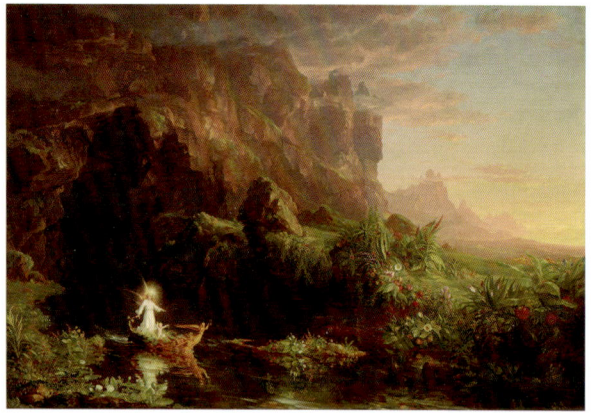 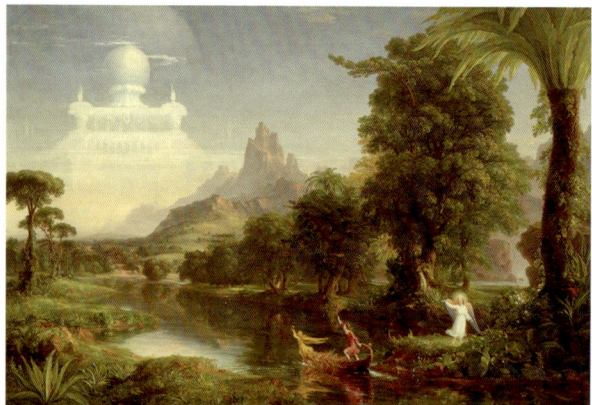

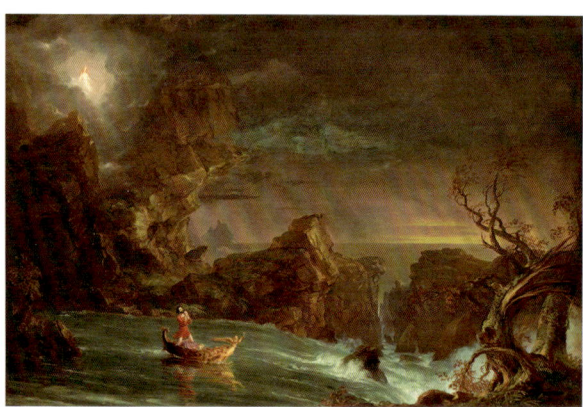 

2.1 Thomas Cole, *The Voyage of Life: Childhood*, 1842. Oil on canvas, 52⅞ x 76⅞ in. (134.3 x 195.3 cm). National Gallery of Art, Ailsa Mellon Bruce Fund (1971.16.1).

2.2 Thomas Cole, *The Voyage of Life: Youth*, 1842. Oil on canvas, 52⅞ x 76¾ in. (134.3 x 194.9 cm), National Gallery of Art, Ailsa Mellon Bruce Fund (1971.16.2).

2.3 Thomas Cole, *The Voyage of Life: Manhood*, 1842. Oil on canvas, 52⅞ x 79¾ in. (134.3 x 202.6 cm). National Gallery of Art, Ailsa Mellon Bruce Fund (1971.16.3).

2.4 Thomas Cole, *The Voyage of Life: Old Age*, 1842. Oil on canvas, 52½ x 77¼ in. (133.4 x 196.2 cm). National Gallery of Art, Ailsa Mellon Bruce Fund (1971.16.4).

The process through which Cole conceived his series began very early in his career. In a sketchbook from 1827 appears a remarkable list of 122 possible subjects for pictures. Most of the ideas have narrative content, and fully 18 of them project narrative-based series, several of which Cole later brought to fruition. His list of ideas from 1827 suggests that even then his powerfully narrative imagination drove him toward their creation.[14] The transformative kind of repetition involved in these series clearly energized Cole, whereas re-creating a discrete landscape view could feel to him like drudgery.

A Series Spanning Cole's Career

As we have anticipated, there is one unified group of landscape paintings that blur this distinction and invite us to consider Cole in a new light. He began his Catskill Creek series in the same year, 1827, that he made his list of ideas for pictures, and the works in this series are very different from most of the ones he projected in his list. In his Catskill Creek paintings he reproduced—apparently without complaint—the same localized scene in at least ten completed landscapes spanning the course of his mature career.[15] These works exhibit no overt narrative development, and when Cole completed the first of them in 1827, he may not have been envisioning a series. But in the end the Catskill Creek paintings became the most sustained sequence of landscapes he ever produced.

They appear intermittently during the 1820s, 1830s, and 1840s, which is to say from the time of Cole's discovery by the New York art world to near his death almost a quarter century later. This period saw major changes in his work and life, as well as radical changes in the political, social, and economic life of the United States during these turbulent antebellum years. The earliest of the Catskill Creek paintings was completed when John Quincy Adams was president and the last of them five presidential terms later, shortly after the election of James K. Polk.

Cole took his vantage points for these works in several locations just outside and to the west of Catskill Village; map 2.1 specifies these locations. He may have passed by the Catskill Creek scene in 1825 during his first visit to Catskill, when he explored the mountains above the village and thereafter made those mountains the first major focus of his landscape art. But even after Cole's focus shifted decisively away from the Catskills at the end of the 1820s, he continued to paint the Catskill Creek scene. He painted it before and after both of his European tours (1829–32, 1841–42), and even during one of them.[16]

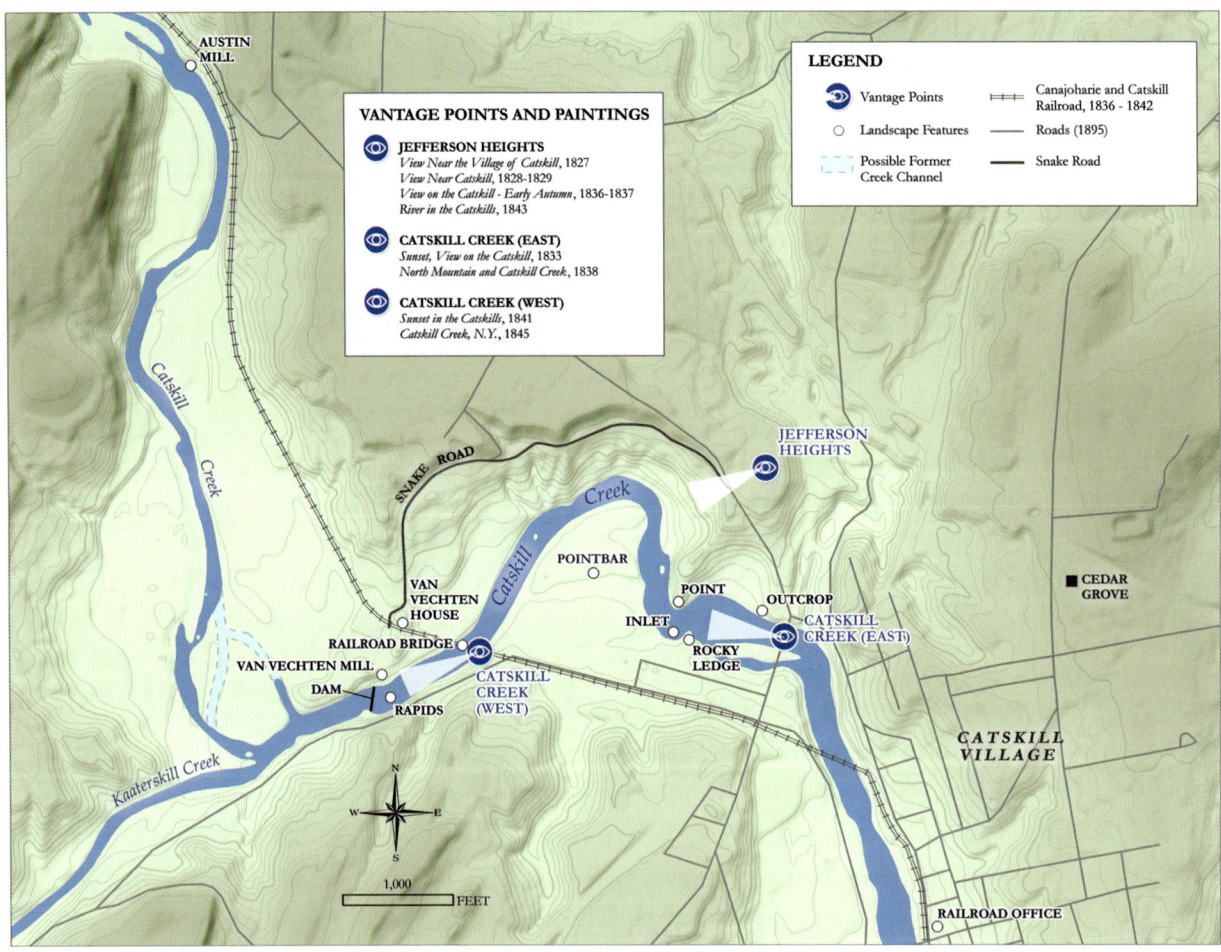

VANTAGE POINTS AND PAINTINGS

JEFFERSON HEIGHTS
View Near the Village of Catskill, 1827
View Near Catskill, 1828-1829
View on the Catskill - Early Autumn, 1836-1837
River in the Catskills, 1843

CATSKILL CREEK (EAST)
Sunset, View on the Catskill, 1833
North Mountain and Catskill Creek, 1838

CATSKILL CREEK (WEST)
Sunset in the Catskills, 1841
Catskill Creek, N.Y., 1845

LEGEND

Vantage Points
Landscape Features
Possible Former Creek Channel
Canajoharie and Catskill Railroad, 1836 - 1842
Roads (1895)
Snake Road

AUSTIN MILL

Catskill Creek

JEFFERSON HEIGHTS

SNAKE ROAD

Catskill Creek

POINTBAR

VAN VECHTEN HOUSE

RAILROAD BRIDGE

VAN VECHTEN MILL

DAM

RAPIDS

CATSKILL CREEK (WEST)

Kaaterskill Creek

POINT

INLET

OUTCROP

ROCKY LEDGE

CATSKILL CREEK (EAST)

CEDAR GROVE

CATSKILL VILLAGE

RAILROAD OFFICE

N W E S

1,000 FEET

Map 2.1 Landforms, landmarks, and Cole's vantage points near and along Catskill Creek. The Hudson River is just to the right (east) of the area shown. Map by Neil Curri.

While the works in the series show interesting and important differences from one another, viewing them together reveals the remarkable stability of their orientation. Four of the ten paintings are panoramic, with high vantage points on a plateau called Jefferson Heights, and six position the viewer along the banks of Catskill Creek. But all look westward from the same wide river bend toward the Catskill Front, or escarpment, and its distinctive ridgelines, shown in the panorama illustrated in figure 2.5.

The works represented in figures 2.6 and 2.7 are Cole's first two Catskill Creek landscapes, created in the 1820s, and the other two, figures 2.8 and 2.9, are his last—from the 1840s. Three of the works illustrated here take panoramic views from Jefferson Heights, and the other one has a vantage point along Catskill Creek. Vantage points for all the works whose position can be verified are illustrated by map 2.1.

While the series illustrates the freedom of imagination that Cole insistently claimed for himself in creating landscape art, it nevertheless organizes a real rather than an imaginary scene (such as those depicted in his allegorical works), one with recognizable landforms and landmarks.[17] As the maps in subsequent chapters illustrate, the Catskill Creek paintings are generally accurate topographically; to a surprising degree, they show us what Cole saw.

What he saw was a rural environment, essentially pastoral and agricultural but exhibiting significant signs of industrialization. Tanneries were operating nearby even when Cole first came upon the scene in 1825 (their smoke is clearly depicted in the very first work in the series), and planning for a railroad line running close to Catskill Village began soon thereafter.[18] The Catskill Creek paintings show only traces of the wilderness sublime that—as depicted in works like *Kaaterskill Falls* (1826) (fig. 1.11)—had first gained him the attention of the American art world.

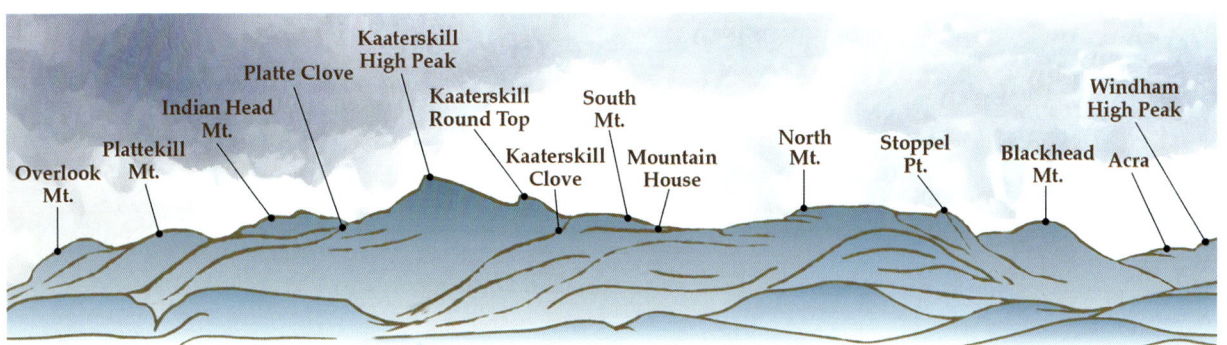

2.5 Illustration of the Catskill Escarpment. Courtesy Thomas Cole National Historic Site, Catskill, N.Y.

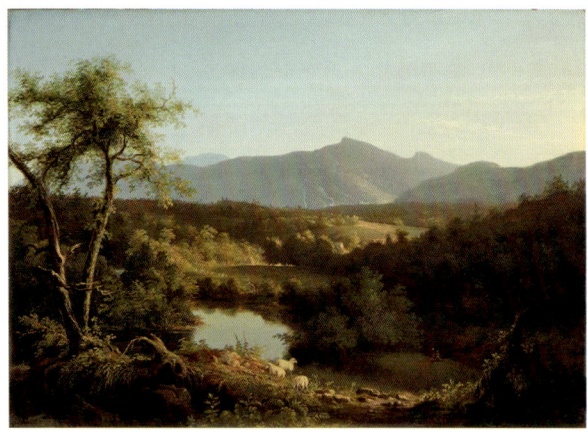
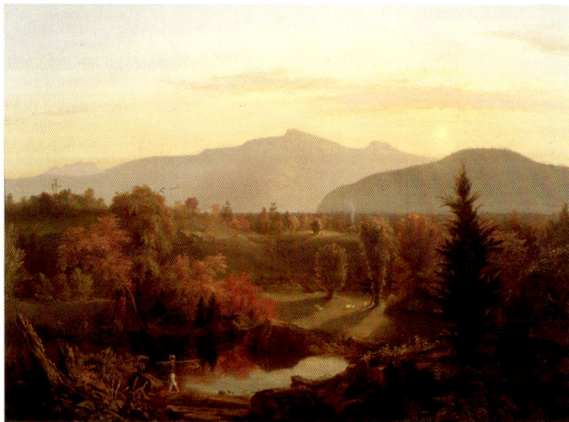

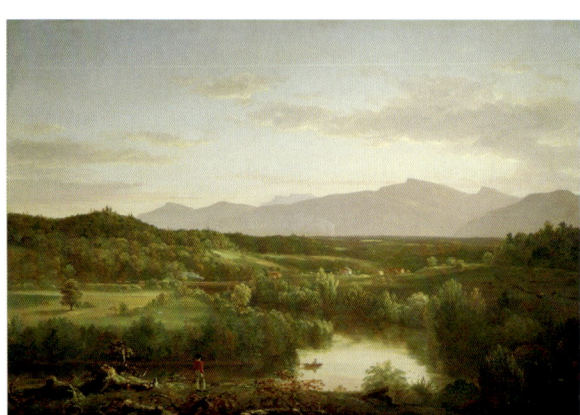
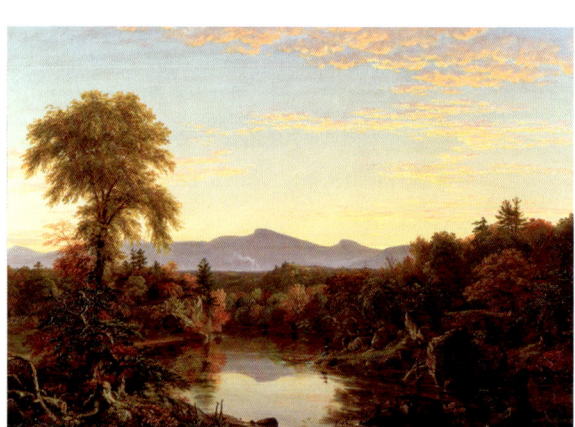

2.6 Thomas Cole, *View Near the Village of Catskill*, 1827. Oil on panel, 24¼ x 35 in. (62.2 x 88.9 cm). Fine Arts Museums of San Francisco, gift of Mr. and Mrs. John D. Rockefeller 3rd (1993.35.7).

2.7 Thomas Cole, *View Near Catskill,* 1828–29. Oil on wood panel, 24½ x 35 in. (62.2 x 88.9 cm). Private collection.

2.8 Thomas Cole, *River in the Catskills*, 1843. Oil on canvas, 27½ x 40⅜ in. (69.85 x 102.55 cm). Museum of Fine Arts, Boston, gift of Martha C. Karolik for the M. and M. Karolik Collection of American Paintings, 1815–1865 (47.1201).

2.9 Thomas Cole, *Catskill Creek, N.Y.,* 1845. Oil on canvas, 26½ x 36 in. (67.3 x 91.4 cm). New-York Historical Society, The Robert L. Stuart Collection, gift of his widow Mrs. Mary Stuart. Digital image created by Oppenheimer Editions (S-157).

Over the course of Cole's career he painted few American rural landscapes (Italy was his focus for such scenes), and the ten Catskill Creek paintings account for a large percentage of them—a fact that in itself distinguishes these works.[19] The apparent modesty of their conception is suggested by their scale. Only one, the Metropolitan Museum's *View on the Catskill—Early Autumn* (39 x 63 inches), executed by Cole in 1836–37, is a large, exhibition-sized painting. Of the other nine, seven are middle-sized works ranging around two by three feet. The remaining two paintings are small, both measuring 16½ x 24 inches. These two works were formatted by Cole for oval frames, suggesting to one scholar that the artist understood them, in part, as ornamentation for domestic settings.[20] This observation points to a quality of intimacy in the Catskill Creek paintings that, as we have seen, is related to his sense of place.

Reasons for Returning

What is it that drew the artist back, again and again, to this rural scene and led him, uncharacteristically, to paint it so many times? One thing, no doubt, is that even after he turned his artistic attention away from the Catskills to other places—first New England and later Italy—his clients' interest in this region did not diminish. One of the first works that Cole sold to his most important patron, Luman Reed, was a Catskill Creek landscape, *Sunset, View on the Catskill* (1833), and his *View on the Catskill—Early Autumn* (1836–37) was commissioned by Reed's business partner, Jonathan Sturges.[21] Painting the Catskill Creek scene may have become something of a staple for Cole, providing him with a reliable source of income as he pursued his more ambitious "higher" landscapes.[22]

But market considerations, in one way or another, informed the subject matter of numerous Cole paintings, not just those in the Catskill Creek series, and professional artists do, after all, work to live. Though the most successful and well-known American landscape painter of the antebellum period, Cole struggled at times during his career to make a living from his art. There are numerous examples of his subject matter being directly influenced by commissions. A notable one involved novelist Cooper's request for a landscape (completed but unlocated) that included his Leatherstocking hero; he wanted it as a gift for his friend the English poet Samuel Rogers.[23]

In any case, there is a rough consensus among scholars that the Catskill Creek paintings were important to Cole for reasons beyond market considerations. By themselves, such considerations do not explain the artist's repeated and sustained attention to the landscape of Catskill Creek, which surely was in large measure an expression of his deep attachment to it. As we shall see in the discussion that follows, this attachment is documented by Cole's letters and journals and even by a notable public address. And it is evoked by several of his poems. In one of them, "The Burial Ground at Catskill," the artist imagines himself among the dead, resting in the "spot of earth that living I have lov'd."[24]

But the paintings themselves are the best guide to the evolution of Cole's response to this beloved landscape. Their stability of orientation expresses his commitment to it, while their variations of composition and reconfigurations of elements dramatize his continuing exploration of the scene. Shaping and reshaping the Catskill Creek landscape in repeated representations was for the artist a creative process in which he tried—over the course of eighteen years—to make himself at home, and indeed to *make* a home.

Much has been written about the profound displacement Cole experienced when, as a seventeen-year-old, he emigrated with his family from England to the United States. And his later removal from urban New York to the Catskill countryside can be understood, in part, as the grounding of a restless soul in an environment that invited him to cultivate a sense of place.[25] The Catskill Creek paintings are place-centered in their nature, and they appear to check Cole's attraction to the potentially boundless and undifferentiated space of the sublime.

Yet these works do not exclude the sublime (or its energy); they contain it within a pastoral framework. The familiar scene they depict is haunted by a sense of the unfamiliar. While Cole's many representations of Catskill Creek successively bring to light different parts and aspects of this landscape, none of them alone illuminates fully the complex and deeply personal meanings it had for him. These meanings reveal themselves incrementally through the works' shared images, images whose significance emerges only when the paintings are seen together—in other words, as a series.

Chapter Three

Discovering Catskill Creek

In the period from 1825 through 1827 Cole's focus in the Catskill region was on "wild" scenes in the mountains, as he portrayed them in works like *Kaaterskill Falls* (1826) (fig. 1.11), *Sunrise in the Catskills* (1826) (fig. 3.1), *The Clove* (1827), and *View of the Round-Top in the Catskill Mountains (Sunny Morning on the Hudson)* (1827). The New York art world's discovery of the artist in 1825 came about in part because of his own discovery of these wild scenes, and because of the distinctive vision of wildness that he developed in response to this mountain landscape.

As for a scene much closer at hand, a wide meander of Catskill Creek just outside the village with the mountains in the deep background, Cole may not have focused on it during his initial tour of the Hudson River Valley. His very first Catskill Creek painting, *View Near the Village of Catskill* (fig. 3.3), does not appear until 1827. And, as I have observed, his list of sketches from his 1825 expedition includes no reference to Catskill Creek, and none of the surviving drawings corresponding to that list shows it.

However, a drawing apparently not associated with Cole's 1825 list—and not previously linked to *View Near the Village of Catskill* (1827)—unmistakably stands behind this work (fig. 3.4).[1] The completed painting follows from this drawing in almost every aspect; the mountain and ridgeline profiles are the same, as are all the middle-distance landscape features, and the boundaries of the composition match. Furthermore, Cole has written "falls" on the drawing in exactly the place where the rapids appear

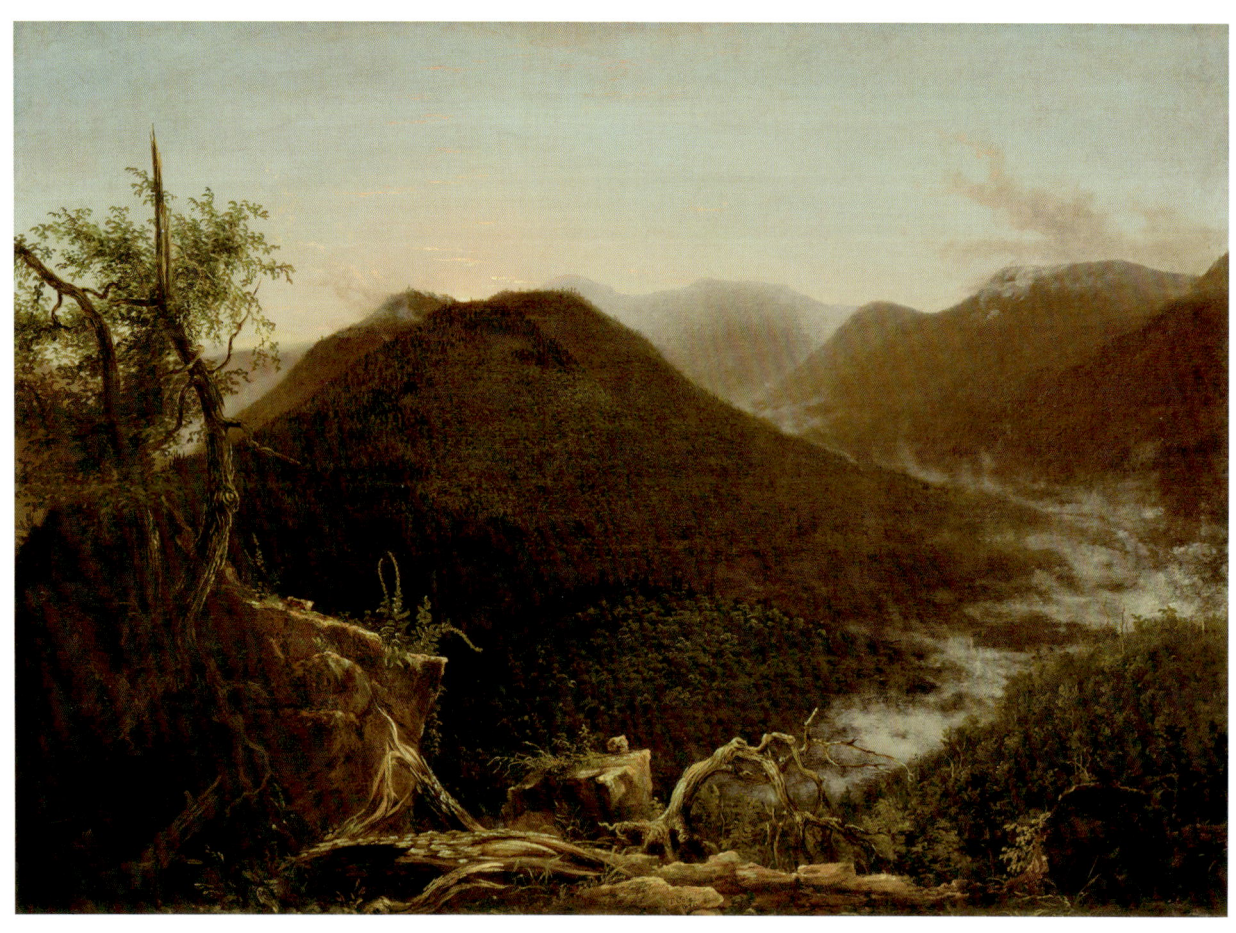

3.1 Thomas Cole, *Sunrise in the Catskills*, 1826. Oil on canvas, 25½ x 35½ in. (64.8 x 90.1 cm). National Gallery of Art, gift of Mrs. John D. Rockefeller 3rd, in honor of the 50th anniversary of the National Gallery of Art (1989.24.1).

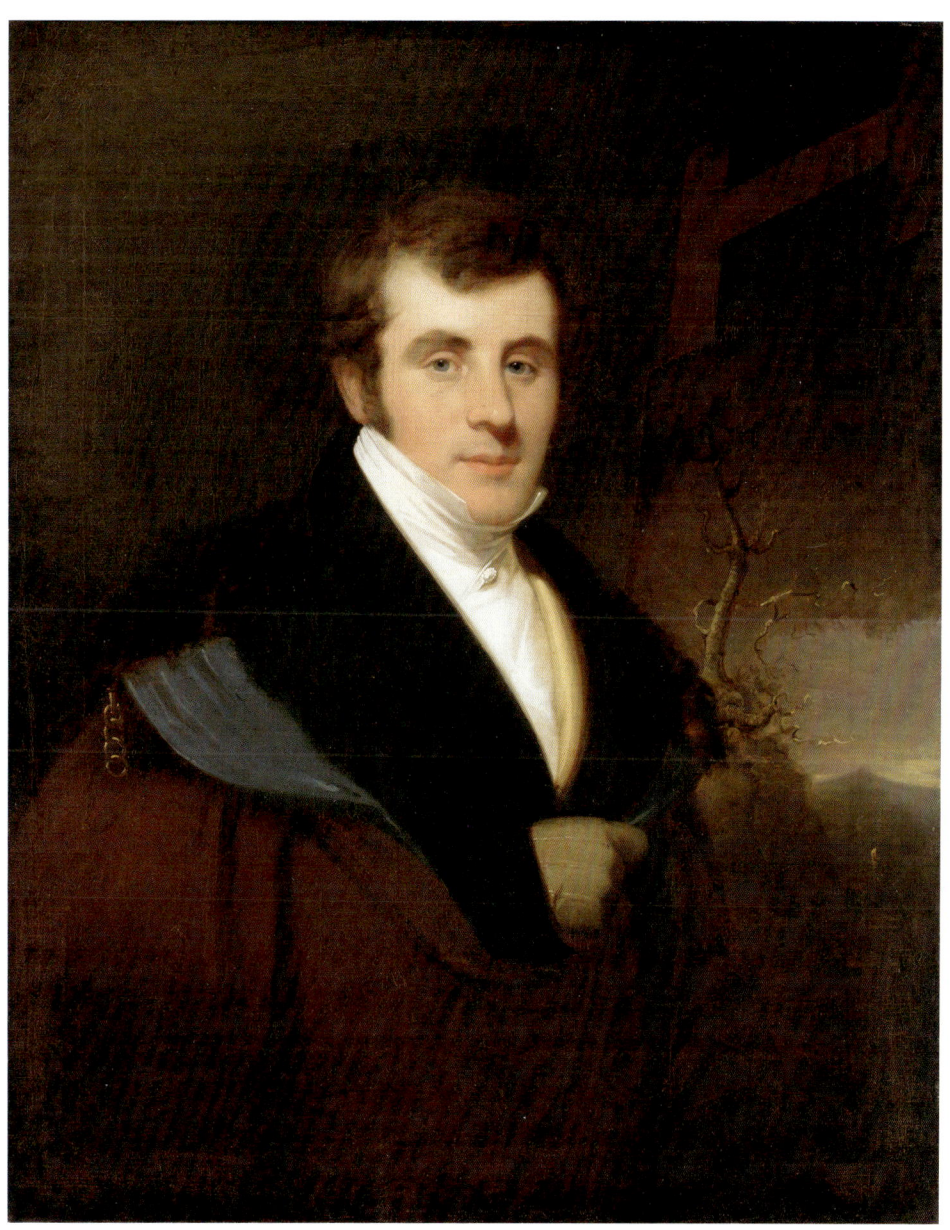

3.2 Thomas Seir Cummings, *Thomas Cole*, 1826–28.
Oil on canvas, 36¼ x 29¼ in. (92.1 x 74.3 cm). Albany
Institute of History and Art, bequest of Mrs. Florence
H. Cole Vincent, granddaughter of Thomas Cole
(1962.51).

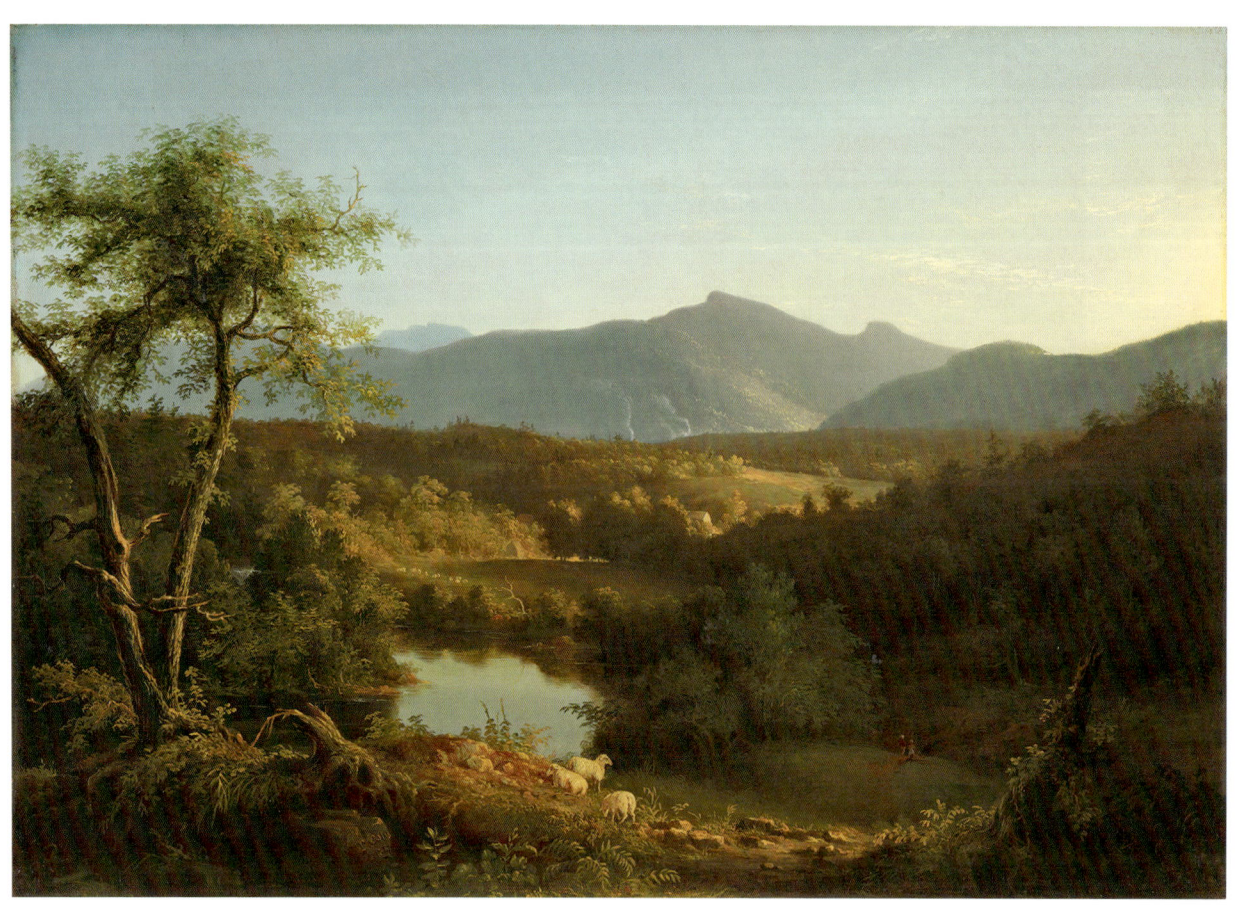

3.3 Thomas Cole, *View Near the Village of Catskill*,
1827. Oil on panel, 24¼ x 35 in. (62.2 x 88.9 cm). Fine
Arts Museums of San Francisco, gift of Mr. and Mrs.
John D. Rockefeller 3rd (1993.35.7).

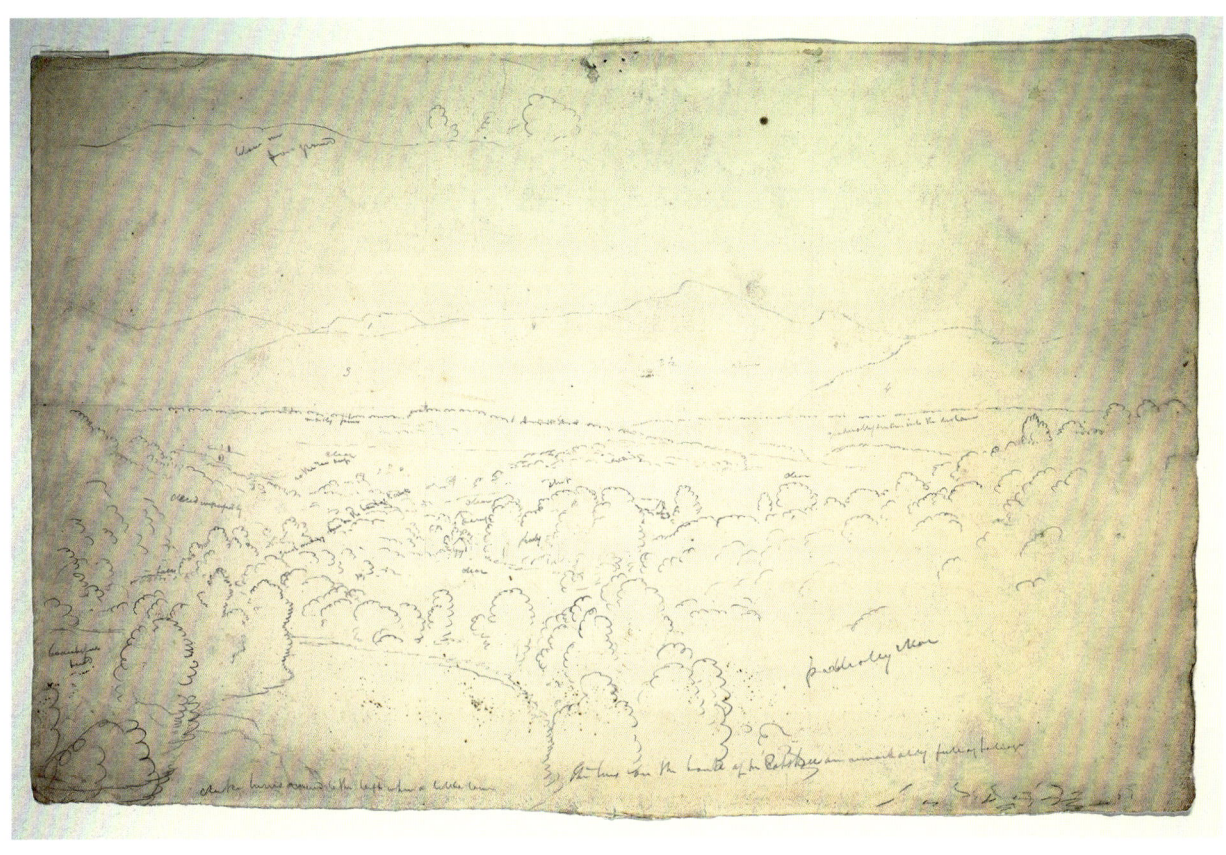

3.4 Thomas Cole, *View in the Catskills,* c. 1825–1848.
Graphite pencil on beige wove paper, sheet (irreg):
11¼ x 17½ in. (28.6 x 44.5 cm). Detroit Institute of
Arts, Founders Society Purchase, William H.
Murphy Fund (39.250.A).

in the completed painting. The only foreground and middle-distance elements from the painting not appearing in the drawing are the large tree on the left and the man and woman at the right. (We will examine both the tree and the couple carefully later in this discussion.) While the drawing is undated, Cole's practices suggest that it was made in the spring or summer of 1827, with the artist executing the oil painting in his studio the following fall.

At the bottom border of the drawing, on the right, the artist has written, "The trees on the bank of the Catskill are remarkably full of foliage," and at the bottom left he noted, "Creek turns around to the left." These are remarkably basic observations, and they suggest a lack of familiarity with the scene. As map 2.1 shows, Jefferson Heights, where Cole would have positioned himself to sketch this panoramic view, is less than a mile outside Catskill Village—hardly a remote location but perhaps for this reason one that did not initially get his attention.

When seen in relation to works like *Sunrise in the Catskills* (fig. 3.1), *View Near the Village of Catskill*—with its pastoral riverside setting and its distant view of the mountains—asserts its independence from Cole's wilderness vision. If it's true that he didn't focus on Catskill Creek until 1827, then his belated attention to it becomes a second discovery—less dramatic than his earlier discovery of the Catskills' mountain scenery but, considered over the long run, a significant one.

The year after painting *View Near the Village of Catskill* Cole began another picture of the scene with a similar title, *View Near Catskill*, and completed it in 1829. These works are almost identical in size (24½ x 35 inches), and both are painted on wood panel. They are two of the four paintings in the larger series that take a panoramic view of the Catskill Creek scene from Jefferson Heights; their shared perspective on the mountains is illustrated by map 3.1.

View Near the Village of Catskill, 1827

The first of these works, *View Near the Village of Catskill*, appeared without the name of its owner in the second annual exhibition of the National Academy of Design; the painting's nineteenth-century provenance remains unknown. It did not come into the public domain until 1993, when a private collector donated it to San Francisco's de Young Museum.[2] *View Near the Village of Catskill* sets forth with astonishing clarity the series' composition and major elements.

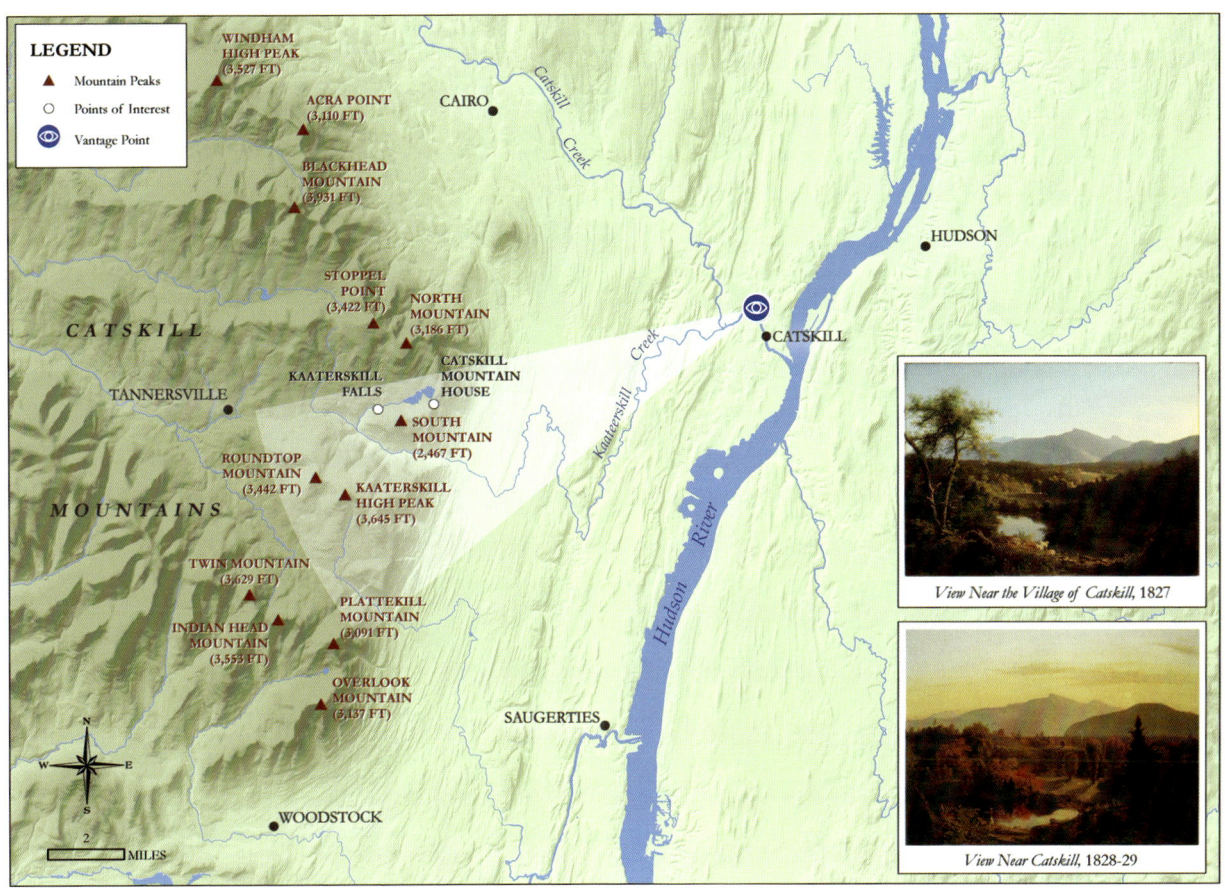

LEGEND

▲ Mountain Peaks
○ Points of Interest
◉ Vantage Point

WINDHAM
HIGH PEAK
(3,527 FT)

ACRA POINT
(3,110 FT)

CAIRO

BLACKHEAD
MOUNTAIN
(3,931 FT)

HUDSON

STOPPEL
POINT
(3,422 FT)

NORTH
MOUNTAIN
(3,186 FT)

CATSKILL

CATSKILL

KAATERSKILL
FALLS

CATSKILL
MOUNTAIN
HOUSE

TANNERSVILLE

SOUTH
MOUNTAIN
(2,467 FT)

ROUNDTOP
MOUNTAIN
(3,442 FT)

KAATERSKILL
HIGH PEAK
(3,645 FT)

MOUNTAINS

TWIN MOUNTAIN
(3,629 FT)

PLATTEKILL
MOUNTAIN
(3,091 FT)

INDIAN HEAD
MOUNTAIN
(3,553 FT)

OVERLOOK
MOUNTAIN
(3,137 FT)

SAUGERTIES

Hudson River

Kaaterskill Creek

Catskill Creek

N
W   E
S

2
☐☐☐☐ MILES

WOODSTOCK

View Near the Village of Catskill, 1827

View Near Catskill, 1828-29

Map 3.1 Viewscape of *View Near the Village of Catskill*
(1827) and *View Near Catskill* (1828–29). Map by Neil
Curri.

Here are the middle-ground landforms and landmarks that will appear in subsequent works. In the distance are the undulating forms of Kaaterskill High Peak (also known simply as High Peak) near the center and Roundtop Mountain to its right, with the nearer, rounded South Mountain superimposed on them. In the farther distance to the left is the broad, shadowy form of Indian Head Mountain, which appears in all of Cole's panoramic versions of the Catskill Creek scene.[3] This configuration of Catskill peaks would become a signature of the series and, indeed, the classical profile of these mountains for a generation of painters. For example, Durand painted the scene; his *Catskill Mountains* (c. 1830) (fig. 3.5) is remarkably similar in composition to Cole's *View Near the Village of Catskill*.[4]

In Cole's painting the stalks of mullein in the foreground, silhouetted against the distant water, is a motif that continues in his series, as does the glimpse of the rapids in the left middle ground, seen through the foliage. The detail in figure 3.6 brings the rapids and the mullein into closer range; the rapids appear as a small gray form.

While introducing several of the series' major elements, however, *View Near the Village of Catskill* exhibits certain distinctive features that make it all the more interesting when viewed in relation to the works that follow it. Its apparent light source is at the upper right, which is to say, in the west. But, strangely, this is not a sunset view, as are almost all the other works in the Catskill Creek series. Nor does it represent, as do several of the other paintings, an autumnal scene. Set in spring or summer and auroral in spirit, it conveys with its bright blue sky a freshness of perception befitting its inaugural role. It's useful to remember, in this regard, that Cole's discovery of the Catskills as a subject for his art in 1825 (his signature on the rock in the left foreground asserts his presence) was followed immediately by the American art world's discovery of him.

Cole's wilderness paintings of the Catskills were, of course, intended to convey a distinctively American vision. In his "Essay on American Scenery," he said that "American mountains are generally clothed to the summit by dense forests, while those of Europe are mostly bare."[5] But the most notably American element appearing in the distant mountains in *View Near the Village of Catskill* is the tiny white form perched on a ridge of North Mountain, seen just to the right of rounded South Mountain. It represents the Catskill Mountain House, constructed only two or three years before Cole painted this picture and for many Americans a symbol of the country's cultural development (fig. 3.7; location identified in map 3.1).

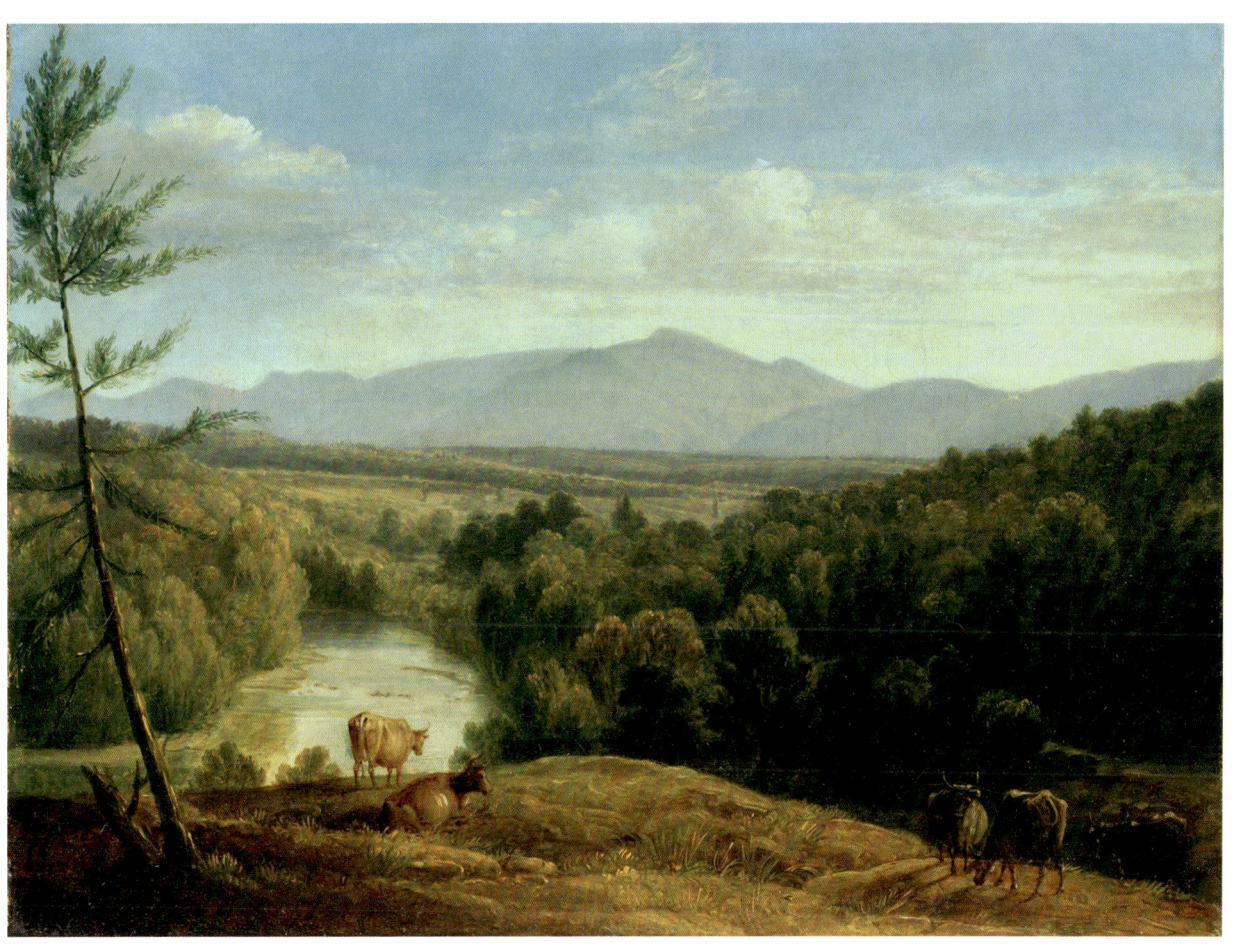

3.5 Asher B. Durand, *Catskill Mountains*, c. 1830.
Oil on canvas, 13¾ x 18 in. (34.9 x 45.7 cm). Albany
Institute of History and Art, gift of Miss Jane E.
Rosell (1987.20.2).

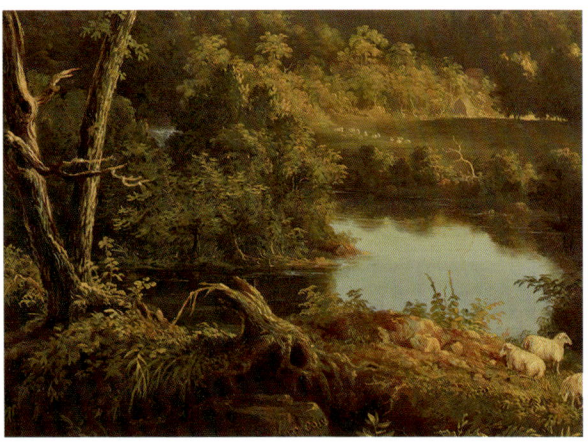

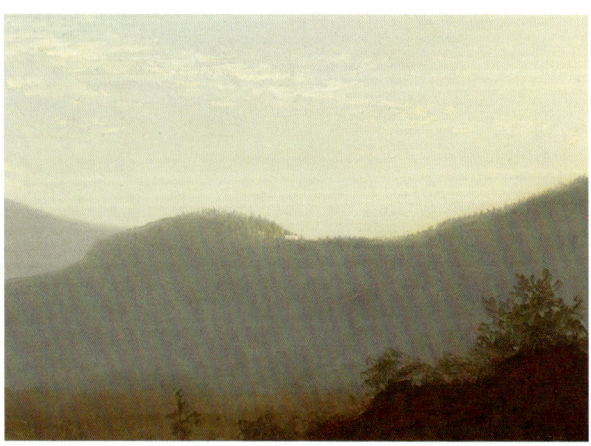

3.6 Detail of figure 3.3, *View Near the Village of Catskill*, 1827   **3.7** Detail of figure 3.3, *View Near the Village of Catskill*, 1827

In more subtle ways, too, *View Near the Village of Catskill* represents a specifically and poignantly American scene. The large framing tree he has placed on the left is, for the only time in the Catskill Creek series, a black locust—native to North America and, because of its hardness and durability, used widely in the United States during the nineteenth century for fence posts.[6] Even the mullein, introduced from Europe during the colonial period, had for Cole a "wild" American aspect, signifying nature's vitality and endurance.[7]

Returning to Cole's sketch for *View Near the Village of Catskill*, we should consider again his notation, "Creek turns around to the left." This notation alerts us to one subtle but significant difference between the drawing and the completed painting. In the drawing Cole has delineated the shoreline of Catskill Creek clearly enough that we recognize the body of water as a river (without the help of his notation), and once we know the larger topography of the scene we can also recognize this part of the river as the farther turn of a wide meander. Map 2.1 shows how this meander forms the broad, oval depositional land formation—what geologists call a pointbar—created by it. In two later Catskill Creek paintings this pointbar will become a stage for human action, such as the man chasing horses in *View on the Catskill—Early Autumn* (fig. 4.24).

In the completed work, *View Near the Village of Catskill*, Cole has disguised Catskill Creek's character as a river. Though a tributary of the Hudson, it is a major one, about two hundred feet across at the point depicted in the painting. But the artist has configured it here more like a lake, a landscape feature, as we saw earlier, that was central to his vision of "American Scenery." Clearly, the river in *View Near the Village of Catskill* has not yet become a river in Cole's imagination. While crossing and voyaging it will figure importantly in later Catskill Creek paintings, the rower who appears in most of them is absent from this landscape.

The blue, sky-reflecting oval of the river's surface is mirrored by the meadow beyond and again by the agricultural field in the farther distance. (The meadow itself has a watery aspect, further unifying the scene.) These three ovals, shading chromatically one into the next, form broad platforms ascending toward the mountains and establish the dominant recessional and skyward movement of the painting. The sense of depth in *View Near the Village of Catskill* is intensified by the rich and lustrous surface created by its medium, oil on wood panel, and by Cole's underpainting of the panel.

Cole would later evoke this vision in "Essay on American Scenery": "The green hills gently rising from the flood, recede like steps by which we may ascend to a great temple, whose pillars are those everlasting hills, and whose dome is the blue boundless vault of heaven."[8] While the artist significantly altered some compositional elements of the Catskill Creek landscape in his subsequent paintings of the scene, his association of the distant mountains with spirituality is expressed in all the works in the series.

The Van Vechten Farmhouse

Understanding Cole's orientation to and perspective on the Catskill Creek scene in *View Near the Village of Catskill* allows us to identify a key human structure appearing in both the drawing and the painting. Located at the lower left-center of the composition, it is the structure angled diagonally leftward that is closest to the shoreline, just to the left of a stand of tall trees. Its position on the river's northern shore and in relation to the rapids identifies it as the seventeenth-century Van Vechten stone farmhouse, part of an estate founded during the colonial era by a Dutch settler named Dirck Teunis Van Vechten—still owned in Cole's time by his descendants.[9] (See the detail in figure 3.8 for a closer view of this structure.) The Van Vechten farmhouse, along the river, was connected to the higher ground of Jefferson Heights—and thereby to Catskill Village—by a winding rural road, Snake Road, as illustrated in map 2.1.

This colonial farmhouse came to represent for Cole the values of an earlier agrarian culture, and it reappears in most of the series' works. It's possible that even in 1827 Cole had already begun to attribute these values to the house, because in his next Catskill Creek painting he clearly saw it as part of an idealized rural landscape. In any case, such an idealized landscape is already fully formed in *View Near the Village of Catskill*.

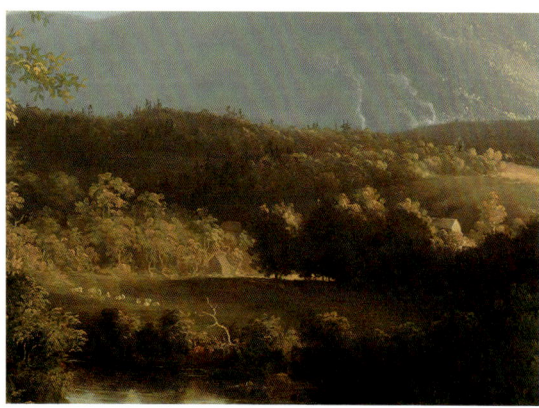

3.8 Detail of figure 3.3, *View Near the Village of Catskill*, 1827

Cole's rendering of Catskill Creek as a pond or lake, with a smooth and reflective surface, emphasizes the painting's specifically pastoral setting, with sheep grazing on both the foreground plateau and at the edge of the meadow below.

As I noted earlier, spires of smoke in the distance proceed from tanneries, but the artist paints them as delicate threads linking the plain to the mountains.[10] In the left foreground to the right of the framing tree, where in some of his other American landscapes we would find a stump, there is instead the natural ruin of a tree.[11] To its right it adjoins other natural forms, including rocks, sheep, foliage, and a second fragmented tree, to draw a long composite arc cradling the entire scene. Most important, as this elongated form curves upward at the far right, it encircles and draws our attention to two small figures almost hidden in shadow. Here we find a man and a woman, striding in unison away from us along what appears to be an earthen path, a path whose location suggests that Cole is referencing Snake Road (fig. 3.9).[12]

Images like this are rare in Cole's work. Human figures when they appear in his landscapes are often isolated or widely separated from one another, and we seldom find two of them in such intimate contact as is this couple.[13] True, Adam and Eve in *Expulsion from the Garden of Eden* (1828), painted in the same period as *View Near the Village of Catskill*, are hand in hand, but their grasp binds them to their mutual woe and shame, emotions seemingly alien to the Arcadian scene depicted in this work.

As in other Cole landscapes, however, the classical motif *Et in Arcadia ego* (Even in Arcadia there is death) makes itself felt here, though very subtly.[14] The lifeless fragment of a tree in the left foreground has its counterpart on the farther shore of the river below, where its leftward grasping shape is mirrored in a fully formed but thoroughly dead tree—painted so distantly and small that, like the couple, it's hard to find

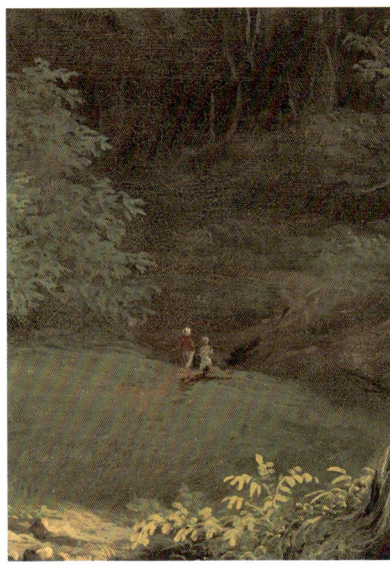

3.9 Detail of figure 3.3, *View Near the Village of Catskill*, 1827

(fig. 3.6; see also fig. 3.8). The doubling of forms is a pervasive feature of the Catskill Creek paintings—another example is the splayed locust in the foreground of *View Near the Village of Catskill*—and it serves in this work to reiterate an image of death. The sight line connecting these dead trees, one near and one far, is downward (though upward on the picture plane), like the path of the couple, who are about to disappear from our view over a mounded hill into the wooded valley below.

The valley itself, with its relatively undifferentiated mass of darkly forested space, is notable. Cole points to it with the curved, elongated form encircling the couple, and, as we will see, Catskill Creek paintings from later in the series contain similar pointers. Abruptly bordering and contrasting with the pond-like river, the smooth meadow, and the rolling field, this darkened sector of the composition—it fills most of the lower right quadrant—may suggest to some the contest between agriculture and wilderness that Cole would later dramatize in *The Oxbow*. As we saw earlier, in that work as here, Cole took a pervasively agrarian setting and introduced into it a *sense* of the wild.[15]

An American Adam and Eve

Given that the only human figures in *View Near the Village of Catskill* are taking long, purposeful strides downward into this landscape's darkened and hidden spaces, we may want to consider them, after all, an American Adam and Eve—and to think about this part of the composition as representing a wilderness of desire.[16] In these subtle ways, Cole brings love and death into his American Arcadia, or, to follow the biblical metaphor, into his Eden.

But if this is Eden, the moment portrayed here is prelapsarian—a kind of threshold moment that, as we will see, is characteristic of the scenes presented in the larger Catskill Creek series. To emphasize the darkness of *View Near the Village of Catskill*, except as an undercurrent, requires overturning the painting's pervading spirit of rural bliss. After all, if the path the man and woman are following leads to the Van Vechten farmhouse—and our map of this landscape suggests that this is the course they are following—then they can be seen to reflect the values of rural simplicity that Cole associated with this structure (map 2.1).

Cole's miniaturizing of the striding couple and of the dead tree in the valley literally diminishes the presence of love and death in *View Near the Village of Catskill* and thereby preserves the dominantly pastoral spirit of the painting. Indeed, the couple, once recognized, becomes an integral part of an idealized rural landscape. As with all the works in the Catskill Creek series, the larger composition holds the view in a pastoral framework, even as complicating motifs are quietly introduced through small embedded images that point in narrative directions without quite telling a story. This is, needless to say, a very different strategy from that of Cole's narrative-driven allegorical series like *The Voyage of Life* (figs. 2.1–2.4).

When *View Near the Village of Catskill* is understood as a pastoral, its figures become strangely premonitory. Seven years after completing this work, Cole met Maria Bartow, marrying her in 1836, and in that year made his home with her in the village, thus realizing in life the intimacy anticipated, or projected, by this painting. This history may bring to mind a later painting in the series, *View on the Catskill—Early Autumn* (1836–37), an overtly autobiographical work in which Cole represented an infant not yet conceived by him and Maria (fig. 4.19).[17] These images point toward an important oneiric dimension of the Catskill Creek paintings, which are, from one point of view, dream spaces—though in a completely different and far more personal sense than in a fanciful work like *The Architect's Dream* (1840).

View Near Catskill, 1828–29

When Cole began to paint the Catskill Creek scene again about a year after he had completed *View Near the Village of Catskill*, he followed the overall composition of the earlier work quite closely and gave it a similar title, *View Near Catskill* (1828–29) (fig. 3.10). But he changed the season from spring or summer to fall—a change whose significance we will consider later in this discussion—and he probably did sketch this scene during the fall of 1828, a year when he remained in Catskill beyond the summer in part to witness the autumnal color.[18] The sketch is unlocated, but on it the artist would characteristically have made descriptive notations about forms and colors, in this case taking special account of the hues of the brilliant red maples.

View Near Catskill, which today is in a private collection, was not completed for several more months, but Cole had it ready for the opening of the spring 1829 exhibition of the National Academy of Design. There it was listed as belonging to the Hudson Valley patroon Stephen Van Rensselaer III, one of Cole's important early patrons and one for whom the scene would have had special meaning. The painting had been commissioned by Van Rensselaer and his wife in the summer of 1828, as a pendant or companion work for Cole's *View on Lake Winnipesaukee* (1828), which they had purchased from him earlier that year. The couple had not been specific in their request for a pendant, asking Cole only for "one of your Catskill views" and mentioning nothing about the Catskill Creek scene.[19]

It's possible that even before the artist received the commission, he had been imagining a second version of this scene and that it came conveniently to mind when he was asked to render a Catskill view. In *View Near the Village of Catskill*, after all, he had painted the river as a lake, and Catskill Creek might have seemed to him especially suitable to place in company with a New Hampshire lake scene. Perhaps he even intended a cross-regional relationship between the paintings. Most important, however, Cole's rendering of Catskill Creek as a lake or pond in *View Near Catskill* links it to its predecessor in the series. Here, as in *View Near the Village of Catskill*, the river's oval surface is mirrored by the meadow beyond, and as before, the artist achieved this effect by limiting our view of Catskill Creek.

But the part of the river being represented in *View Near Catskill* is different from that of the earlier painting. Cole appears, in this second work in the series, to have shifted his vantage point significantly leftward (on the picture plane) to a more southern position on Jefferson Heights. In the earlier work we were looking up the meander's far (western) turn, and here we are seeing a portion of its near (eastern) side. After the river goes out of sight at the center right of the composition, in *View Near Catskill*, its upstream course sweeps rightward and then curves back to the left in the farther distance to form the pointbar. (See map 2.1.) Our view of the river at this farther point is blocked by intermediate landscape features,

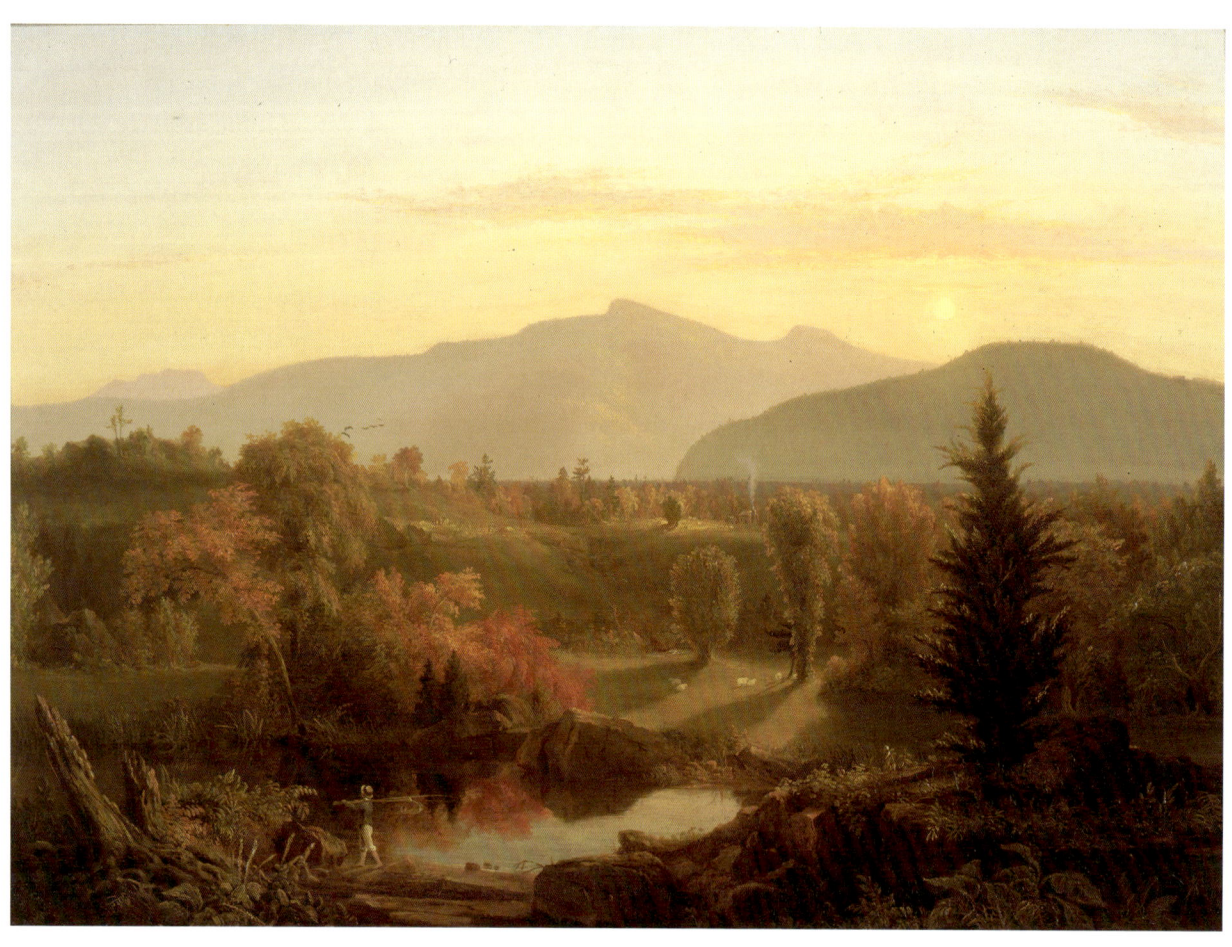

3.10 Thomas Cole, *View Near Catskill,* 1828–29. Oil on wood panel, 24¼ x 33¾ in. (61.6 x 85.7 cm). Private collection.

beyond which appears a rustic structure, positioned more or less where the Van Vechten farmhouse is located.

Map 2.1 shows the location of this farmhouse at the far westward end of the river's wide meander—where the house remains, beautifully restored, today—on the north shore. The pointbar, where sheep are grazing, is relatively shapeless in this painting, but it would gain full definition in the artist's two subsequent panoramic views of the scene, *View on the Catskill—Early Autumn* (fig. 4.19) and *River in the Catskills* (fig. 5.14).

Another later work in the series, *Settler's Home in the Catskills* (1842), will provide a close-up of the riverside scene where the Van Vechten farmhouse is located, just across the river from the pointbar (fig. 5.9). In that work, as in *View Near Catskill*, Cole hides the course of the river and thereby creates the illusion that the farmhouse is situated *on* the pointbar rather than across the river from it. This effect is very difficult to see in *View Near Catskill*, where the farmhouse is rendered distantly and small, but the detail in figure 3.11 gives a sense of it. In this detailed view we also find, to the left of the farmhouse, one of the Catskill Creek series' important motifs, a free-standing large tree with a broad, rounded crown. A maple or an oak, it will appear prominently in *View on the Catskill—Early Autumn* near the woman and infant in that work (fig. 4.19).

View Near Catskill thus begins to focus the Catskill Creek scene and it makes a clearer relation to later works in the series than did Cole's previous (1827) rendering of the scene, *View Near the Village of Catskill*. Nevertheless, in its freedom of expression and its lyricism *View Near Catskill* participates in the vision expressed by its predecessor and even extends that vision by simplifying its forms. For example, the multiple spires of smoke from tanneries in the earlier work are replaced in *View Near Catskill* by a

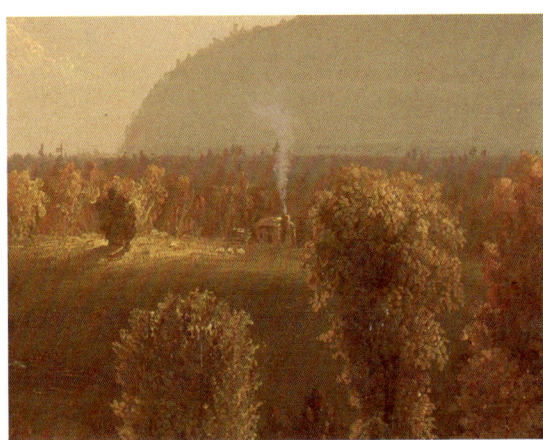

3.11 Detail of figure 3.9, *View Near Catskill*, 1828–29

single spire from the chimney of the farmhouse, flagging this structure as a symbol of American rural order and effacing signs of disruptive industry.

Crossing Over

Amplifying the idealized rural vision of *View Near Catskill* is a boy, at first hardly noticeable, with a fishing rod over his shoulder (fig. 3.12). His form is cradled by foreground elements in the same way as was the couple in the 1827 painting; a tall hemlock now rises up where they had strolled. He is crossing a plateau—again, Jefferson Heights—above the river, but because of the way Cole has telescoped his position, he is aligned with its shoreline. Of both land and water, the boy integrates the scene and belongs to it.

Yet in another way he does not. He is a transplant from another place, the Allegheny Mountains that Cole had traversed several years earlier (1819–23), soon after his emigration to the United States, when he himself was not much beyond boyhood. By his own account, his life in this period was ungrounded and deeply unsettling, and as Nancy Siegel has perceptively written, he appears to have been reviewing that experience in 1827. That year, as he was beginning to paint the Catskill Creek scene, the artist created from memory a drawing of a crude wooden bridge spanning a river in the Alleghenies; a boy with a fishing rod over his shoulder is crossing it. As Siegel has explained, the 1827 oil painting for which this drawing was preparation is lost.[20] But an extant work completed in the same year, with somewhat altered landscape features and titled *Crossing the Stream*, may have been inspired by the same scene (fig. 3.13). The

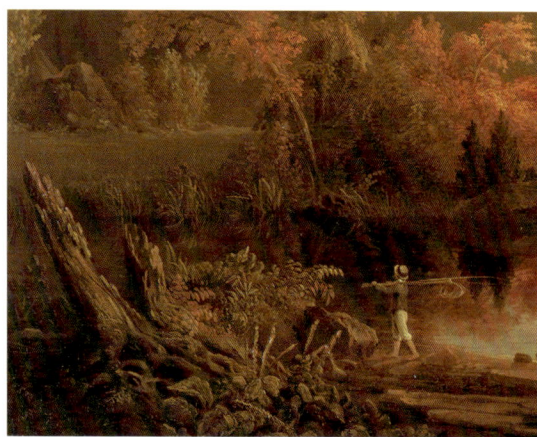

3.12 Detail of figure 3.10, *View Near Catskill*, 1828–29

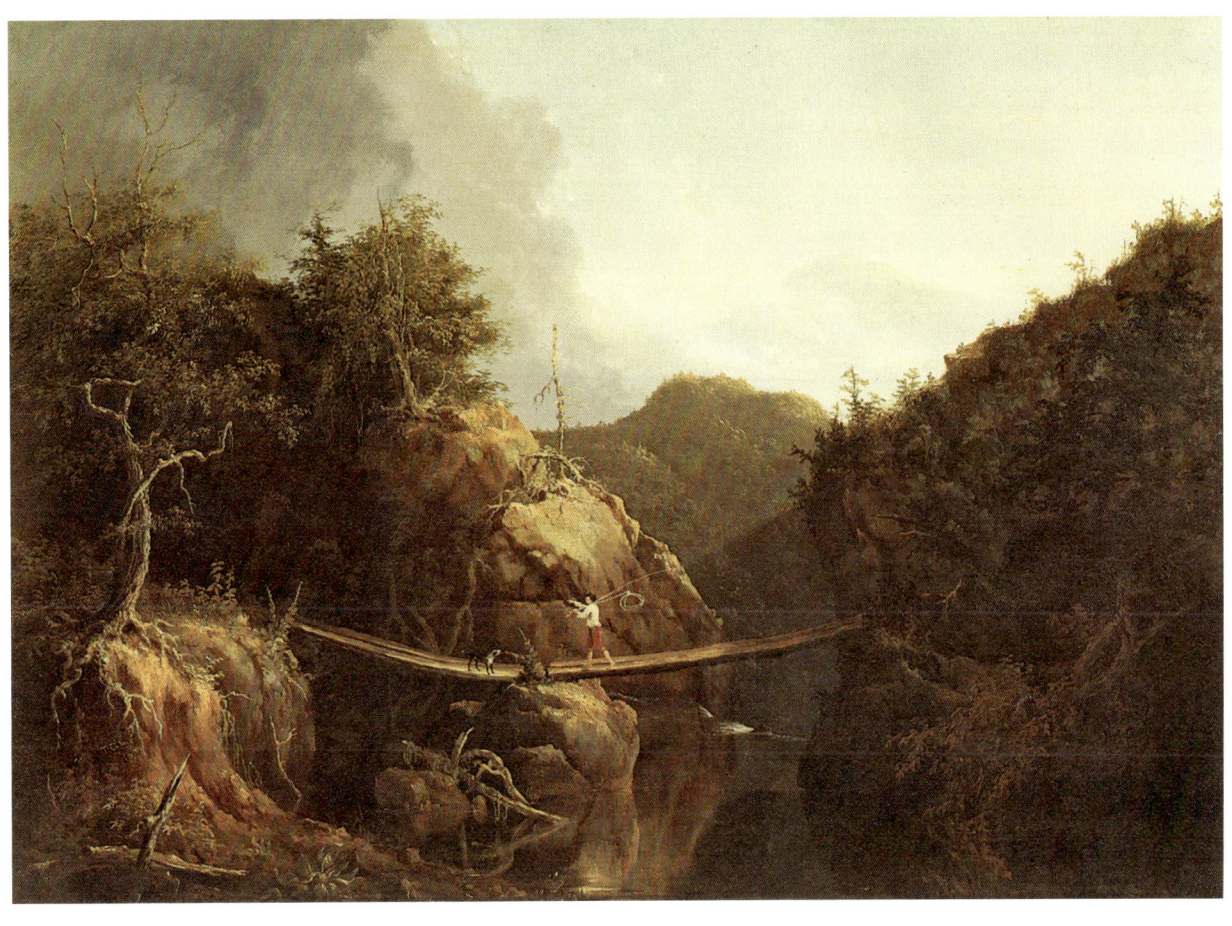

3.13 Thomas Cole, *Crossing the Stream*, 1827. Oil on wood panel, 24½ x 35 in. (62.2 x 88.9 cm). Jamee and Marshall Field Collection.

young fisherman in this work, as in *View Near Catskill*, is moving right to left and in almost every other aspect—including the fishing hoop dangling from the end of his pole—he mirrors the figure in the Catskill Creek painting.

The boy in *Crossing the Stream*, as the title of the work makes clear, is central to the meaning of the painting, whereas his counterpart in *View Near Catskill*—rendered so much smaller in relation to the surrounding landscape—could be considered but one of several rural motifs. Yet Cole's transplanting of this boy on a bridge in the Alleghenies into his Catskill Creek scene may be significant. Bridges and bridge-like structures appear frequently in his work—in his poems and prose sketches as well as his paintings—and they are most often associated with peril. They are bridges of fear, to call up the titles of two drawings that Cole made in the same period that he was painting *Crossing the Stream*, and they bring attention more to the chasms they unreliably span than to their support.[21]

The gracefully dipping, sunlit bridge in *Crossing the Stream* seems secure, but it is leading the boy into an uncertain realm. The side of the river toward which he is moving so eagerly and expectantly has a cavern-like aspect (is his dog barking a warning?) and is overarched by a gnarled tree, with storm clouds overhead. These elements of the sublime in a landscape otherwise characterized by the beautiful may represent a transition from one state of being to another whose darker meanings the boy, in his innocence, does not yet recognize.

The experience of "crossing over" had intensely felt meanings for Cole, and every one of the subsequent Catskill Creek paintings has a rower—almost always crossing the stream rather than following its course, as does the figure in his allegory *The Voyage of Life*. Crossing and voyaging were closely related in the artist's religious imagination; both could dramatize the idea of departure and arrival along a spiritual journey. But crossing for Cole was inflected somewhat differently than voyaging was; as later paintings in the Catskill Creek series suggest, crossing a river—and especially being at midstream—was for him a kind of threshold experience, an experience of uncertainty or expectation without the linear clarity of a voyage toward a final end.

A European Presence

Both *Crossing the Stream* and *View Near Catskill* have specifically American landscapes as their subjects, and, as we have seen, the 1820s was a period when Cole was learning how to give national meaning to his works. Like its predecessor in the series, *View Near*

Catskill references the Catskill Mountain House—this time with just a tiny uplift along the darkened profile of South Mountain (very near the painting's right-hand border), a subtle but an unmistakable cultural marker.

There is one element in *View Near Catskill*, however, that does not seem American. This is the formal row of Lombardy poplars, casting long shadows, in the meadow near the river's shoreline and to the right of the red maples. Such poplars were introduced into the United States only forty years before Cole painted this picture, and they bring into his American scene a European presence. Their appearance in this painting can be read as a reference to Claude Lorrain's pastoral landscapes and perhaps to the artist's pleasurable anticipation of his approaching grand tour (1829–32), which he would undertake in June of 1829 soon after exhibiting *View Near Catskill*—providing a glimpse into his future.

These mature poplars do not appear in *View Near the Village of Catskill*, painted the previous year, nor does the large hemlock growing in the spot where the couple in the earlier work had strolled. Both the poplars and the hemlock are probably fanciful. They belong to the work's freedom of conception and suggest a level of improvisation unusual among the Catskill Creek paintings. For example, unique to this work among these paintings is its subordination of the undulating profile of Kaaterskill High Peak and Roundtop, in the left distance, to South Mountain—rendered here as a dark, imposing, and monolithic form. Part of the effect is caused by the fact that in this painting, as compared with *View Near the Village of Catskill*, Cole has drawn the boundaries of the composition inward and thereby proportionately made all its landscape features larger. But this effect is most pronounced with South Mountain.

Cole appears to have "discovered" South Mountain while creating *View Near Catskill*—on many days of the year its outline against the more distant and taller mountains, as viewed from Catskill Village, is hard to see—and experimented with making it the dominant feature of his composition. Never again in the series, however, would he so dramatically foreground and deeply shadow this mountain. In these various ways, *View Near Catskill* is more deliberately experimental, even playful, in its treatment of individual elements—especially its inventions and substitutions—than was the earlier work.

But the most pronounced differences in the treatment of landscape between Cole's 1827 and 1828–29 renderings of Catskill Creek are the season and the time of day. In the latter work, the fiery maples and the long shadows of the poplars depict a sunset in early autumn. The sun itself, which does not appear in *View Near the Village of Catskill*, is visible now, set in the notch separating Roundtop from South Mountain—and advancing along its southward march toward the winter solstice. The dramatic contrast between South Mountain's dark tone and the surrounding landscape may have been inspired by the painting's sunset motif.

This movement from spring or summer into fall and the transition from an ambiguously auroral setting to an explicitly sunset view suggest the possibility that Cole was considering the development of a series based upon diurnal and seasonal progression, a possibility supported by individual elements in the two works. For example, the large splayed locust on the far left of the 1827 painting has been replaced in the later work by a foreshortened dead tree with the same doubled structure (fig. 3.12). (That this transition involved the virtual elimination of a Claudian framing tree shows just how experimental *View Near Catskill* is.) And the mullein whose vigorous spring or summer growth was highlighted in the earlier work are here diminished and visually subdued by background elements, appearing near a large rock just to the left of the young fisherman (fig. 3.12).

Cole's 1827 sketchbook list includes a number of ideas for seasonal and diurnal series, and the concept is clearly one that interested him. One of these notations reads in full, "Seasons—each picture represents the same scene."[22] Had he continued to paint Catskill Creek in the later 1820s and the early 1830s, he might have left behind a full revolution of its days and seasons. But soon after the 1829 exhibition that included *View Near Catskill*, Cole departed on his first European tour, lasting three and a half years and transforming his life and art. When he painted Catskill Creek again in 1833, more than four years after his previous treatment of it, whatever ideas he might have had about such a progression had been abandoned.

Chapter Four

Taking a Different View

On June 1, 1829, Thomas Cole departed for England on the first of his two European tours. Fewer than four years had passed since his discovery by the American art world, yet he sailed out of New York Harbor a cultural hero for his achievements in landscape painting. The moment was not unlike that of his friend Cooper's three years before when the novelist—fresh from the enormous success of his *Last of the Mohicans* (1826)—sailed to Europe on his own extended tour. The degree to which Cole, by now, was perceived as a thoroughly American artist (despite his emigration to the United States just eleven years earlier) is expressed in a sonnet written to him at this time by Bryant, "To Cole the Painter on his Departure for Europe":

> Thine eyes shall see the light of distant skies:
> Yet, COLE! thy heart shall bear to Europe's strand
> A living image of thy native land,
> Such as on thy own glorious canvass lies.
> Lone lakes—savannas where the bison roves—
> Rocks rich with summer garlands—solemn streams—
> Skies, where the desert eagle wheels and screams—
> Spring bloom and autumn blaze of boundless groves.

Fair scenes shall greet thee where thou goest—fair,
But different—everywhere the trace of men,
Paths, homes, graves, ruins, from the lowest glen
To where life shrinks from the fierce Alpine air.
Gaze on them, till the tears shall dim thy sight,
But keep that earlier, wilder image bright.[1]

Cole's two years in England (June 1829–May 1831) appear to have disappointed him. The fame he had won in the United States did not impress an artistic world dominated by the great English painters John Constable and J. M. W. Turner, and Cole felt unappreciated. But his subsequent year and a half in Italy (May 1831–October 1832) were deeply rewarding and productive. In Florence and in Rome he found supportive communities of American artists, he took drawing classes that improved his ability to render the human form, and he painted a wide range of subjects including biblical scenes and Italian landscapes. The high point appears to have occurred for him during the summer of 1832, which he later reported to Dunlap was the happiest and most productive time in his life up to that point.[2]

Not long thereafter, however, Cole's worries about his parents during a cholera threat in New York drew him home. When he arrived there in late November of 1832 the votes that would elect Andrew Jackson to his second presidential term were still being counted, and it must have seemed to the artist that the United States of the 1830s was a very different place from the country he had left at the end of the 1820s. Indeed, the previous summer Jackson had vetoed the renewal of the Second Bank of the United States, causing many to fear destabilization of the national economy.

One important dimension of the social and economic changes occurring in this period is a shift in Cole's patronage relationships.[3] As we have seen, the Hudson Valley patroon Stephen Van Rensselaer III had purchased the artist's second Catskill Creek painting in 1829, the year he traveled to Europe. But the purchaser of Cole's next work in the series, completed soon after his return, was a dry goods merchant, Luman Reed. Cole made the most of his relationship with Reed, who supported the artist with numerous important commissions, including that for *The Course of Empire*. Eighteen thirty-six was the year in which Cole completed both *The Course of Empire* and *The Oxbow*, and in 1839–40 he painted *The Voyage of Life* (first set). These and many other notable works from the 1830s show that this decade, despite the uncertainties of the times, was an immensely productive period for Cole.

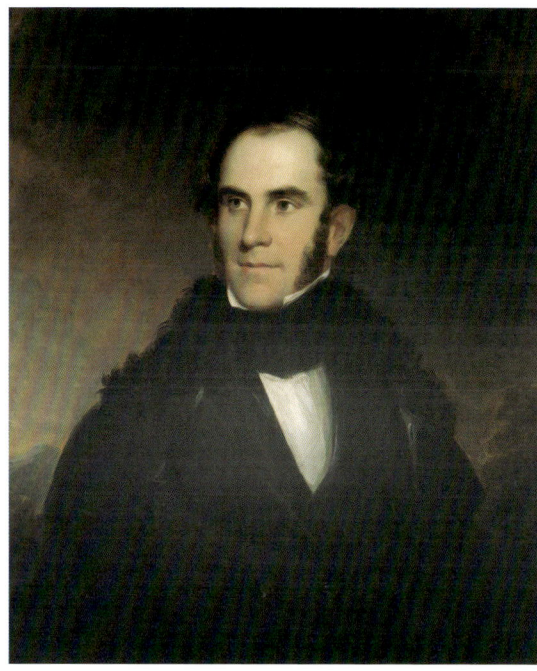

The four Catskill Creek paintings completed during this decade reflect both the uncertainties of these years and the artist's achievement during them. *View on the Catskill—Early Autumn* (1836–37) is the most notable and ambitious of these works, but alongside Cole's conception and development of this important painting came a striking subset of the Catskill Creek landscapes—a three-part series within the larger series. Two of these works precede *View on the Catskill—Early Autumn* and the other one follows it, but they form an integral unit, even as they project and reflect upon the larger painting.

Sunset, View on the Catskill, 1833

The first of these three works, *Sunset, View on the Catskill*, was completed in 1833 not long after Cole's return from Europe and, as I have noted, was among the first paintings that the artist sold to Reed. It is now in the collection of the New-York Historical Society. *Sunset, View on the Catskill* is painted on wood panel, linking it to the Catskill Creek landscapes of the 1820s (and other works from that decade), though this is his last painting in the series on this surface (fig. 4.2). A more enduring continuity between

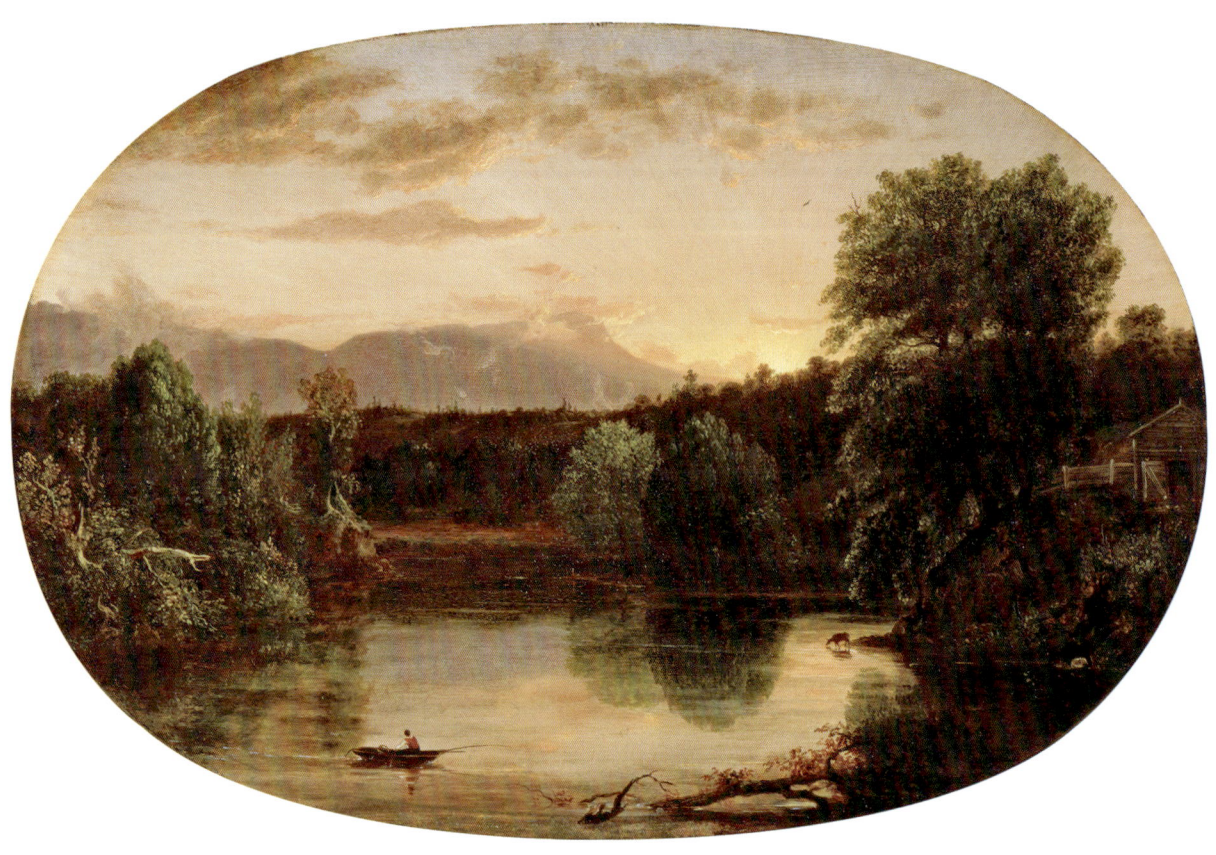

4.2 Thomas Cole, *Sunset, View on the Catskill*, 1833.
Oil on wood panel, 16½ x 24½ in. (41.9 x 62.2 cm),
New-York Historical Society, gift of the New York
Gallery of the Fine Arts (1858.44).

Cole's works of the two decades is his depiction, in the 1833 painting, of a sunset scene, which had characterized the 1828–29 *View Near Catskill*.

But the scene is now more formally organized than in the earlier work, reflecting the artist's direct exposure abroad to the art of Claude Lorrain. Perhaps it is the Claudian influence that fixed the Catskill Creek landscape in a sunset mode, which characterizes most of the subsequent works in the series. The title *Sunset, View on the Catskill* makes the mode explicit, not only in its naming of the time of day but also in its shift of prepositions. Rather than the place-oriented phrase "view near Catskill" in the titles of the series' first two paintings, we have "view *on* the Catskill," a change that implies a more framed and distanced, European view of landscape than was true of the 1820s works.

What may be surprising is that Cole, soon after rapturously experiencing the art and dramatic scenery of Italy, applied his Claudian vision to so modest an American scene as Catskill Creek. It didn't have the historical associations he found in some other American landscapes and would celebrate in his "Essay on American Scenery," nor did it express the intense drama of his earlier scenes of the American wilderness. Nevertheless, Catskill Creek held its place in Cole's imagination.

As if to underscore the point, he created—probably also in 1833—another Catskill Creek scene virtually identical, in both size and composition, to Reed's (fig. 4.3). At about 16½ x 24 inches, these are the two smallest of the Catskill Creek paintings; both, as noted earlier, were formatted by the artist for oval frames. Unsigned, undated, and untitled, the replica was found in Cole's studio after his death. Nothing in the existing provenance information for this work, which now resides in the Albany Institute of History and Art, explains why it was created and why it may never have been sold.[4]

Cole probably painted the replica while the original was still in his possession, in 1833, rather than later, when he would have had to borrow it back from Reed. One difference between the works is that Reed's is painted on wood panel, whereas the other one is on composition board, a difference that could suggest that the latter is a preliminary study and not a replica. But it seems unlikely that Cole would have made so careful an oil study for so small a landscape, scaled identically.

However the Albany painting came into being, its mere existence, given the degree to which Cole resisted copying his own works, is notable. As one commentator has suggested, it may have been produced out of the artist's special satisfaction with the

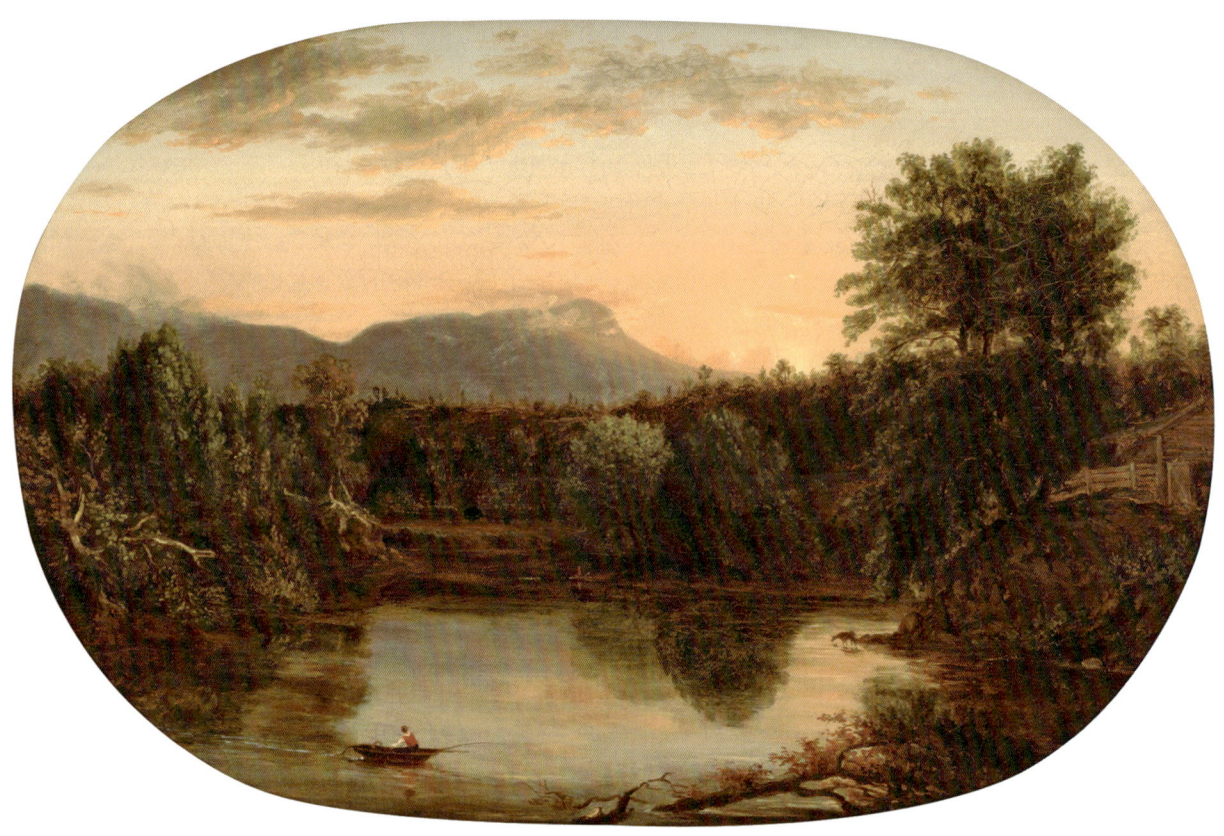

4.3 Thomas Cole, *View of Catskill Creek* (formerly *Distant View of Roundtop*) c. 1833. Oil on composition board, 17 x 25 in. (43.2 x 63.5 cm). Albany Institute of History and Art Purchase, Evelyn Newman Fund (1964.70).

composition; perhaps he wanted one for himself, an explanation that accords with what we know of his attachment to the scene represented in the original painting.[5]

But a functional purpose for this work also comes to mind: as a careful model for future depictions of the same scene. In 1838, five years after Cole painted *Sunset, View on the Catskill* and its replica, he produced another, more accomplished and significantly larger work (26⁷⁄₁₆ x 36⁷⁄₁₆ inches) unmistakably based on their composition. Its arched frame also links it to the earlier works, with their oval frames (fig. 4.4).

This painting is now in the collection of the Yale University Art Gallery, and David Steinberg, who oversaw Yale's acquisition of it in 1981, makes a compelling argument that the two 1833 paintings and this one from 1838 are tightly interwoven parts of the same project. He believes that the Yale painting was developed for a commission (the original owner is unknown), as an "assemblage of elements from [these] earlier versions," and it is certainly true that the three paintings form a group compositionally distinct within the Catskill Creek series.[6]

A Riverside Perspective

One important aspect of these paintings' distinctiveness, however, has gone unnoticed: they are the only works in the series that take a northwesterly view of the Catskill Front, and the mountain profile they depict is entirely different from that of the other seven paintings. All the others look southwesterly toward Kaaterskill High Peak, Roundtop, South Mountain, and the southern end of North Mountain. While the sharp bend of Catskill Creek and the broad pointbar created by this meander remain Cole's compositional anchor in these works—as they are in all ten of the Catskill Creek paintings—his view of the mountains has swiveled northward along the escarpment almost ten miles. The peak in the background of the two 1833 works and Yale's 1838 painting is Blackhead Mountain. Its distinctive leftward slope is delineated with special clarity in the Yale painting and in an 1833 Cole sketch (fig. 4.5) that, along with another of his drawings (fig. 4.6), may stand behind Reed's version of the scene.

This shift involved the artist's finding a vantage point along the shore of Catskill Creek, a third of a mile southward from and considerably lower than the panoramic Jefferson Heights perspective he had taken in the 1820s works; the two vantage points are illustrated by map 2.1. Map 4.1 (which does not illustrate the replica) shows how Cole's new, shoreline view looked upriver toward the northern part of the Catskill

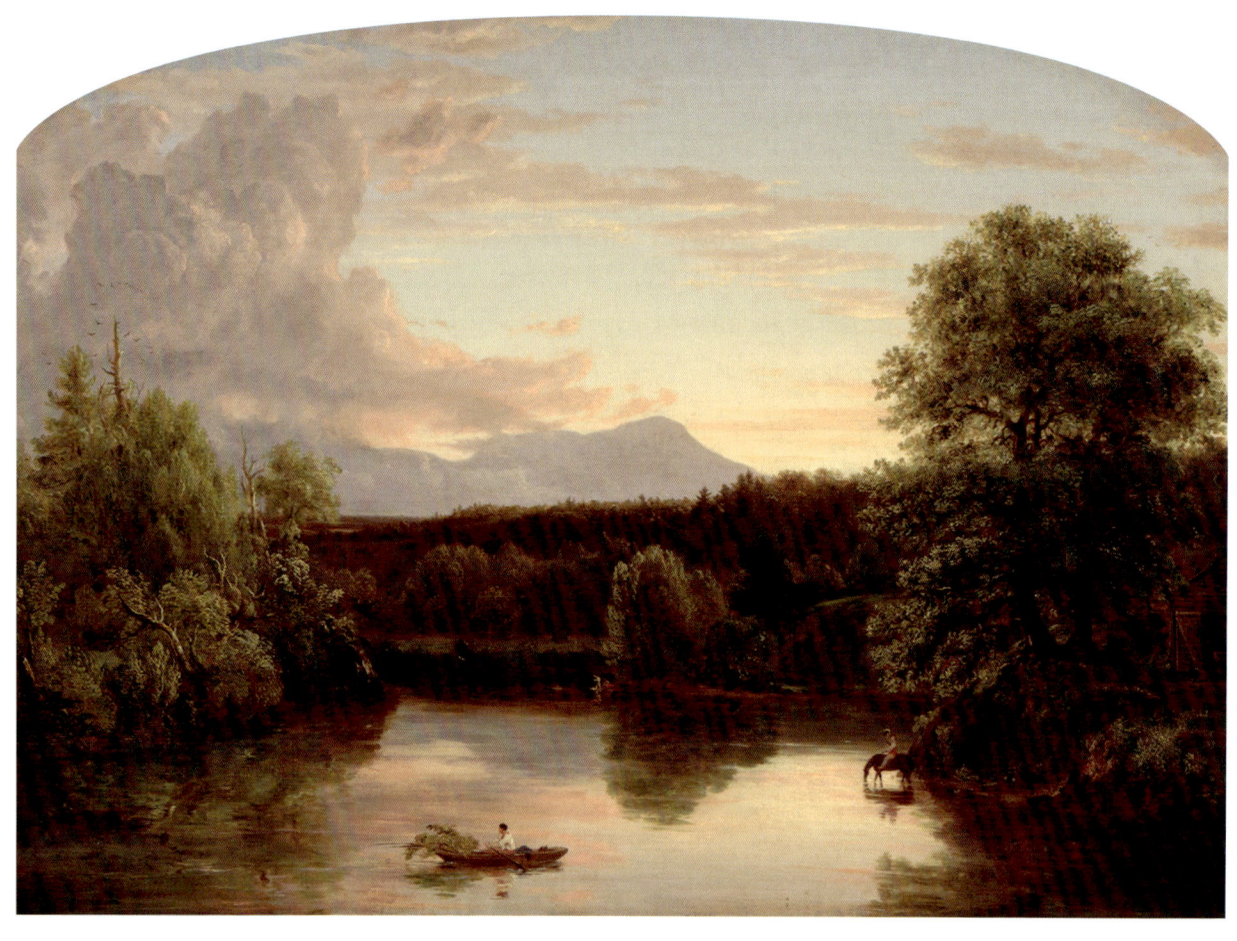

4.4 Thomas Cole, *North Mountain and Catskill Creek,*
1838. Oil on canvas, 26⁷⁄₁₆ x 36⁷⁄₁₆ in. (67.2 x 92.6 cm).
Yale University Art Gallery, gift of Anne Osborn
Prentice (1981.56).

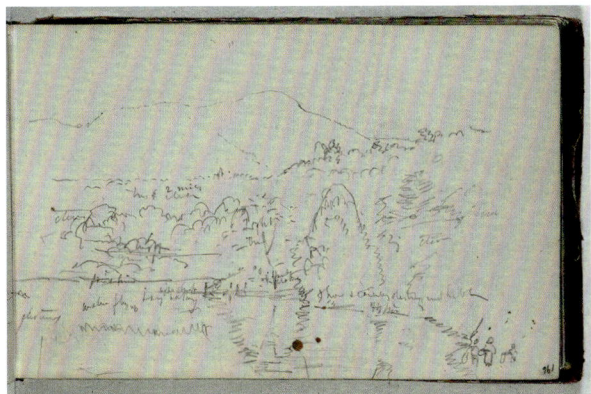

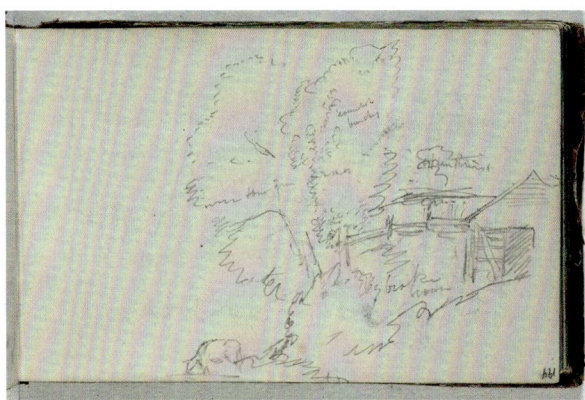

4.5 Thomas Cole, (Untitled, landscape study), c. 1833. Graphite pencil on off-white wove paper, sheet: 4⅛ x 6½ in. (10.5 x 16.5 cm). Detroit Institute of Arts, Founders Society Purchase, William H. Murphy Fund (39.567.196).

4.6 Thomas Cole, (Untitled), c. 1833. Graphite pencil on off-white wove paper, sheet: 4⅛ x 6½ in. (10.5 x 16.5 cm). Detroit Institute of Arts, Founders Society Purchase, William H. Murphy Fund (39.567.194).

Front, with Blackhead at its center and Windham High Peak curving eastward and farther northward beyond it.[7] Today tall trees block the artist's view from this riverside location, but the photograph in figure 4.7, taken from a drone above the tree line, approximates it.

Most subsequent paintings in the Catskill Creek series continue to have a shoreline perspective, resulting in a more intimate and less panoramic vision than that of works with Jefferson Heights as their vantage point. This vision may have been inspired, in part, by the "picturesque" landscape aesthetics of William Gilpin, whose influence on Cole we considered earlier in relation to his first sketches of scenes in the Hudson River Valley. As Earl A. Powell III has written, Gilpin, who proposed the picturesque as an alternative to Edmund Burke's dichotomous categories of the sublime and the beautiful, "believed that the most worthwhile place to search for picturesque scenery was along the banks of rivers."[8]

Cole's altered, northward view of the Catskills in the 1833 and 1838 paintings has gone unnoticed perhaps because of the mistitling of both the replica of Reed's painting and the Yale painting. When the replica was first exhibited in the 1960s, the title *Distant View of Roundtop, Catskill* was attributed to it, and when the Yale painting later came to light, it was given the title *North Mountain and Catskill Creek*. But the mountains named in these titles are nowhere to be seen in these works.[9] Perhaps interpretations from the mid-twentieth century linking Cole's career closely with American

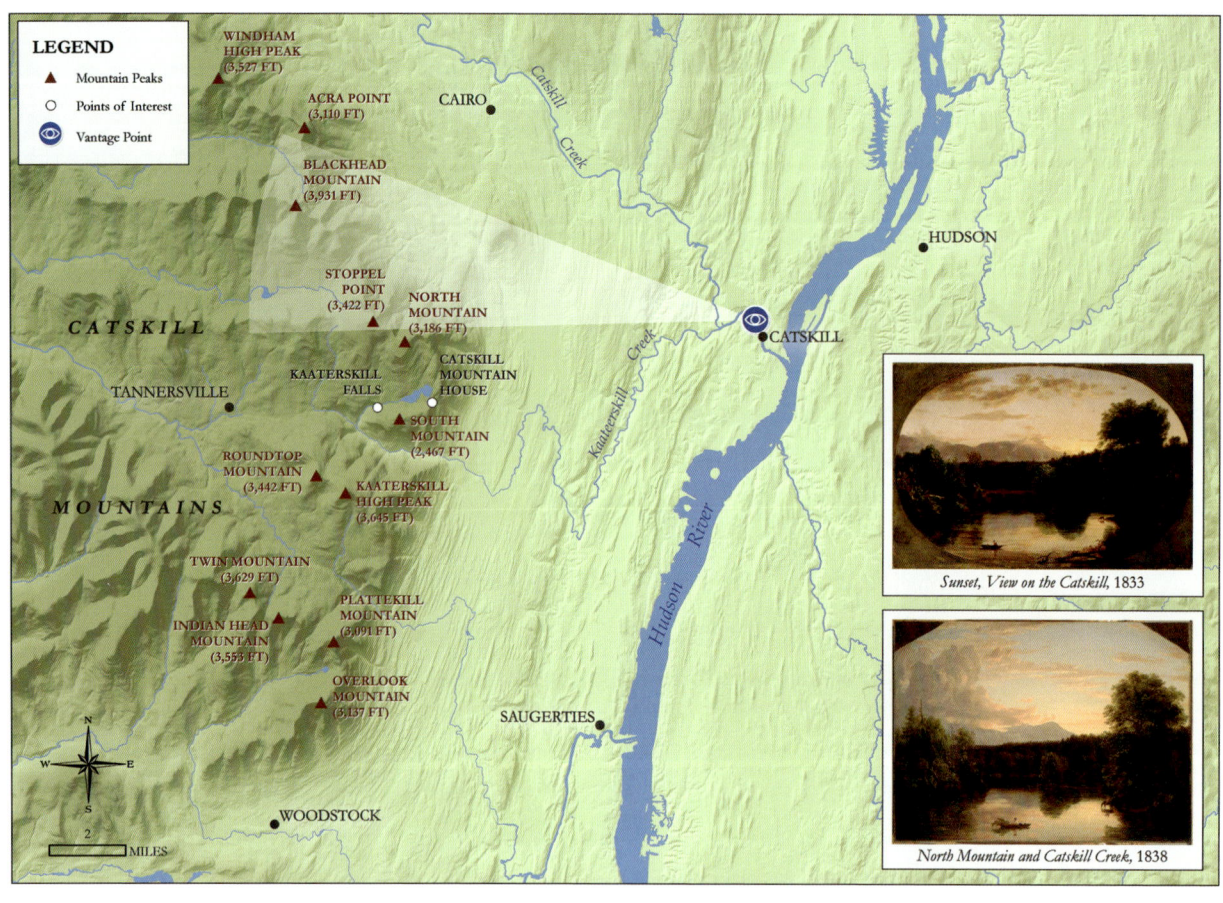

Legend:

LEGEND
- ▲ Mountain Peaks
- ○ Points of Interest
- ◉ Vantage Point

WINDHAM
HIGH PEAK
(3,527 FT)

ACRA POINT
(3,110 FT)

CAIRO

Catskill Creek

BLACKHEAD
MOUNTAIN
(3,931 FT)

HUDSON

STOPPEL
POINT
(3,422 FT)

NORTH
MOUNTAIN
(3,186 FT)

C A T S K I L L

CATSKILL

KAATERSKILL
FALLS

CATSKILL
MOUNTAIN
HOUSE

TANNERSVILLE

SOUTH
MOUNTAIN
(2,467 FT)

Kaaterskill Creek

ROUNDTOP
MOUNTAIN
(3,442 FT)

KAATERSKILL
HIGH PEAK
(3,645 FT)

M O U N T A I N S

TWIN MOUNTAIN
(3,629 FT)

PLATTEKILL
MOUNTAIN
(3,091 FT)

Hudson River

INDIAN HEAD
MOUNTAIN
(3,553 FT)

OVERLOOK
MOUNTAIN
(3,137 FT)

SAUGERTIES

N
W   E
S

2
MILES

WOODSTOCK

Sunset, View on the Catskill, 1833

North Mountain and Catskill Creek, 1838

Map 4.1 Viewscape of *Sunset, View on the Catskill* (1833), *View of Catskill Creek* (not shown) (c. 1833), and *North Mountain and Catskill Creek* (1838). The works are not scaled to size. Map by Neil Curri.

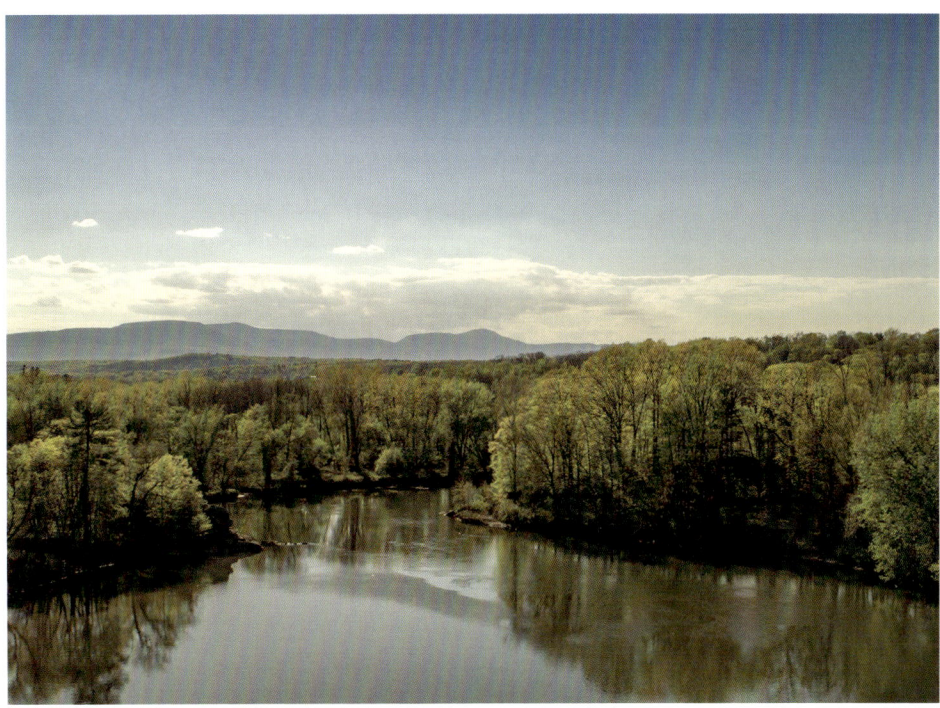

national identity led viewers, in that period, to see the mountain forms in the 1833 and 1838 paintings as imprecise renderings of Roundtop and North Mountain. The latter borders the Catskill Mountain House, located on the bluff from which Cooper's Leatherstocking hero in *The Pioneers* (1823) claimed he could see "all creation." Cole's accurate rendering of an entirely different mountain confirms, for one thing, that in creating the Catskill Creek paintings he was being faithful to the landforms he saw, and that a certain kind of realism is embedded in their conception and execution.

Despite the compositional departure of the 1833 and 1838 Catskill Creek paintings from those of the 1820s, they are linked—across the divide of Cole's first European tour—by their enigmatic and complicated deployment of human figures in the landscape. Now the couple and the young fisherman are gone, having been replaced in the foreground by a rower. He will appear in all the subsequent Catskill Creek paintings, and the repetition of his form lends to the series a figural continuity. In other words, what might have been understood before as mere staffage asserts itself through repetition as a motif. In fact, there is little in the Catskill Creek paintings—or in Cole's work overall—that is incidental or solely conventional. We should take very seriously what he wrote to his patron Daniel Wadsworth in 1828: "It is always my intention to introduce nothing in a picture for which I cannot give a good reason."[10]

The Experience of Rivers

With the introduction of the rower into the series comes a clarification of the river's form. In the two Catskill Creek paintings from the 1820s, the body of water, ambiguously a pond or lake or river, was but one of several discrete topographical features of more or less equal compositional weight. Now it has found its distinctive form as a river and in doing so has opened an exploration into human experience associated with rivers. As I have noted, however, the mode of experience explored in the Catskill Creek paintings is very different from that of Cole's allegorical river series, *The Voyage of Life*. In all but one of the eight Catskill Creek paintings in which the rower is present, he is crossing—or in one case has just crossed—from one shore to the other, rather than voyaging the stream. (*View on the Catskill—Early Autumn* is the significant exception.) His lateral movement conveys a different set of meanings than does *The Voyage of Life*, where the figure in the boat, having no motive power of his own, is carried inexorably downriver to the sea (figs. 2.1–2.4).

This is the difference between freedom and fate, desire and destiny. The solace of Cole's allegory, despite the vicissitudes dramatized by its serial development, is the inevitability of its outcome; the river's currents run in only one direction. In contrast, the Catskill Creek series depicts a world of crosscurrents. The rower can be found in various postures and positions—purposefully pulling at his oars as he crosses the stream (in both directions), drifting in apparent contemplation on its surface, and landing on its shore; variability is part of the series' meaning. His reappearances from one painting to the next—always on the same reach of water, the same field of action—can be characterized as creative reiteration rather than as narrative development.

In both the 1833 and 1838 works, the rower is crossing the stream left to right. The 1833 paintings show him looking over his shoulder toward his destination on the northern shore, where there is a cow drinking from the river. Hanging off the prow is a fishing pole, and at the rower's feet is a basket (with a hooped handle and a beaded rim), an object whose meanings will aggregate during the course of the Catskill Creek series. In the 1838 work the rower, like his counterpart in the 1833 paintings, is positioned at the midpoint of his river crossing, and he too is pulling strenuously on his oars. The 1838 painting shows, in the same position as the cow in the 1833 works, an unsaddled horse drinking from the river, and astride the horse is a man waving his hat in a greeting to the rower (figs. 4.8–4.11). Both versions of the scene include, on the northern shore, a shed or small barn on a steep, rounded outcrop—a landscape feature Cole has rendered with topographical accuracy (figs. 4.2 and 4.4).[11] Map 2.1 identifies the location of this outcrop.

Just forward of the rower in the work from 1838 are a jug and a blue jacket; at the other end of the boat is a full load of willows, misidentified in some commentaries as rushes, which do not have long stalks such as those protruding off the stern in this picture.[12] Willows were used widely in rural America during the nineteenth century—and indeed for millennia by Native Americans—for making baskets; as we saw, a carefully delineated basket is represented at the rower's feet in the 1833 painting.

In that work and the one from 1838 as well, large willow trees centered in the middle distance on a point projecting from the right shoreline are highlighted in light green against the darker background foliage. With our attention drawn to them, we are asked implicitly to consider a relationship between these willows and the rower, and his role in synthesizing them into an artifact. On one level, he represents the simple, agrarian life that Cole wanted to associate with Catskill Creek, but on another he may stand in for the artist and for the activity of making art. Thoreau's well-known parable of the Indian basket in *Walden* ("I too had woven a kind of basket of a delicate texture") comes to mind.[13]

These willows, given so central a position in the composition, are made even more prominent by the magnifying effect of their deep reflections; the Catskill Creek paintings of the 1830s are notable for the way they introduce reflections, as an important motif, into the series. They are, in part, an aspect of the heightened Claudian aesthetic that Cole brought back from Europe, but they also reinforce the pervasive doubling of forms in these works. Reflections intensify the meanings of key images by mirroring them. For example, all the works in the series beginning with those from 1833—there is one telling exception, a work titled *River in the Catskills* (1843)—show reflections of the distant mountains in the river and thereby deepen the spirituality that Cole attributed to these Catskill peaks.[14] At the same time, through the traditional association of reflectivity with contemplation, reflections work to quiet this landscape—to stabilize the artist's emerging vision of Catskill Creek.

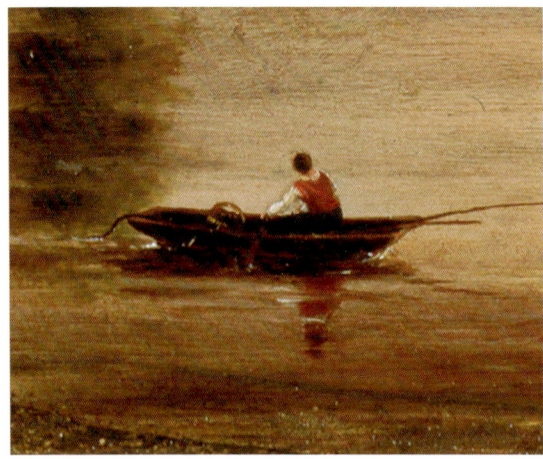

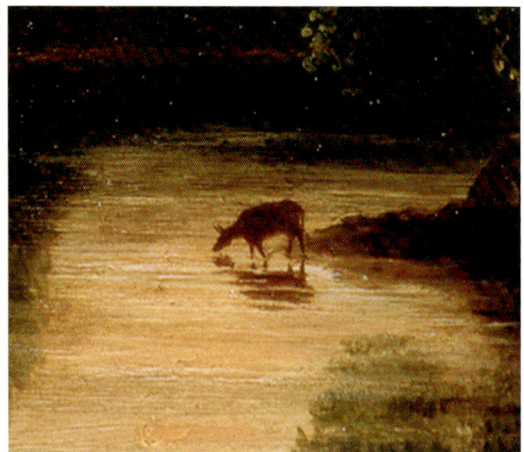

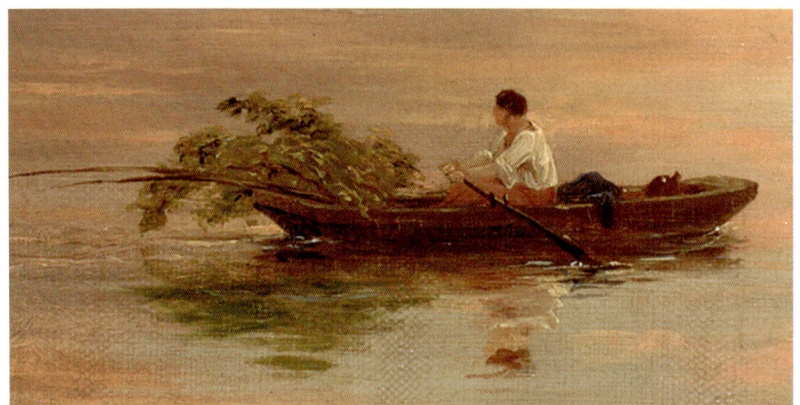

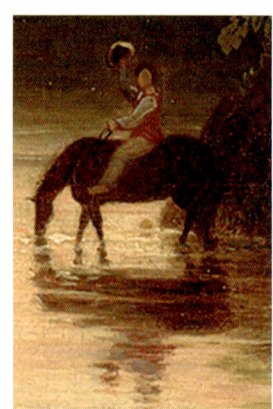

4.8 Detail of figure 4.2, *Sunset, View on the Catskill*, 1833

4.9 Detail of figure 4.2, *Sunset, View on the Catskill*, 1833

4.10 Detail of figure 4.4, *North Mountain and Catskill Creek*, 1838

4.11 Detail of figure 4.4, *North Mountain and Catskill Creek*, 1838

Figures from the Past

The rowers in the 1833 and 1838 paintings are linked, through their identification with American rural life, to the strolling couple and the young fisherman of the 1827 and 1828–29 Catskill Creek paintings. Like those figures, these rowers belong to Cole's own present experience of Catskill, at least to an idealized version of this community as the artist envisioned it in the 1820s and early 1830s. But on a point farther up the river in the 1833 painting (see the location designated as "Point" in map 2.1), painted in miniature, we find another human figure who does not belong to Cole's present. Here, standing alone on this point overhung by willows, and looking out over the water, is the haunting image of a woman in colonial dress (fig. 4.12). Her Martha Washington-style mobcap places her historically, and her yellow bodice covering her full red dress associates her with rural life. (In the rougher 1833 replica, this figure is but a dash of color.) The woman's distance from the rower—he is not looking toward her nor she toward him—can be read as the historical distance separating them.

In exactly the same place in the 1838 painting we find a man, his breeches identifying him too as a colonial figure, and immediately behind him is a Native American clad in loincloth, squatting, with a red blanket behind him (fig. 4.13).[15] All the Catskill Creek paintings depend for their organization on spatial recession, but in

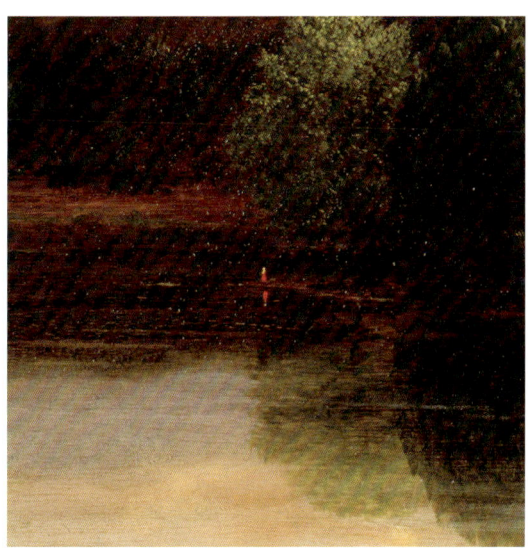

4.12 Detail of figure 4.2, *Sunset, View on the Catskill*, 1833

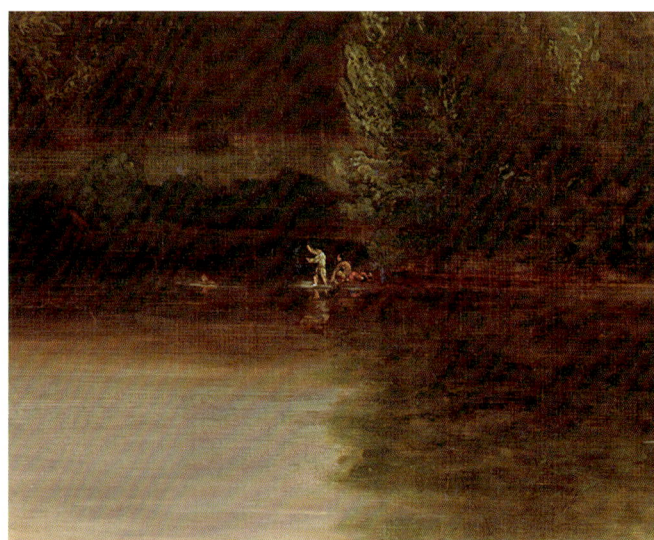

4.13 Detail of figure 4.4, *North Mountain and Catskill Creek*, 1838

these works we have temporal recession as well. To look upriver is to look into the past of this landscape, toward both the era of Dutch colonial settlement (the Van Vechten house is a short distance upstream from the point on which these figures are positioned) and its deeper Native American past. According to a local legend that Cole may have known, a large Iroquois settlement preceding the Dutch lay just upriver, at the nearby confluence of Catskill and Kaaterskill Creeks.[16] (See map 2.1.) Thus, the 1833 and the 1838 paintings work in two temporal dimensions; the trajectory of their (lateral) river crossings, in the present, intersects their recessional alignment with the past.

The figures in the deep background of these works are rendered so small—smaller even than the couple in the 1827 painting—that it's hard to see what they're doing. The white man on the distant point, in the work from 1838, has his right arm raised, in the manner of the horseman's greeting (another instance of doubling), and he appears to be holding a fishing rod and trying to haul in a very large catch, perhaps one of the gigantic sturgeons for which the Hudson River and its bays were once famous. What appear to be two huge, bulging eyes suggest that the artist meant to depict something nonhuman. In some of Cole's works, miniature figures serve clear thematic purposes. An example is the boy drawing a figure on the surface of a stone bridge in *The Pastoral State* of *The Course of Empire* series (fig. 4.14). He is rendered very small, but once we see him and what he is doing, he augments for us the idea of a civilization in the beginning stages of the arts and sciences.[17]

With such images, Cole was following in a tradition, long established in Western art, of accessory motifs, or *parerga*, which indirectly supported an art work's central

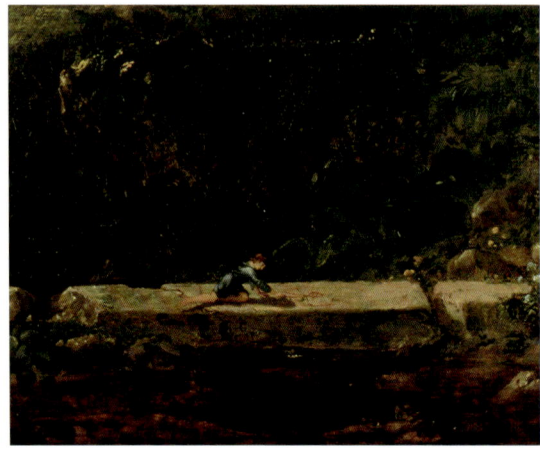

4.14 Detail of figure 1.3, *The Course of Empire: The Arcadian or Pastoral State,* 1834. Oil on canvas, 39¼ x 63¼ in. (99.7 x 160.7 cm). New-York Historical Society, gift of the New York Gallery of the Fine Arts. Digital image created by Oppenheimer Editions (1858.2).

theme. But such motifs were meant to be recognized and understood by viewers, at least the most learned and sensitive of them, and their experience of the work was to be enriched and deepened by their presence.[18] In the Catskill Creek paintings, however, Cole's miniaturized human and animal figures seldom function as accessories to a unified, central theme. They sometimes complicate, challenge, or even contradict it, and their presence is as much about concealing, through diminution, as revealing.

A strategy of concealment in the paintings from 1833 and 1838 is found in Cole's depiction of the foreground figures as well as those in the background. In the 1833 works we cannot see the rower's face because his head is turned away from us, and in the one from 1838 the faces of both the rower and the horseman are blank. In an accomplished painting in which everything else appears finished, these blank faces, which resemble featureless masks, must be read as deliberate and meaningful portrayals. Once we notice them, we experience them as erasures of identity.

One way of reading these erasures is to understand them as broadly symbolic; in this view, the two figures' blank faces conjoin them into a rural type, and Cole's willow gatherer and horseman certainly do have typological significance. But when we regard them in relation to figures with overt autobiographical meaning in other Catskill Creek paintings—especially the next one to be considered in this discussion—their mystery returns. Who are these men without faces? What is the nature of their relationship to one another and of both of them to the colonial figures in the deep background?

The small barn or shed, which in the sketch for *Sunset, View on the Catskill* Cole appears to have labeled "broken house," belongs to these mysteries (fig. 4.6). In both the 1833 and 1838 works its slatted door opens into a darkened space where there appears, ever so faintly, a reddish form that can be read, in the case of Reed's 1833 work (left), as a man kneeling right to left and pushing a heavy object. In the 1838 painting (right), we may see the shadowy outline of a standing human figure just to the left of a wagon (figs. 4.15 and 4.16).[19]

We are not meant to fully recognize the forms we (barely) see, and in this case to discern what else may lie hidden in the shadows of this little barn. Hiddenness seems to be the point, but hidden from whom? Cole must have known, and even intended, that the viewers of these landscapes would not take particular note of his miniaturized figures, and contemporary reviews suggest that they did not. Instead, they would have been engaged by the "view," a term used in this era to describe pleasing and undemanding landscapes.[20]

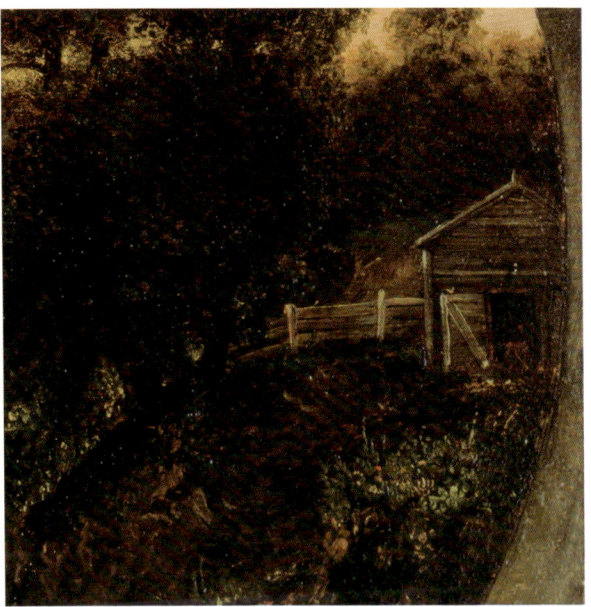
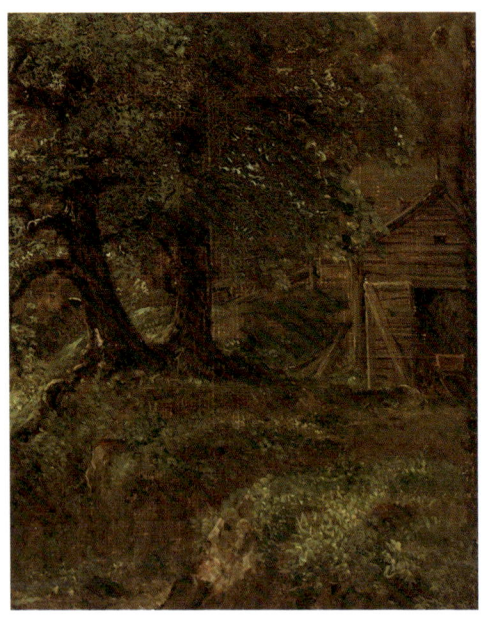

4.15 Detail of figure 4.2, *Sunset, View on the Catskill*, 1833

4.16 Detail of figure 4.4, *North Mountain and Catskill Creek*, 1838

Meanings of the Hidden

The poet Jane Hirshfield, in a chapter on the "hidden," finds the word's origins in Old German and Sanskrit terms for protection, and argues that in its protective function "hiddenness itself has meaning."[21] For Cole it certainly did. His figures appear to be elements in a personal code, or the fragments of a private narrative, with meanings that the artist needs to express but does not want to signify overtly. That Cole sometimes encoded his paintings has been known since the early 1980s, when scholars discovered that clear-cuts on a distant, forested hillside in *The Oxbow* inscribed on that hillside the Hebraic letters spelling "The Almighty."[22] One remarkable thing about this discovery is that it took so long, that the code remained unbroken for almost 150 years.

Breaking the code of the more private 1833 and 1838 paintings may not be possible, but certain differences between them are suggestive. In both, a long, receding triangle aligns their human and animal figures; the distances separating them, however, are significantly shorter in the work from 1838. Here the cow is replaced by a horseman waving a greeting to the rower—a gesture of social exchange that shortens the space separating them still further. And in the deep background of the 1838 painting we find not a motionless lone figure but an animated fisherman and his Native American companion. Together they form an assemblage from a living past associated for Cole with Catskill, New York.

Whether these figures were imagined by him, based on local legend, or derived from literary sources like Cooper's Leatherstocking novels—Natty Bumppo and his Indian companion, Chingachgook, certainly come to mind—they are phantoms, spirits of the place. In this regard, they are linked to Irving's ghostly Dutchmen in "Rip Van Winkle," a story with which the mountains above Catskill were intimately associated by the time Cole arrived on the scene.[23]

Thus the 1838 Catskill Creek painting amplifies the works from 1833 in ways beyond its literally greater size, its enhanced tonal and pictorial balance, and its increased level of accomplishment. In presenting a more harmonious landscape, it works to repair a broken relation with the past. Still, for all the ways in which this painting shortens spatial and temporal distances, those distances remain central to its composition. The triangle, with its widely spaced vertices, holds its basic shape. Cole's American landscapes characteristically describe separation rather than connection, and this work is no exception. At the center of the composition is still our rower, at midstream, and the painting is more about his strenuous efforts to make his crossing than about the encounter that awaits him when he does. As viewers, we may anticipate his arrival at the shore—when two faceless figures should meet face to face—but Cole himself is more interested in the crossing.

Faceless men, apparitional forms, miniaturized figures from a ghostly past—all of these images introduce into the 1833 and 1838 Catskill Creek paintings an element of the gothic, a mode that for Cole was associated with the sublime.[24] At first glance, however, these works don't seem sublime at all. Only in focusing on one of their "eccentric detail[s]," to use Naomi Schor's term describing the power of details to subvert a larger composition, do we begin to feel a sense of strangeness, even of the uncanny. As one draws in, elements of the landscape become defamiliarized, and in this way the sublime comes in through the back door.[25] This process of drawing in, or of being drawn in, is recessional but not panoramic. It leads our vision not outward toward the broader landscape but "across" and "into" the landscape's discrete and delimited spaces, into its darkened doorways. As we shall see, all the Catskill Creek paintings that take a low vantage point have secrets to hide. The mysterious quality of these works is related to the way in which their "picturesque" riverside vision, inspired in part by the aesthetics of William Gilpin, is unsettled by its enigmatic figural images.

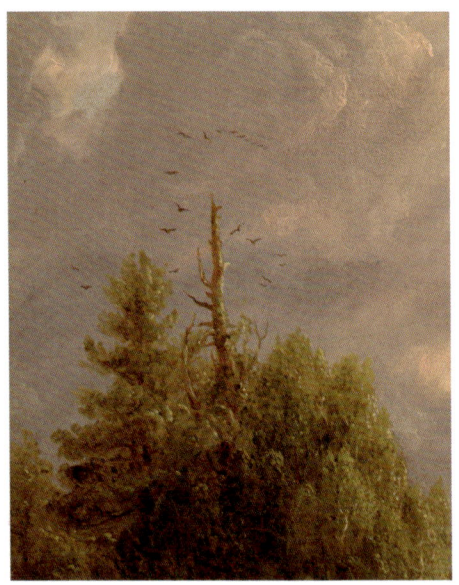

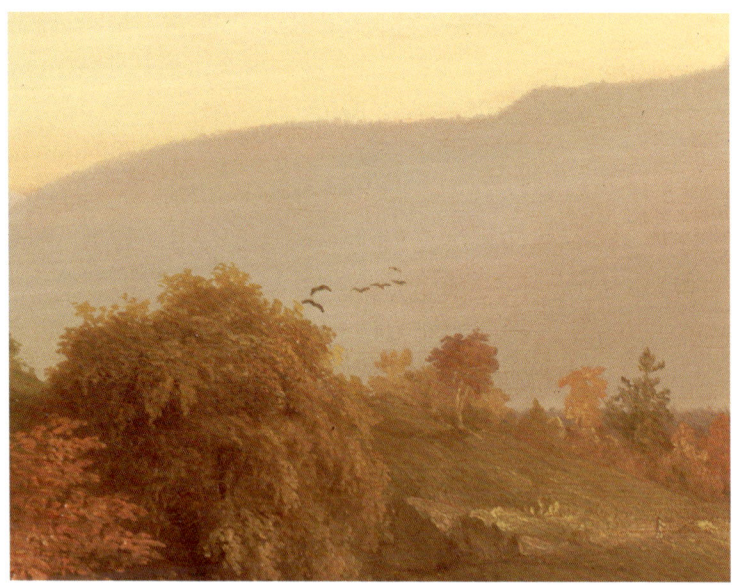

4.17 Detail of figure 4.4, *North Mountain and Catskill Creek*, 1838

4.18 Detail of figure 3.9, *View Near Catskill*, 1828–29

Not until we come upon such images in the work from 1838, perhaps, do we notice the swarm of vultures circling a dead tree in the left background (with dark clouds above), though it is quite clearly delineated (fig. 4.17).[26] Birds in the same formation and the same part of the composition appear distantly in *View Near Catskill*, painted fully a decade earlier, and only in retrospect do we recognize them as vultures in this otherwise buoyant and sunny landscape (fig. 4.18). Here is a reminder that death is never very far away in Cole's American Arcadia, and it is another example of the ways in which the Catskill Creek paintings illuminate one another, whether we run them forward or backward.

A Poem in the Painting

The painting from 1838 is the end point of this version of the Catskill Creek landscape. While Cole would render the scene from a low vantage point several more times in the series, never again in one of its completed oil paintings would he take this northwesterly view of the mountains with Blackhead in the center background.[27] He may himself have understood the 1838 work as a culmination (of a series within a series), because this is the only one of the ten Catskill Creek paintings—and possibly the only such case in Cole's career—in which he embedded a poem in the work itself, perhaps placed there as a summarizing gesture. On the wooden backing of the painting, written in chalk in a large, free-flowing hand that virtually fills the space of the backing, we find this:

> The valleys rest in shadow and the hum
> Of gentle sounds and low toned melodies
> Are stilled, and twilight spreads her misty
>   wings
> In broader sadness oer their happy scene
> And creeps along the distant mountain sides
> Until the setting sun's last lingering beams
> Wreathe up in many a golden glorious ring
> Around the highest Catskill peak.[28]

These verses have been ascribed to Cole himself, and they do resemble his own poetry. But the artist found them in *Godey's Lady's Book*—an influential and popular magazine of the period—where the author is identified as Anna H. Dorsey. Under her name appears "Baltimore, March 27, 1838," and her poem, written specifically "for the Ladies Book," appeared in the September 1838 issue of the magazine.[29] Because the poem was both written and published in 1838, the same year Cole completed his painting, he probably made the inscription on the artwork himself, and the handwriting appears to be his.

The lines he recorded are the first nine of this hymn-like poem—its refrain is "Praise ye the Lord"—titled "Sunset Among the Alps." One can see why the religious sentiment appealed to Cole but also why he selected out the least didactic and most purely descriptive lines in the poem. His few changes appropriated a European landscape for his own beloved Catskill landscape, turning "the highest Alpine peaks" into "the highest Catskill Peak." In a similar vein he converted the poet's plural "scenes" into his own "scene," thereby creating a more unitary and focused sense of this mountain landscape.

Yet Cole's changes do not rescue the poem. Like much of his own poetry, when he used it to paraphrase his art, these verses are disappointing because they depend so much on the vocabulary and prosody of romantic sentiment. In this case, the poem's familiar paean to melancholy beauty and its hurry to bring closure with the setting sun rob the painting of its complexity. It's all about the "broader" harmony of its "happy scene" and does not speak to the picture's haunting landscape features and its strangely idiosyncratic figures. But the key point to make about this poem is that it exists—that Cole chose in this rare if not unique instance to broadly inscribe it onto the artwork, and, of equal importance, that he chose to hide it. Parchment may have covered the wooden backing from Cole's time until twentieth-century curators pulled it away. Like the Hebraic letters in *The Oxbow*, the poem may have gone unnoticed—literally hidden from view in this case—for more than a century.

View on the Catskill—Early Autumn, 1836–37

In every way, *View on the Catskill—Early Autumn* is the central work in the Catskill Creek series (fig. 4.19). Executed during the winter of 1836–37, it is the fifth-painted of the ten works, and it was completed at the midpoint of the eighteen-year period spanning them. By far the largest of these paintings, and the first on canvas, *View on the Catskill—Early Autumn* is also the most ambitious, perhaps the only one Cole intended for a conspicuous place in a major exhibition. It appeared in the National Academy exhibition of 1837 as a companion to his identically sized *View of Florence from San Miniato* (also completed in 1837), and contemporary critics saw in the pairing a contrast between a "humble" but beautiful American rural setting and a "lovely" European city with a history of "despotism."[30]

Cole's pairing of *View on the Catskill—Early Autumn* and *View of Florence from San Miniato* is an interesting illustration of what we might call the Catskill Creek paintings' lateral relationships. Our emphasis here has been on the vertical, or internal, trajectory of these works as we have followed a paradigmatic landscape through multiple versions—each work responding to and revising those that went before while anticipating those that are to come. But at every stage elements, images, and aspects of these paintings point outward to worlds beyond the localized setting of Catskill Creek and can be found in numerous other works by Cole.

The nationalist feelings that *View on the Catskill—Early Autumn* inspired in contemporary viewers are a significant part of its history, but it has a private history too—beginning with the way in which it was conceived. In this work, Cole returned to the high vantage point on Jefferson Heights from which his two Catskill Creek paintings of the 1820s were based and which afforded him a panoramic, southwesterly view of High Peak, Roundtop, and South Mountain, with Indian Head in the distant background. The viewscape of this painting is illustrated in map 4.2. From Jefferson Heights

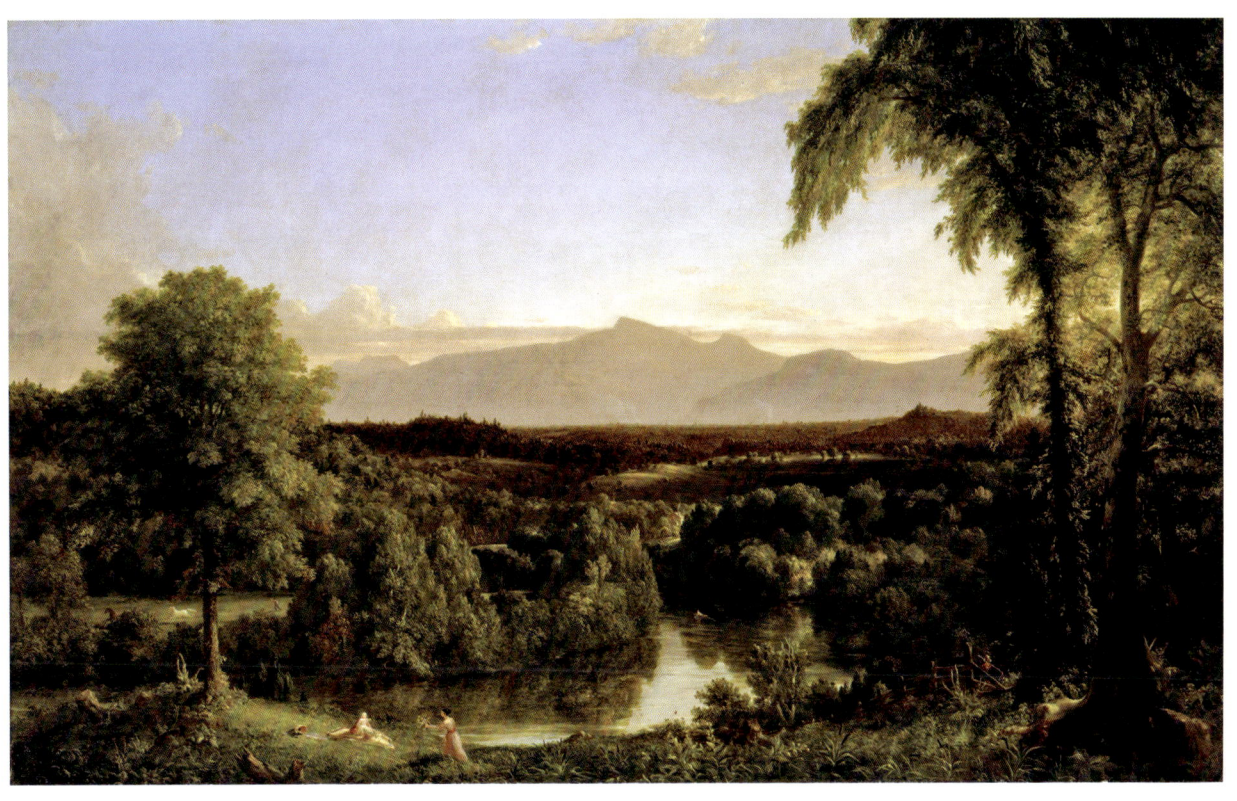

4.19 Thomas Cole, *View on the Catskill—Early Autumn*, 1836–37. Oil on canvas, 39 x 63 in. (99.1 cm x 160 cm). Metropolitan Museum of Art, gift in memory of Jonathan Sturges by his children, 1895 (95.13.3).

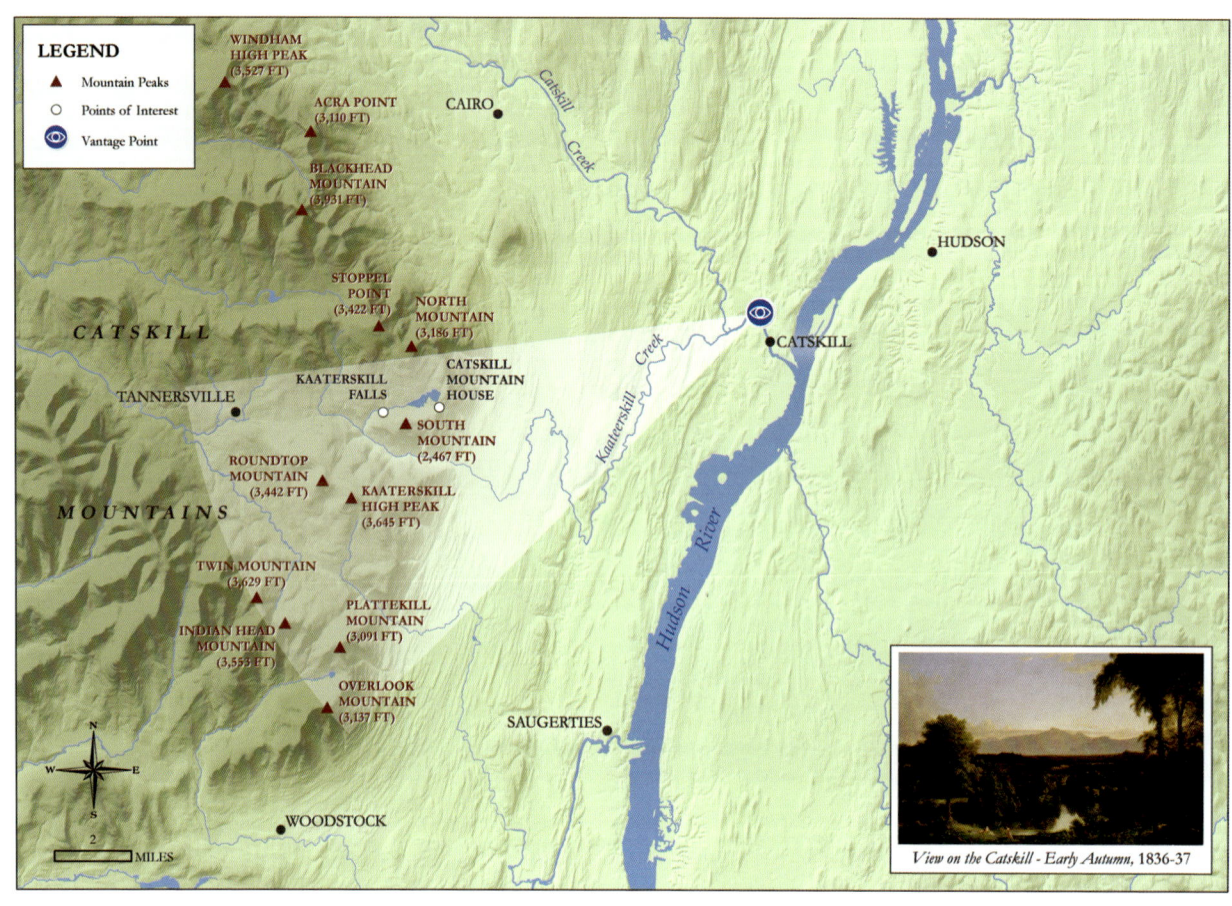

▲ Mountain Peaks

○ Points of Interest

◉ Vantage Point

WINDHAM
HIGH PEAK
(3,527 FT)

ACRA POINT
(3,110 FT)

CAIRO

BLACKHEAD
MOUNTAIN
(3,931 FT)

STOPPEL
POINT
(3,422 FT)

NORTH
MOUNTAIN
(3,186 FT)

CATSKILL

KAATERSKILL
FALLS

CATSKILL
MOUNTAIN
HOUSE

CATSKILL

TANNERSVILLE

SOUTH
MOUNTAIN
(2,467 FT)

HUDSON

ROUNDTOP
MOUNTAIN
(3,442 FT)

KAATERSKILL
HIGH PEAK
(3,645 FT)

MOUNTAINS

TWIN MOUNTAIN
(3,629 FT)

PLATTEKILL
MOUNTAIN
(3,091 FT)

INDIAN HEAD
MOUNTAIN
(3,555 FT)

OVERLOOK
MOUNTAIN
(3,137 FT)

SAUGERTIES

N
W · E
S

2
MILES

WOODSTOCK

View on the Catskill - Early Autumn, 1836-37

Map 4.2 Viewscape of *View on the Catskill—Early Autumn* (1836–37). Map by Neil Curri.

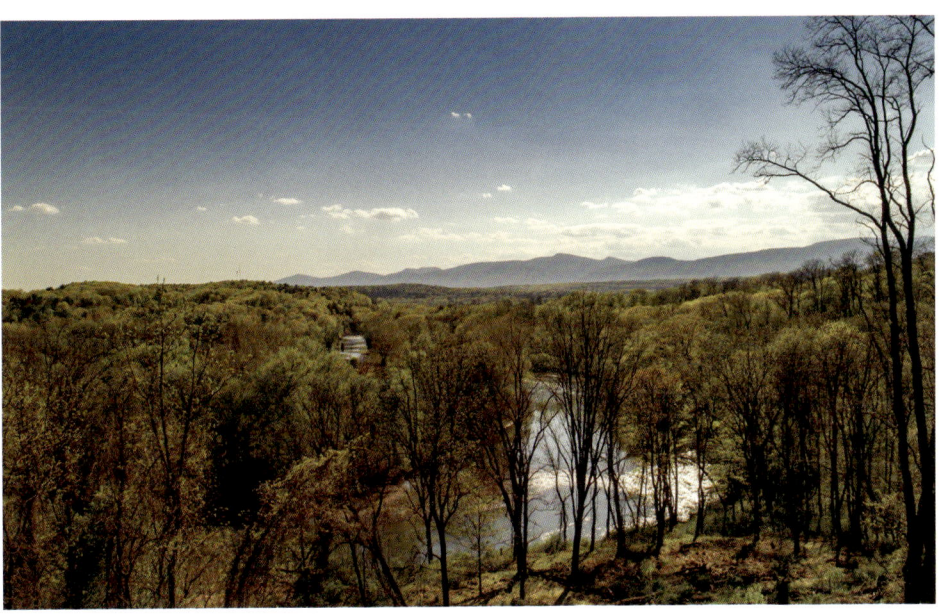

4.20 Approximate view taken by Cole's *View on the Catskill—Early Autumn* (1836–37), looking southwest from Jefferson Heights toward Kaaterskill High Peak, Roundtop, and South Mountain, 2018, Catskill, NY. Photo by Alon Koppel Photography.

today, as is true for Cole's riverside perspective in the 1833 and 1838 Catskill Creek paintings, trees obscure the artist's view of the mountains; the drone photograph in figure 4.20 partially restores it.

This panorama includes the glimpse of the rapids, in the left middle ground, that had appeared in the very first Catskill Creek painting, and it presents the series' first fully delineated view of the Van Vechten house—with its distinctive east extension—near the center of the composition. The graceful curl of smoke issuing from its chimney may remind us of the same form in the 1828–29 painting; as in that work and its 1827 predecessor, this farmhouse in *View on the Catskill—Early Autumn* sits at a diagonal relationship to the viewer (fig. 4.21). Looking back at those more generalized compositions with this one in mind can bring some of their features into focus.

Reclaiming a Landscape

Cole had resumed sketching the Catskill Creek scene in the months following his return to New York from Italy late in 1832, and Oswaldo Rodriguez Roque argues

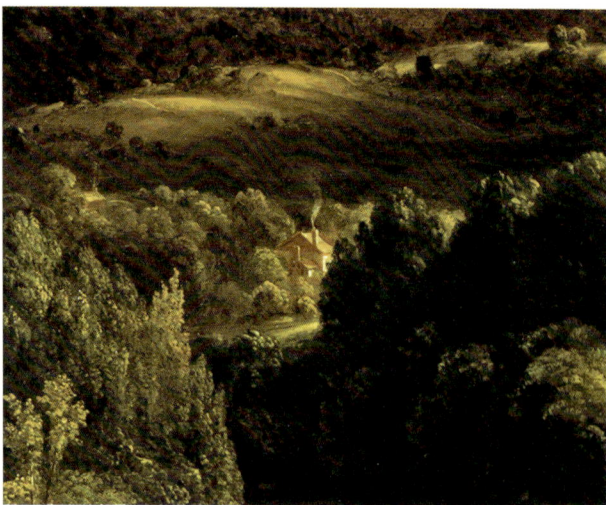

4.21 Detail of figure 4.19, *View on the Catskill—Early Autumn*, 1836–37

convincingly that one particular sketch from this period is the basis for *View on the Catskill—Early Autumn*. He explains that Cole, when beginning to work on the picture late in 1836, deliberately turned to a sketch made several years earlier because he wanted to visually reclaim a landscape that had been altered dramatically that year by the construction of the Canajoharie and Catskill railroad line.[31]

Rodriguez Roque considerably strengthened his argument by quoting from a letter of March 23, 1837, written to Cole by Jonathan Sturges, who had commissioned the work. Here Sturges appeared to be echoing Cole's plans for the painting, as expressed in an unlocated letter from the artist.[32] This letter by Cole has been discovered; he wrote it on February 24, and it confirms Rodriguez Roque's understanding—linking the artist's sadness about the destruction caused by the railroad with his mournful feelings about the recent death of his primary patron, Luman Reed. Here is the relevant passage:

The picture is an American View, which I believe you desired, & it is the richest I have been able to select—It is a view in the valley of the Catskill near this place. Mr. Reed and myself have several times together gazed on the scene & with mutual delight. The vicinity of the site from which the view is taken was a favourite haunt of mine—but its beauty has passed away—the same season that took away Mr. Reed found the valley desolate & the magnificent woods had all been felled—I take a pleasure in thinking that my picture may for years to come—tell what the Valley of the Catskill was before what is called "improvement" blasted the scene.[33]

Regarding *View on the Catskill—Early Autumn* as a landscape reconstructed from memory led Rodriguez Roque to view it as a nostalgic and uncomplicated work in which broken harmonies of the natural world have been mended. One thing about the painting, however, surprised him: "the many small-scale figures that at first appear out of place in such a panoramic landscape." But, in his discussion, surprise quickly gave way to an understanding of these figures as "symbols of a happy and sane relationship with the environment."[34] Absorbing them into the larger landscape has become the prevailing, even singular, way of regarding their presence in *View on the Catskill—Early Autumn*: "Tiny figures carefully set into the minutely detailed landscape add to the overall feeling of harmony," as another scholar put it.[35]

But when we examine this work in the context of the other Catskill Creek paintings, two important points come to mind. First, Cole's human and animal figures in these works are never merely part of the larger composition; they are meaningful in their own (often mysterious) ways. Second, when the figures in *View on the Catskill—Early Autumn* are compared with some of their miniaturized counterparts in other Catskill Creek paintings, they are hardly tiny. In fact, they are so relatively prominent, and numerous, that they cannot be ignored. Their numbers complicate their meaning, as does their presence in almost every part of the composition.

Obviously, one reason for the size of these figures is that the work itself was executed on a much larger scale than were earlier paintings in the series. But Cole had to have known that the effect of working on this scale would draw attention to his figures, thus making interpretation of their meanings an implicit challenge to the viewer. The risk he may have felt in issuing such a challenge is suggested by his February 24 letter to Sturges, in which he appears to be advising his client not to search the painting too deeply: "I hope you will not anticipate too much in this picture—remember it is a *view* & it is impossible to introduce in a view the richness of composition & variety of objects that can be clustered together in a composition."[36] In calling up the distinction his era made between "views" (pleasing and undemanding landscape scenes) and "compositions" (landscapes with moral import), he may have been trying to draw attention away from his enigmatic figures.

Figures Coming out of Hiding

View on the Catskill—Early Autumn is, in fact, the Catskill Creek painting in which the figures come out of hiding. In doing so, they highlight and interrogate the process of miniaturization at work in the series as a whole and thereby confirm the significance of human and animal figures in the other paintings.[37] We have seen how, in those other works, figures have both public and personal, sometimes hidden, levels of meaning, and the relationship between these levels can be discordant. We might say that their public meanings (e.g., the willow gatherer as a rural type) are symbolic, whereas their personal meanings are, in a very particular sense, emblematic—dense, riddling or parabolic, and unfixed.[38]

To sharpen the contrast, we could point to the overtly symbolic meanings of the figure in Cole's allegory *The Voyage of Life* (figs. 2.1–2.4). The voyager's singular role—there are no other figures, except angels—is that of Everyman, and if the (universal) meanings attached to his voyage were to become unfixed or unstable, the allegory would collapse. This symbolic voyager is painted large (large for Cole) on imaginary landscapes that shift one to another, like stage sets, as the serial narrative unfolds. The relationship between figure and ground in the Catskill Creek series is just the opposite. Here the setting holds (more or less) steady through its repeated renderings and becomes a template onto which several diverse figures are drawn. Some, like the rower, appear more than once in the series but always within the circumscribed world of Catskill Creek, itself a landscape characterized—on the surface at least—by the familiar rather than the exotic and by the beautiful rather than the sublime.

Cole created numerous paintings devoted to the sublime, and he had a place for miniaturized figures in them. For example, the third and fourth works in his series *The Course of Empire* (*The Consummation of Empire* and *The Destruction of Empire*) contain what appear to be thousands of such figures, densely overpopulating a Roman-like city in one painting and experiencing its destruction in the other (figs. 1.4 and 1.5). It is the aggregate force of these small figures (in the collective they become immense, gigantic) that contributes to the sublime, and powerfully narrative, aspect of these works.

Cole's use of miniaturized figures in the Catskill Creek paintings is very different. Idiosyncratic and usually separated from one another by wide spaces (and sometimes so small they can barely be seen), they suppress rather than encourage perceptions of narrative development. Susan Stewart's reflection on the essence of miniature comes to mind: "The miniature always tends toward tableau rather than toward narrative, toward silence and spatial boundaries, rather than toward expository closure."[39] As we have learned from earlier works in the series, the Catskill Creek landscapes do, in fact, contain encoded narrative elements, and so does *View on the Catskill—Early Autumn*. We might say that in the Catskill Creek paintings miniature, working on different levels, functions *both* to stabilize and to unsettle its landscape, subtly expressing narrative relationships while also rendering the sense of a tableau.

Into such a tableau, or what I'm calling a template, Cole embeds his figures into sectors of the composition already made meaningful by their prior configurations in earlier Catskill Creek paintings.[40] In *View on the Catskill—Early Autumn*, the hunter in the right foreground emerges from the dark space of the woods below him, following roughly the same course—in reverse—of the striding couple in the very first Catskill Creek painting. In the central foreground, a woman and an infant take their places on a meadowed plateau that was crossed, in the series' second work, by a young fisherman. These first and second paintings in the series both depict in the valley below pastureland that belongs to the broad, oval pointbar emerging clearly, for the first time, in *View on the Catskill—Early Autumn*. It becomes in this painting the scene of a young man chasing horses. Finally, distantly portrayed on the river is the rower who appears in the other Catskill Creek paintings of the 1830s. As in those works, the arrangement of compositional sectors in *View on the Catskill—Early Autumn* is both lateral and recessional, and, as we will see in the following discussion, the recessional dimension of the painting is temporal as well as spatial.

The broad spaces separating the figures in this landscape can be bridged thematically if we accept the prevailing understanding of it as happy and harmonious. Following this understanding, interpreters have emphasized the rustic aspects of the picture, characterizing, for example, its foreground scene as a hunter "returning to his family."[41] Certainly, Cole intends that his viewers should see a familial relation among the painting's foreground figures, and indeed should see them participating in a narrative of homecoming. But other elements that we will explore in the larger work, and in the Catskill Creek paintings that precede it, suggest a more complicated relationship.

In any case, to summarize *View on the Catskill—Early Autumn* as depicting a hunter returning to his family links him implicity to the figures in Cole's late and somewhat sentimental wilderness paintings *The Hunter's Return* (1845) and *Home in the Woods* (1847). But the setting of *View on the Catskill—Early Autumn* is hardly a wilderness; it is a refined, indeed pastoral landscape, and all its most prominent figures are marked by their clothing and activities as rural gentry.[42]

The man advancing up the hill is coming home from a day of sport, not subsistence hunting. And the elegantly bodiced and ribboned woman (and bonneted infant) is his female counterpart. The young man in the valley is wearing a dashing red vest, and the horses he is pursuing are not beasts of burden. Rather, their fleet and graceful forms identify him as a person whose means and station involve owning horses, animals emphatically associated with social class in the England of Cole's youth. It could be argued, therefore, that the most obvious quality linking the figures in *View on the Catskill—Early Autumn* to one another is their common status as gentry.

Pursuing Objects of Desire

Still, a shared attribute like social class is an external rather than an integral association and does not, by itself, bridge the wide spaces separating these figures. To echo Rodriguez Roque's initial puzzlement—a response to be trusted—who are these strange little people, and what are they doing here? Perhaps the best place to start answering this question is with the wide spaces themselves. The hunter advancing upward from the dark woods is separated from the woman and infant, and from their meadowed plateau, not only by a wide expanse but also by a slatted fence; he is literally fenced off from them. But in the moment depicted in this painting, he has turned his head toward them, noticed them, and just above him a downed slat of the fence opens his view into their sunlit sphere and potentially provides a passageway to it (fig. 4.22).

The woman, too, is afoot, running toward the infant, who in turn reaches out to her; the bouquet of wildflowers she extends to the baby signifies her attachment and also bridges some of the space between them (fig. 4.23). Given the subject matter of this scene, Cole might well have represented the mother and child in a (static) embrace.

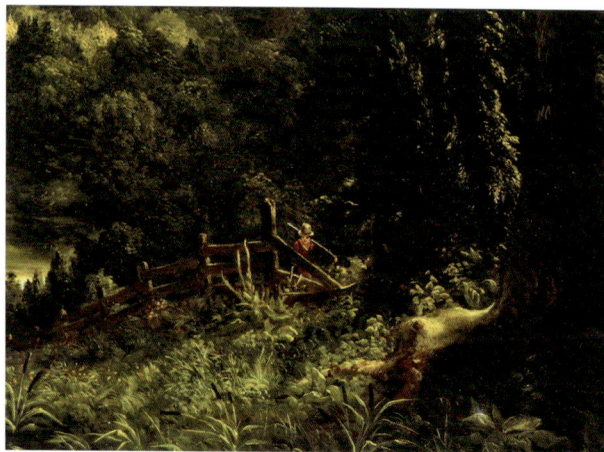

4.22 Detail of figure 4.19, *View on the Catskill—Early Autumn*, 1836–37

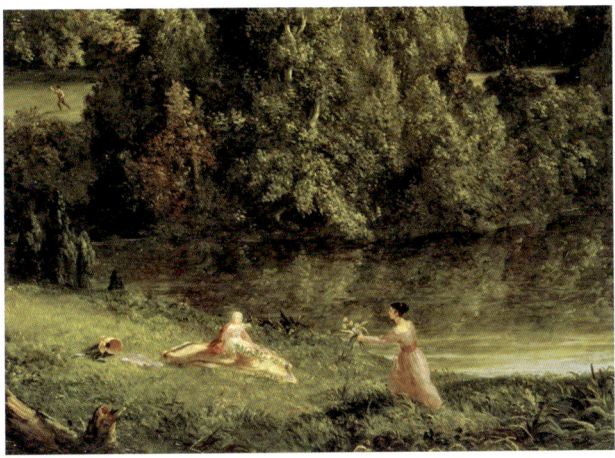

But it is central to the meaning of *View on the Catskill—Early Autumn* that its figures are in motion, with almost everyone moving (or about to move) leftward—a choreography led by the galloping horses and following the course of the river. All of them, at different speeds and in different postures, are attempting to close the space between themselves and their objects of desire.

This is certainly true of the young man in the valley running after the escaped horses. If these horses, one brown and one white, can be said to represent his alternative dreams or possible destinies, they both appear to be getting away from him. The scene is a particularly interesting example of doubling in the Catskill Creek paintings; while the horses are distinguished from one another by color (though in size and form they are identical), one is running directly behind the other, following exactly the same course and racing toward the same finish line.

As we know from Cole's allegory *The Cross and the World* and other of his works, he was intensely interested in the idea of diverging pathways, in part a legacy from his Bunyanesque religious background. But the dynamic of this scene, the thing that energizes it, is not a set of polar destinations; rather, it is the horses' flight from the young man, from whom the composition sharply divides them. For the viewer, a large maple or oak in the middle distance separates him decisively from the horses, fencing him, like the hunter, into a separate sphere (fig. 4.24). (Here is a Claudian framing tree with an unusually specific purpose.) What is it they are fleeing from, and what, in turn, is it that has escaped him? While horses in Anglo-American culture during the nineteenth century carried certain clear symbolic values, such as power and sexuality, these

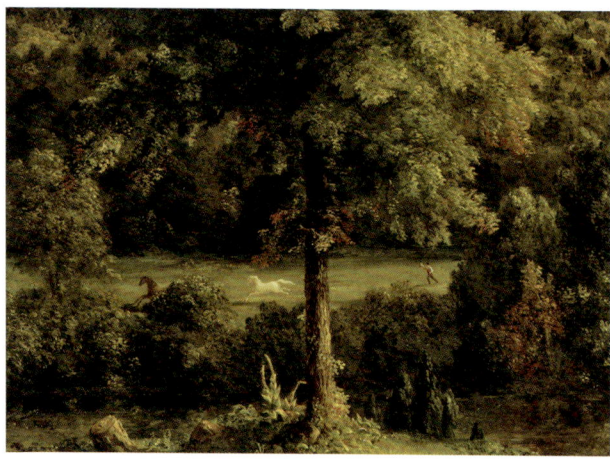

4.24 Detail of figure 4.19, *View on the Catskill—Early Autumn*, 1836–37

horses—like so many animal and human figures in the Catskill Creek paintings—seem more emblematic, their meanings more obscure. In this way, they may remind us of the lost bay horse, hound, and turtledove in Thoreau's famous parable.[43]

The rower in the far distance, moving leftward around a bend of the river, is part of this mysterious drama (fig. 4.25). He is the only rower in the Catskill Creek series who is clearly following the course of the river rather than crossing it (or, in subsequent works, contemplating it and landing on its shore), and his destination therefore is unknown.[44] The Van Vechten farmhouse lies immediately upstream from his position, and given that a later work in the series unmistakably shows a rower heading for it, he may divert from his course and make his landing there.[45] On the other hand, he may be embarking

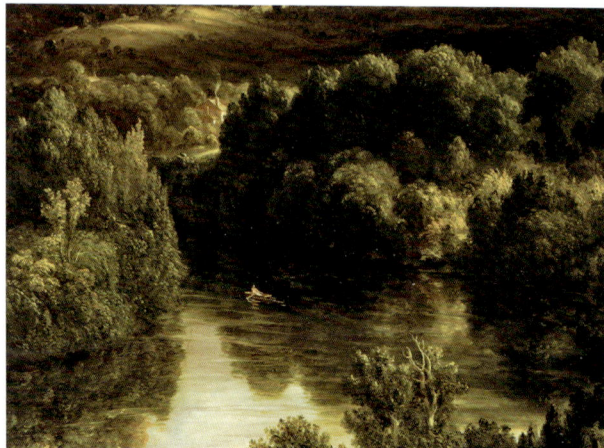

4.25 Detail of figure 4.19, *View on the Catskill—Early Autumn*, 1836–37

94

on an upriver voyage. We are not given to see what may lie around the bend, except for the challenge of the rapids, but the rower's arched back, as he pulls hard on his oars, links him to the other figures' pursuits. Because he is rowing upstream (unlike the figure in *The Voyage of Life*) toward the river's source in the mountains, perhaps his dreams lie there. Many of Cole's poems, including his adaptation of the one he copied onto the backing of the 1838 Catskill Creek painting, describe these mountains as an ethereal realm—a land of dreams—and he certainly paints them this way in all the works in the series. If they are sublime, they belong to a distinct version of this aesthetic category that John Conron has called "softened sublimity."[46]

About to disappear from our view, the rower is very distant from the other figures, and his line of sight to most of them is blocked. The woman on the plateau and the young man in the valley—separated by elevation as well as distance, not to mention their intense preoccupations—are not aware of one another; they exist on different levels, in every sense. Among the figures, only the hunter shows an awareness of others, as he turns his head toward the woman and infant. And he is the only figure whose ascending motion associates him with the landscape's lower and upper levels; he potentially bridges different sectors of the composition, recessionally through his movement from the forested valley below and horizontally through his vision.

While the hunter cannot, from his position, see the young man in the valley, he is connected to him through our eyes. The bright red of the hunter's cape that first alerts us to his presence in the shadows of the trees is the same color as the young man's vest. And the young man's jet-black hair—a full head of it trailing into long, bushy (youthful) sideburns—corresponds to that of the older hunter, his own black hair spilling out from under his hat brim and coloring his brows. As we look still more closely at the young man, we see something else—an extreme example of miniaturization that until now has gone unobserved—linking him to the hunter. His right arm extended upward is thickened by a falconer's glove, and the bird, facing in the direction opposite to the horses' movement, is about to launch in pursuit of prey (fig. 4.26). The young man is a hunter too and, like his older counterpart on the hill, a sport hunter.

Catskill Creek as a Voyage of Life

Once we grasp the subtle, encoded linkage of these two figures—younger and older versions of the self—we see how recession in *View on the Catskill—Early Autumn*, as in

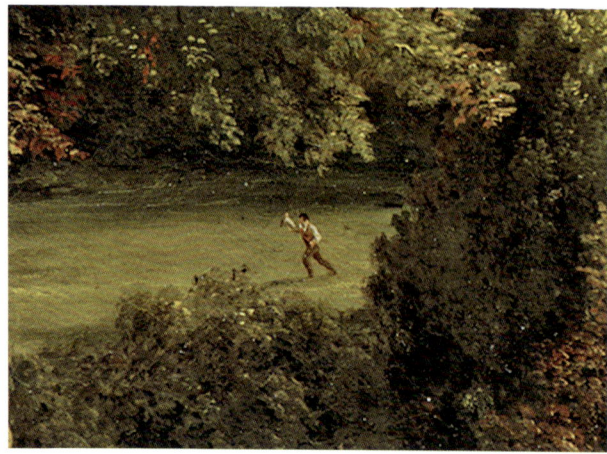

4.26 Detail of figure 4.19, *View on the Catskill—Early Autumn*, 1836–37

the other Catskill Creek paintings of the 1830s, has a temporal dimension. The linkage also reminds us of one of Cole's favorite themes, the passage of time as it informs and differentiates the stages of life. His conception for *The Voyage of Life* took final shape during exactly the same period—the closing months of 1836—that he began painting *View on the Catskill—Early Autumn*.[47]

The two works can be thought of as companions, one public and one private, dramatizing their shared theme through different modalities: a serial narrative on the one hand and, on the other, a matrix of elements that I have called emblems. The serial format of *The Voyage of Life* allows its narrative to flow (its cinematic quality) to its predetermined and fateful end, whereas the emblematic approach of *View on the Catskill—Early Autumn* conveys the sense of a world momentarily brought to a standstill. While its figures are portrayed in postures of motion—running, climbing, rowing—this motion appears suspended, with everyone caught in midstride or, in the case of the rower, with his oars locked in place. There are narratives here, to be sure, but they are interrupted, incomplete narratives.[48]

None of the painting's suspended moments is so poignant as the one in which the hunter is caught looking over the fence at the woman and infant (fig. 4.22). Unlike his implicit connection to the young man in the valley, this connection is direct and visual; he is eyeing them, which, in the temporal logic of the work, means he is eyeing his own imagined future. Cole married Maria Bartow in November of 1836, in the period when he was beginning to work on *View on the Catskill—Early Autumn*, but, as I noted earlier, they had not conceived a child by the time he completed the painting.[49] Because of the proleptic nature of this scene, we might say that the woman in the meadow, like the infant, *also* belongs to the hunter's future, and, in turn, the infant belongs to hers as well as his. This is to see the woman not only as a static symbol of "natural fecundity," in the words of one commentator, but as a figure as much in motion as everyone else in the painting.[50] Her running posture and her raised arm share the animation of the young man chasing horses in the valley. All the figures in this painting are aspiring, all are resisting fixity, and all are looking beyond their spheres.

The hunter's look has a sexual dimension, linked here specifically to procreation, or insemination, by a planter's basket with a beaded rim resembling that of the basket at the rower's feet in *Sunset, View on the Catskill* (fig. 4.8). Its arrowed form is aimed at the woman and infant and toward the woman's deeply funneled hat—its interior the same color as her dress—lying on the ground nearby. Like several of Cole's other encoded images, the planter's basket is virtually hidden by miniaturization and in this case, as well, by an illusion: he has framed it into the triangular shape formed by the downed slats of the fence, and it comes into focus only when we recognize that its base sits considerably higher than the ground.

Strangely, the basket contains shoots of mullein, a vigorous, wild growing plant that needs no cultivation. In fact, the right-hand third of the painting, unlike the rest of the composition, has an unruly, disordered aspect. While vine-encircled trees are a common sight in the Hudson River Valley, the one that appears in this part of *View on the Catskill—Early Autumn* seems almost tropical. Of the two tall trees in this sector, the one on the left appears particularly out of place in this otherwise bucolic scene. It would be more at home in one of Martin Johnson Heade's or Frederic Church's Central and South American settings.[51] Likewise, the rounded, fleshy roots of the tree at the far right have an unmistakably exotic aspect (fig. 4.27). In a landscape composition divided into several distinct sectors or zones, perhaps this darkened one occupied by the hunter can be understood, in part, as a source of erotic energy, an understanding consistent with certain nineteenth-century associations of the tropics with exoticism and sexuality.[52]

Immediately in front of the planter's basket there are mature mullein growing in the ground, and as we look left all the way across the picture—beyond the woman and infant—we find a cluster of substantial mullein stalks growing just to the left of the large framing tree (fig. 4.24). This is the same general position in the composition where mullein appear prominently in the first two Catskill Creek paintings (both of them panoramic views like *View on the Catskill—Early Autumn*), from almost a decade earlier. Here, along with the mullein near the hunter, they frame the composition, but

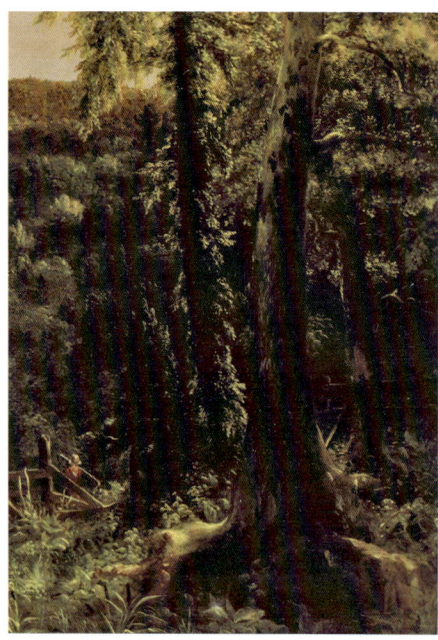

4.27 Detail of figure 4.19, *View on the Catskill—Early Autumn*, 1836–37

hardly in the classic, elevated Claudian fashion; rather, they do so in a literally grounded way. Their position immediately adjacent to the framing tree highlights the contrast.

In mid-nineteenth-century American literary culture it was Walt Whitman who, in the first edition of *Leaves of Grass* (1855), most notably drew attention to the undoubtedly widespread erotic associations of the mullein, with its phallus-shaped terminal spike.[53] Cole, with his deeply Puritan background, could not have done so openly. Were he to have written about the mullein in one of his own poems, he might have reflected on its botanical lineage. As the painter surely knew, the mullein is a plant introduced to the Hudson Valley during the colonial period by the Dutch. One way to read the image of the planter's basket is to see it as a link between the hunter and the settlers who appear in the deep background of the other Catskill Creek paintings from the 1830s and will appear again later in the series.[54] Nineteenth-century (and earlier) cultural associations of settlement and procreation have been widely documented by feminist scholarship.[55] And it's useful to remember that Cole himself was transplanted from the Old World, an experience central to his identity, and in this way the mullein can also be associated with him.

Here, then, are stages of life—mating and reproduction—that could not be included in the solitary and masculine *Voyage of Life*. In that work, a maternal presence pervades the first painting, *Childhood*, as the infant emerges from a womb-like cave—an image cognate with the woman's funneled hat in *View on the Catskill—Early Autumn* and, of course, with the baby on the blanket. But following this emergence, there is no place for a woman on this voyage, except for the feminine-looking angel who oversees his passage. The voyage's adventures and challenges—following one's dreams, surviving the perilous rapids—were culturally defined for Cole and his era as male, and they were understood, especially by the Byronic Cole, as solitary.

Like *The Voyage of Life*, *View on the Catskill—Early Autumn* does represent youth, through the young man in the valley and the rower in the distance, and of course it represents manhood through the hunter. But whereas *The Voyage of Life* defines these stages as monolithic and distinct (youth is all about idealistic dreams and manhood is full of trouble), *View on the Catskill—Early Autumn* presents a more complex view. As we noted earlier, the doubled horses may project alternative futures for the young man; he might not realize either of them. In any case, his fate is far less certain than the predetermined destinies of Cole's pilgrims in *The Cross and the World*. And there's no telling where the rower in *View on the Catskill—Early Autumn* is headed on his upstream voyage. As for manhood, it is represented here as an uphill trek, but it does not appear particularly troubled in this moment. And unlike its representation in *The Voyage of Life*, manhood in this Catskill Creek painting is pictured in relation to a woman and child.

Notably, *View on the Catskill—Early Autumn* does not include old age and imminent death, as does *The Voyage of Life* in its final scene. Cole's omission of the end of life from this work is in its character as a pastoral. While it complicates the voyage of life through the deeply encoded strategies we have examined, at the same time it contains these complications within the stabilizing framework established and reinforced by the template of Catskill Creek. As in other paintings from the series, death is nearby, though it's held at bay through various visual strategies. Stumps appear in the middle distance on the plateau, but the ones on the left are angling toward the edge of the composition, and the one in the center is surrounded by lush foliage, their presence thus minimized.

The Artist and the Hunter

The Cole scholar Ellwood C. Parry III noticed the autobiographical elements in *View on the Catskill—Early Autumn*. As he wrote, the hunter unmistakably resembles Cole's representation of himself in the contemporaneous *Oxbow*, and the artist's wife Maria, Parry adds, "might have been the model for the woman with the flowers."[56] The relationship between the artist and the hunter, however, can be understood in ways beyond their similar features. It is a common trope of Romanticism that the artist *is* a hunter, a hunter after truth and beauty.[57] In *The Oxbow*, he commands the landscape before him through the prospect view he has taken, and much has been written about how, in looking back toward the viewer, he negotiates for Americans the polar visions of wilderness and agrarian abundance.[58]

In *View on the Catskill—Early Autumn*, the hunter's movement upward from the valley can be understood as an ascent toward such a prospect view, the one that we as viewers already have. But like almost every other figure in the painting the hunter is in medias res, on his way to a different position in time and space—a condition familiar to the restless Cole. Unlike the artist in *The Oxbow*, planted firmly in the central lower part of the composition, the hunter is still (literally) on the margin, not yet situated. Will he ever be? If *The Oxbow* asserts the artist's centrality to culture, does *View on the Catskill—Early Autumn* quietly cast doubt upon his capacity to assume this role, to capture the beauty he hunts? Or, to put the question differently, will the hunter, or any of the figures in this painting, close the gap between themselves and their objects of desire? What are the nature and meaning of the spaces that divide them from one another and separate them into different spheres? And, finally, does *View on the Catskill—Early Autumn* promise to close these spaces or does it fix them into unbridgeable sectors? The remaining paintings in the Catskill Creek series may help us answer these questions.

CHAPTER FIVE

LIVING THROUGH TRYING TIMES

Cole's first European tour (1829–32) had decisively marked off the dramatic beginning of his career in the 1820s from its mature development in the 1830s. With Andrew Jackson's reelection occurring in November of 1832, in the very moment of the artist's return to the United States, the nation too was undergoing a significant transition. The artist's second (and last) European tour (1841–42) also occurred near the turning over of a new decade and, like his first tour, it roughly marked a divide in both his life and his times.

Cole left for Europe on a year-long tour on August 7, 1841. Earlier that year, in February, he had turned forty, and there are several indications that this birthday prompted in him an assessment of his career, including his acknowledgment of some acute disappointments. In a poem written on this fortieth birthday, titled simply "January 31, 1841," Cole described himself as being "disconsolate" and "lost in gloom." A few months later, in his journal of May 1841, he lamented his career in this way: "I am not the painter I should have been had there been a higher taste." The passage includes the artist's concern about the uncertain fate of his major series *The Voyage of Life*, executed in 1839–40, which he feared would be broken up and dispersed.[1]

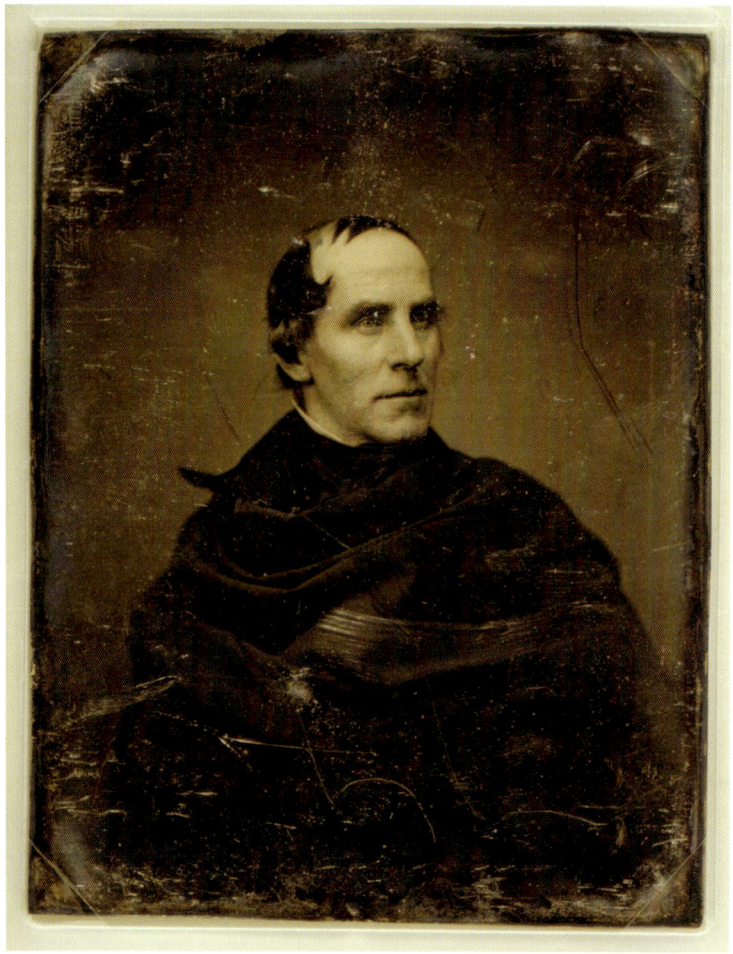

5.1 Matthew B. Brady, *Daguerreotype of Thomas Cole*, c. 1844–48. Daguerreotype, Library of Congress, Prints and Photographs Division, LC-USZC4-8981 DLC, DAG no. 057.

During the 1840s Cole continued to paint the Catskill Creek scene—four works in all—and to the degree that they can be understood as a pastoral response to the complications and troubles of his own life, they were also a pastoral response to the troubled times he lived in. The late 1830s had been marked by extreme social and economic turbulence. There were back-to-back financial panics in 1837 and 1839, and the resulting recession lasted until the mid-1840s. The period included many other social and economic dislocations—including urban riots—associated with an unruly and unpredictable market economy. As others have documented, these forces directly affected Cole's career.[2]

Sunset in the Catskills, 1841

Not long before Cole departed on his second European tour in early August of 1841 he completed his seventh Catskill Creek landscape, *Sunset in the Catskills*. This beautiful work has its present home in the Museum of Fine Arts, Boston (fig. 5.2). Like *View on the Catskill—Early Autumn*, it was painted for Sturges, who may also have purchased the 1838 Yale work; the donor of that painting to Yale descended from his son-in-law. And, as we will see in the discussion that follows, Sturges may have purchased from Cole still another Catskill Creek landscape from this period—*Mill Dam on the Catskill Creek* (1841). Like his business partner Luman Reed, he appears to have had a special fondness for the Catskill Creek scene, and his support of Cole during a sustained period after Reed's death is an aspect of the series' continuity.[3]

One of the most important unifying motifs of *Sunset in the Catskills* is identified by its title, similar to that of Reed's 1833 painting, *Sunset, View on the Catskill*, but generalizing the sunset motif and making it the central subject rather than an aspect of the "view." The work's dominant browns and yellows heighten the autumnal atmosphere that, early in the development of the Catskill Creek series, had also become one of its essential features.[4]

While the relatively low vantage point of *Sunset in the Catskills* resembles that of the Catskill Creek paintings from 1833 and 1838 (its arched frame, like that of the 1838 work, is another link), the mountain profile centered in the distance is no longer north-lying Blackhead Mountain. Instead, it is the undulating form of High Peak and Roundtop to the southwest, which previously had appeared only in the series' panoramic works. In making his composition for *Sunset in the Catskills*, Cole synthesized his prior renderings of the Catskill Creek landscape. He combined the intimacy of the canopied riverbank from the 1833 and 1838 paintings with the profile of the distant mountains that characterizes his panoramic view of the scene and that, by now, had become fixed for him almost as a paradigm.

The degree to which the profile of High Peak and Roundtop, with rounded South Mountain superimposed on them, had gained this status for Cole is evident in one of his sketches, where it appears all by itself—a pure form, as central to his vision of the Catskills as Mont Sainte-Victoire would later become to Paul Cezanne's vision of Provence, and Cerro Pedernal would become to Georgia O'Keeffe's vision of northern New Mexico (fig. 5.3). All subsequent Catskill Creek paintings, whether they assume a low or a high vantage point, would show this mountain profile.

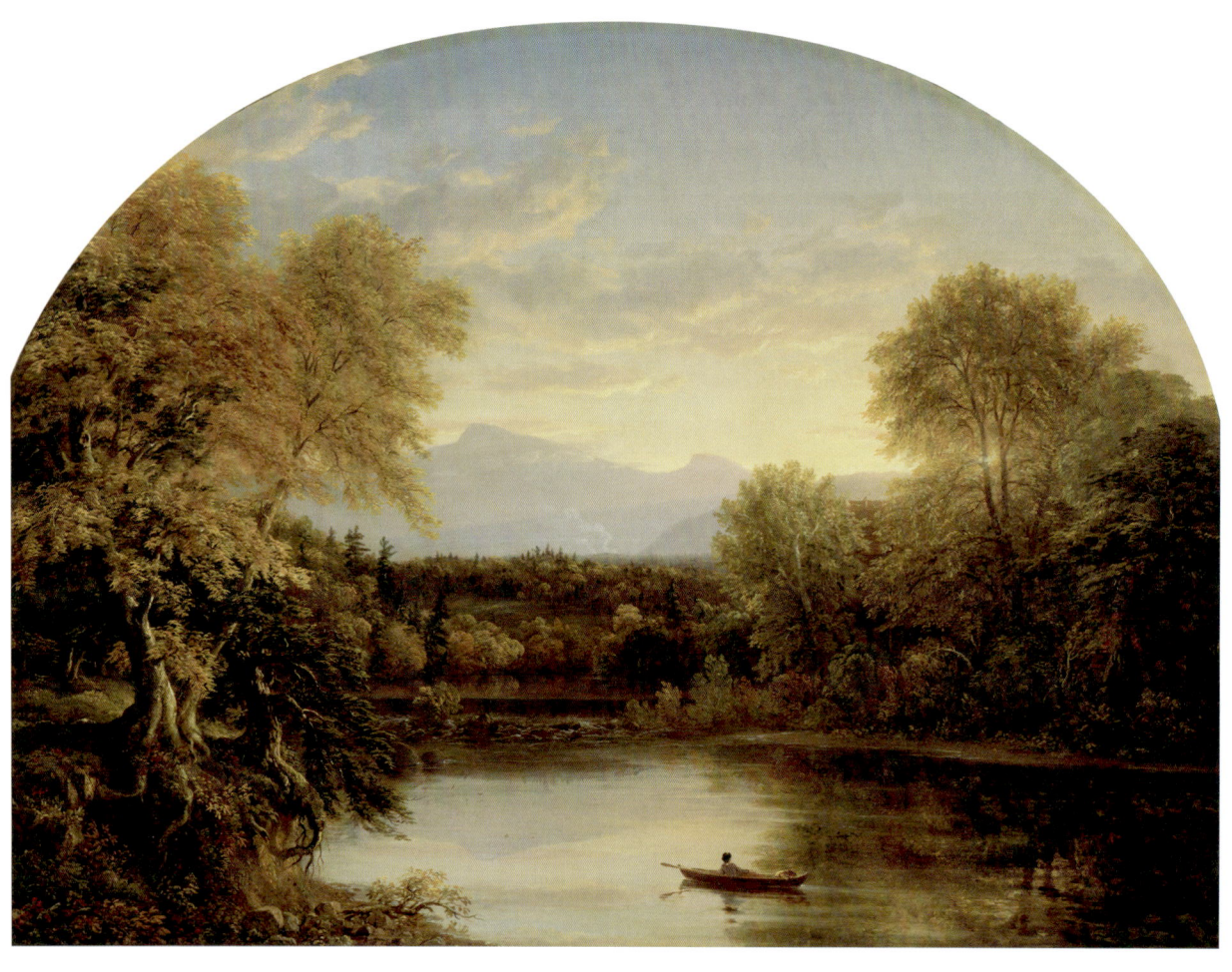

5.2 Thomas Cole, *Sunset in the Catskills*, 1841. Oil on canvas, 22½ x 30 in. (57.15 x 76.2 cm). Museum of Fine Arts, Boston, bequest of Mary Fuller Wilson (63.271).

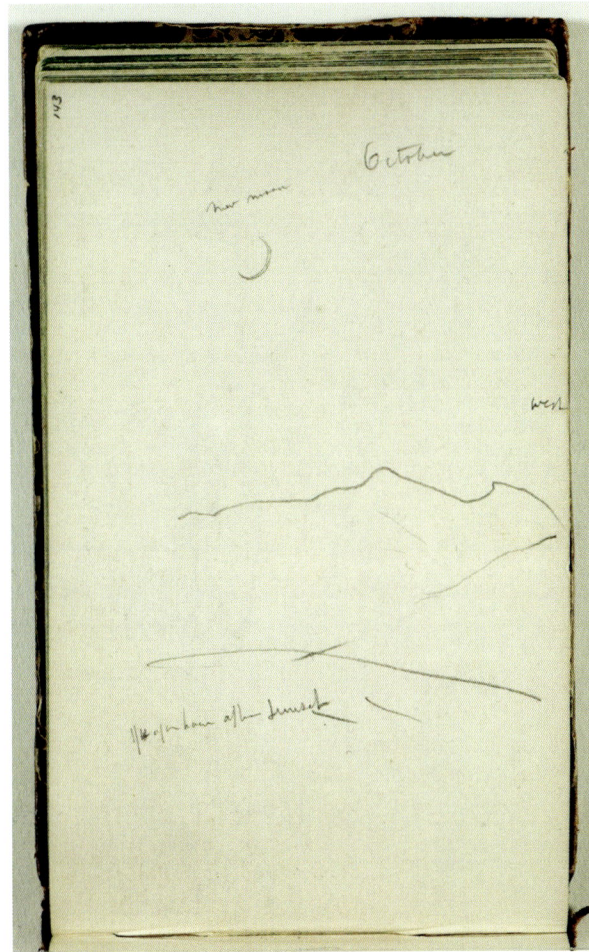

5.3 Thomas Cole, *New Moon October*,
c. 1833–34. Graphite pencil on off-white
wove paper, sheet: 4⅛ x 6½ in. (10.5
x 16.5 cm). Detroit Institute of Arts,
Founders Society Purchase, William H.
Murphy Fund (39.567.143).

To obtain a view of High Peak and Roundtop from the low position represented in
Sunset in the Catskills, Cole moved half a mile upstream from his vantage point for the
1833 and 1838 paintings, as seen in map 2.1. The river's course at this point, near the
Van Vechten farmhouse and its mill, is in alignment with High Peak and Roundtop
and thus opens a channeled view of these mountains. Map 5.1 shows the viewscape of
Sunset in the Catskills and also illustrates its shared perspective with a later work in the
series, *Catskill Creek, N.Y.* (1845), discussed at the end of this chapter.

Cole's new perspective on the mountains gave him a direct view of the rapids,
which had appeared only in glimpses in his panoramic views of Catskill Creek, and
of the dam that in his time lay just above the rapids. As with other Catskill Creek

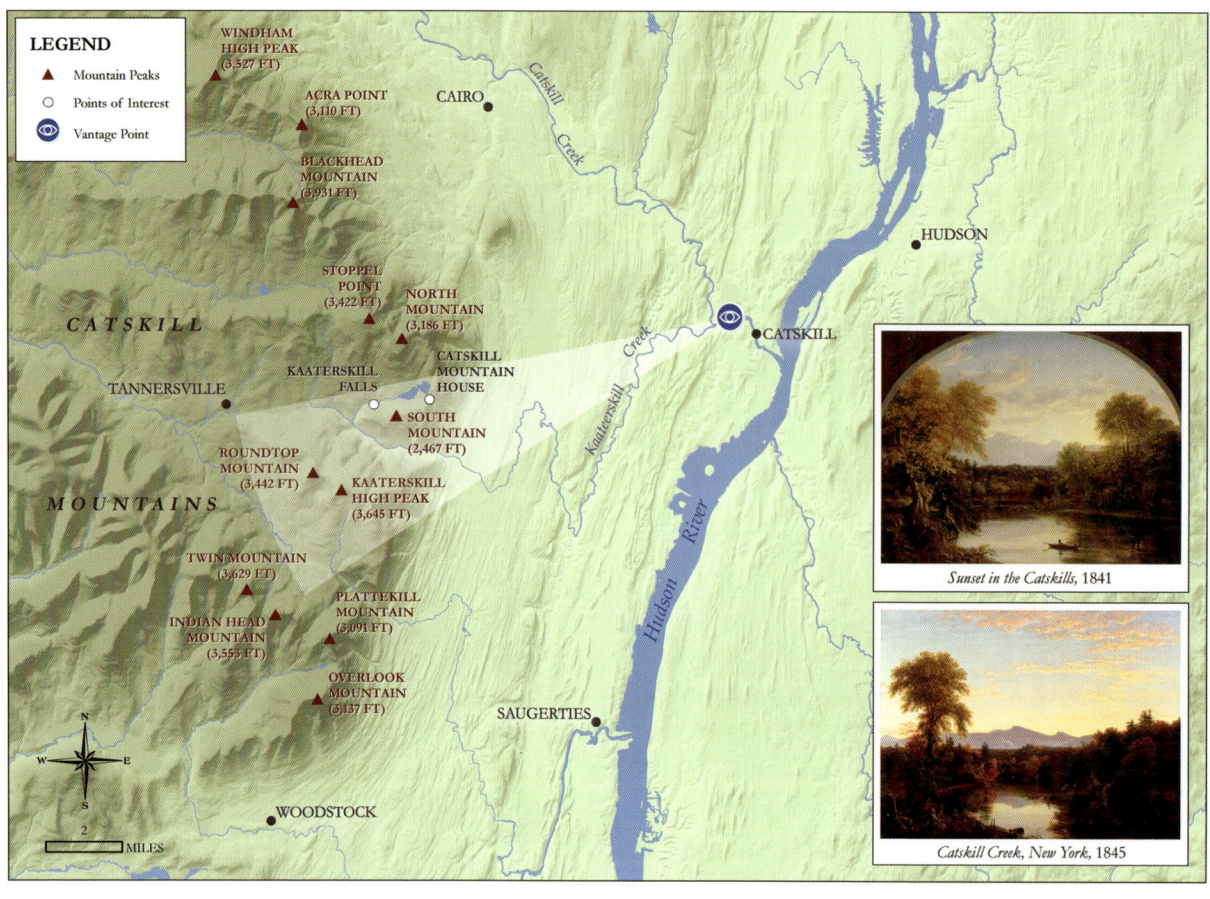

LEGEND

▲ Mountain Peaks
○ Points of Interest
◉ Vantage Point

WINDHAM
HIGH PEAK
(3,527 FT)

ACRA POINT
(3,110 FT)

CAIRO

Catskill Creek

HUDSON

BLACKHEAD
MOUNTAIN
(3,931 FT)

STOPPEL
POINT
(3,422 FT)

NORTH
MOUNTAIN
(3,186 FT)

CATSKILL

CATSKILL

KAATERSKILL
FALLS

CATSKILL
MOUNTAIN
HOUSE

Kaaterskill Creek

TANNERSVILLE

SOUTH
MOUNTAIN
(2,467 FT)

ROUNDTOP
MOUNTAIN
(3,442 FT)

KAATERSKILL
HIGH PEAK
(3,645 FT)

MOUNTAINS

Hudson River

TWIN MOUNTAIN
(3,629 FT)

PLATTEKILL
MOUNTAIN
(3,091 FT)

INDIAN HEAD
MOUNTAIN
(3,553 FT)

OVERLOOK
MOUNTAIN
(3,137 FT)

SAUGERTIES

N
W   E
S

2
MILES

WOODSTOCK

Sunset in the Catskills, 1841

Catskill Creek, New York, 1845

Map 5.1 Viewscape of *Sunset in the Catskills* (1841) and
Catskill Creek, N.Y. (1845). Map by Neil Curri.

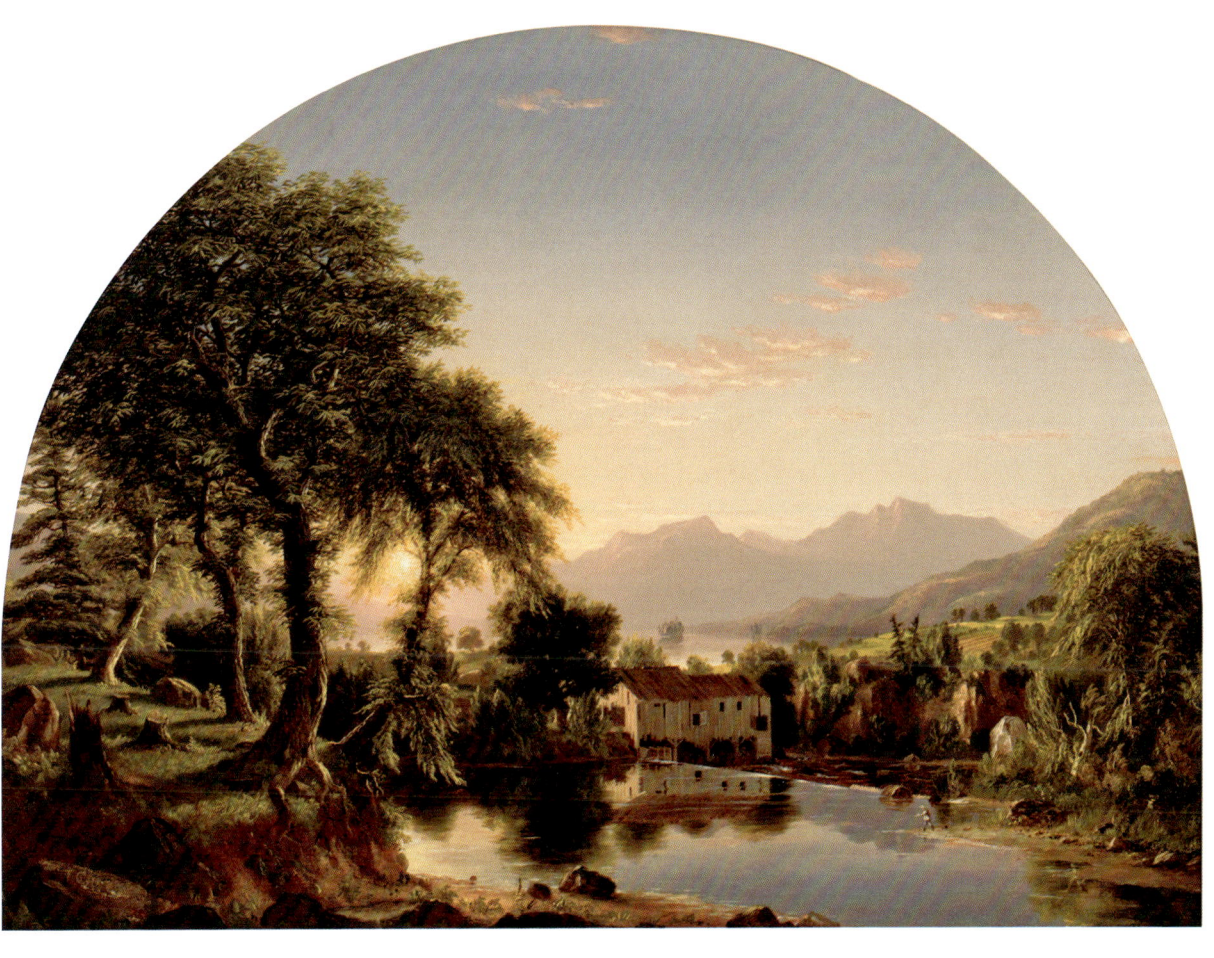

5.8 Thomas Cole, *Mill Dam on the Catskill Creek*,
1841. Oil on canvas, 22¼ x 30¼ in. (56.62 x 76.84 cm).
Currier Museum of Art, bequest of Henry Melville
Fuller (2002.20.19).

Creek a part of the Catskill Creek series; rather, it might be thought of as an experiment conducted within the series, and an experiment that illuminates the series' issues.

In this painting the artist depicts still water held back by a dam in the foreground, with the dam itself and the rapids in the middle distance. We know that Cole had long been interested in the idea of taking different perspectives on the same scene; he had done so ingeniously in his most famous allegorical series *The Course of Empire*, completed in 1836, and shortly thereafter in his 1837–38 two-part series *The Departure* and *The Return*.[8]

Mill Dam on the Catskill Creek, like *Sunset in the Catskills*, was formatted for an arched frame highlighting the sunset motif shared by these paintings. They are the same size (22½ x 30 inches), which raises the interesting possibility that Cole conceived of them as pendants. While they have not been linked in this way, at least in modern times, the fact that they were completed in the same year and perhaps for the same client makes such an intentional pairing seem a serious possibility.[9]

If the stretch of river shown in *Mill Dam on the Catskill Creek* is indeed the same as the one in *Sunset in the Catskills*, except viewed from the opposite direction, then the mill represented so prominently in the former picture must be the Van Vechten mill. It has the same ungainly, rectangular shapes as those the nineteenth-century photograph portrays and that also appear in this mill's representation in a later Cole painting, *River in the Catskills* (fig. 5.14). In *Mill Dam on the Catskill Creek*, as map 2.1 illustrates, the Van Vechten farmhouse would be located to the right, just off the view shown in the painting.

The pairing of *Sunset in the Catskills* with *Mill Dam on the Catskill Creek*, intentional or not, serves to compare two versions of a river landscape—one pastoral (its mill almost invisible and its dam miniaturized) and the other the site of a prominently depicted working mill. In this sense, the paintings render before and after images that could be considered in relation to Cole's earlier portrayal, in Sturges's *View on the Catskill—Early Autumn*, of a bucolic scene that had been altered by the construction of a railroad line. As the artist's "Essay on American Scenery" makes clear, this was a comparison between a rural past and an industrialized present whose issues deeply concerned him.[10]

There were many mills along Catskill Creek in Cole's time. In his angry journal entry from August 1, 1836, that we examined in the prologue, he reports having walked the previous evening to and beyond Austin's mill, which was a mile upriver from the Van

Vechten mill (map 2.1). But Cole does not appear to have been troubled by such mills. As we saw earlier, American mills had for him a picturesque aspect—personified in *Mill Dam on the Catskill Creek* by a fisherman near the dam. They did not represent for him the same industrial threat that the large textile mills of England had. This was a difference of scale, of course, but also a difference between a small American mill's relation to a local economy and the distant markets of England's mills. The Van Vechten mill, for example, was a grist mill. As for the railroad, on the other hand, it most decidedly did not belong to a picturesque vision for Cole, and, as we have seen, it makes its threatening presence felt in *Sunset in the Catskills* by the eroded shoreline depicted in the painting.

Again, assuming that *Sunset in the Catskills* and *Mill Dam on the Catskill Creek* represent the same stretch of river, Cole's experiment in reversing his point of view was challenging because it involved the paintings' important shared motif of the sun setting over the Catskills. The view of the mill in *Mill Dam on the Catskill Creek* is toward the northeast, and Cole needed therefore to pull both the sunset and the mountains far from the west into his composition. The mountain profile in this picture cannot be found anywhere along the Catskill escarpment as seen from the site of the mill; these peaks are imaginary or imported from another place, but they do bring some mountain grandeur to a prosaic scene. And this would not be the first time that Cole moved mountains; he had done so in the 1820s in two of his *Last of the Mohicans* paintings, where he imported New Hampshire's Mount Chocorua into the Lake George region of New York State.[11]

Catskill Creek in Retrospect

If *Mill Dam on the Catskill Creek* was a departure, in orientation, from Cole's usual rendering of his favorite landscape, *Sunset in the Catskills* is remarkably faithful to his original conception of it, including, as I have observed, his return to High Peak and Roundtop as his mountain backdrop. This painting summarizes and reflects upon Cole's views of the Catskill Creek landscape, which is to say his constructions and reconstructions of it over the previous fourteen years.

The rower appears to participate in this reflection. Usually pulling on his oars, here, for the first and only time in the series, he is reclining and taking in the view. The sunset glinting through the trees toward which he is looking, along with the painting's autumnal setting, casts the entire landscape in a retrospective light. The rower is drifting back toward the river's southern shore, from which he began his crossing in the works from 1833, and through him Cole re-views the Catskill Creek scene—what it had become for him—from the perspective of 1841.

Part of what it had become, of course, was a damaged landscape. One aspect of the new era of the 1830s and 1840s was rapid industrial growth. *Sunset in the Catskills* takes indirect though powerful account of this development, and not only with the trails of smoke from tanneries that appear here in the distance, just as they did in the very first Catskill Creek painting. Returning our attention to the rower, with these observations in mind, we see that he is looking not only toward the sunset but also directly at the Van Vechten mill. In the part of Cole's "Essay on American Scenery" where he is describing the recuperative power for city dwellers of certain rural landscapes, he gives special attention to the sunset: "Let him be transported to those favored regions, where the features of the earth are more varied, or yet add the sunset, that wreath of glory daily bound around the world."[12]

The mill's alignment with the sunset in this painting may be understood as its participation in this "glory," that is, as a rustic structure in keeping with its pastoral setting. But in the Romantic imagination of Cole's time, sunsets were not always glorious; they could be melancholy and even tragic, representing the utter end of things; *Desolation* is the title of the sunset scene in Cole's final picture in the *Course of Empire* series.[13]

As we will see in our discussion of *River in the Catskills* (1843), the construction of the Canajoharie and Catskill railroad line almost destroyed the foundation of the Van Vechten farmhouse. The farmhouse and its mill, as real architectural structures and as symbols of an older, rural way of life, were for him endangered, even doomed. There are no vultures circling here (at least none that I can see), but through other means the artist has greatly complicated the meaning of this autumnal scene.

Settler's Home in the Catskills, 1842

Cole did not leave Catskill Creek behind as he departed for Europe in the summer of 1841. He took with him his vivid memory of it, and while abroad the following year he translated this memory into the eighth painting in the series, *Settler's Home in the Catskills*. The artist signed and dated it on a rock in the foreground (fig. 5.9).[14] This work, which measures $22^{15}/_{16}$ x $28\frac{1}{2}$ inches, is in a private collection, and its provenance is unknown.

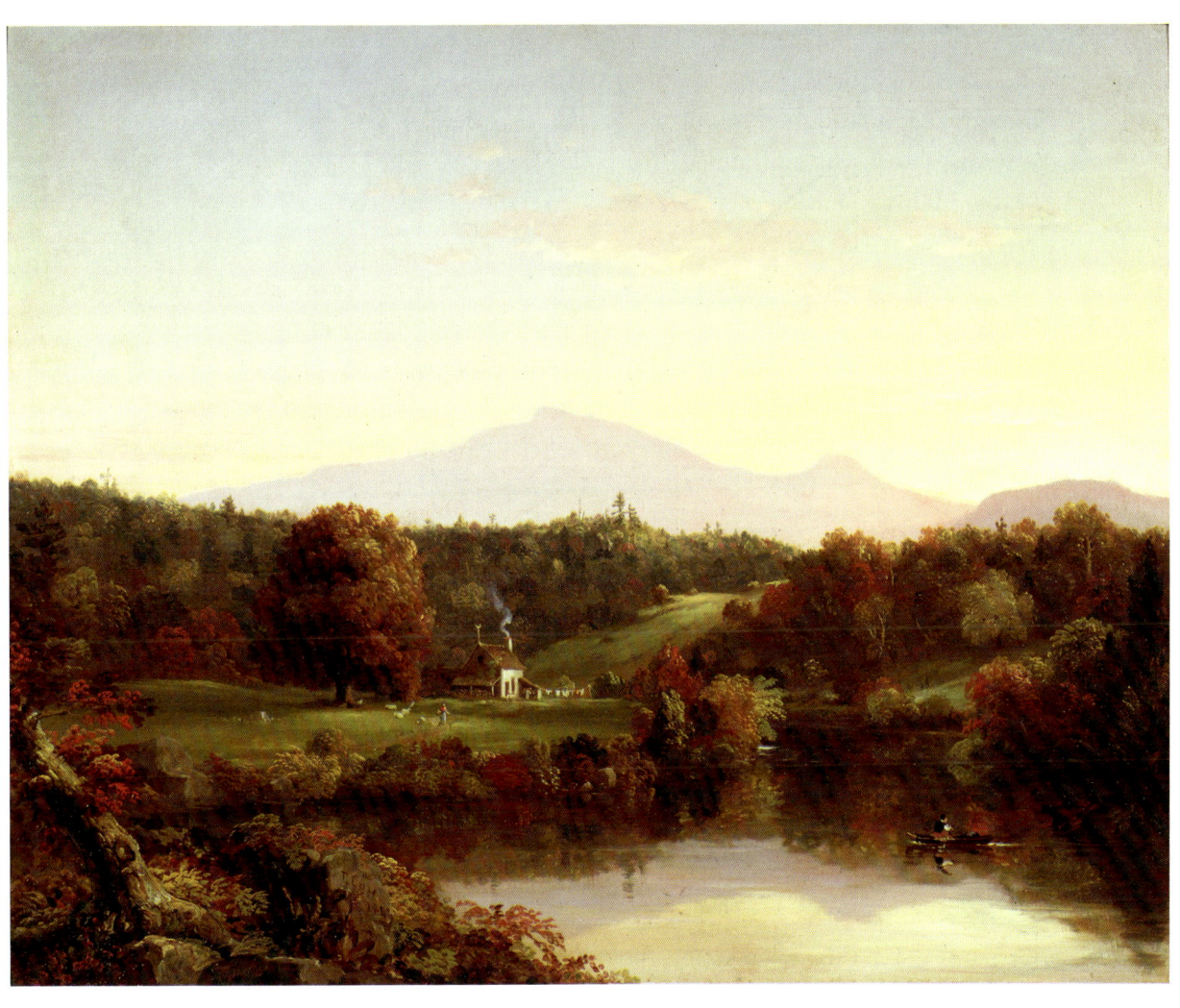

5.9. Thomas Cole, *Settler's Home in the Catskills*, 1842. Oil on canvas, 22¹⁵⁄₁₆ x 28½ in. (58.4 x 72.4 cm). Private collection.

A sketch in the collection of the New-York Historical Society, which has not previously been associated with *Settler's Home in the Catskills*, locates Rome as the place where Cole painted it (fig. 5.10). Identical in composition to the completed work, and almost certainly the basis for it, the sketch has its own title, *On the Catskill*, inscribed by the artist, and a dedication as well: "T. Cole, Roma, May 24 / 1842 / to T. P. Rossiter." A formal sketch with a lined border, it probably was presented as a gift to Thomas Prichard Rossiter, a member of Cole's Rome circle of American artists.[15]

That *Settler's Home in the Catskills* was conceived and executed abroad helps explain why I have been unable to fix its vantage point in the actual landscape of Catskill Creek. While all the individual elements of the painting, including High Peak, Roundtop, and South Mountain in the distance—not to mention the Van Vechten farmhouse, with its half-moon weathervane—belong to that landscape, there is no shoreline position from which their relationships to one another make sense; for this reason map 2.1 does not assign a vantage point to *Settler's Home in the Catskills*.[16]

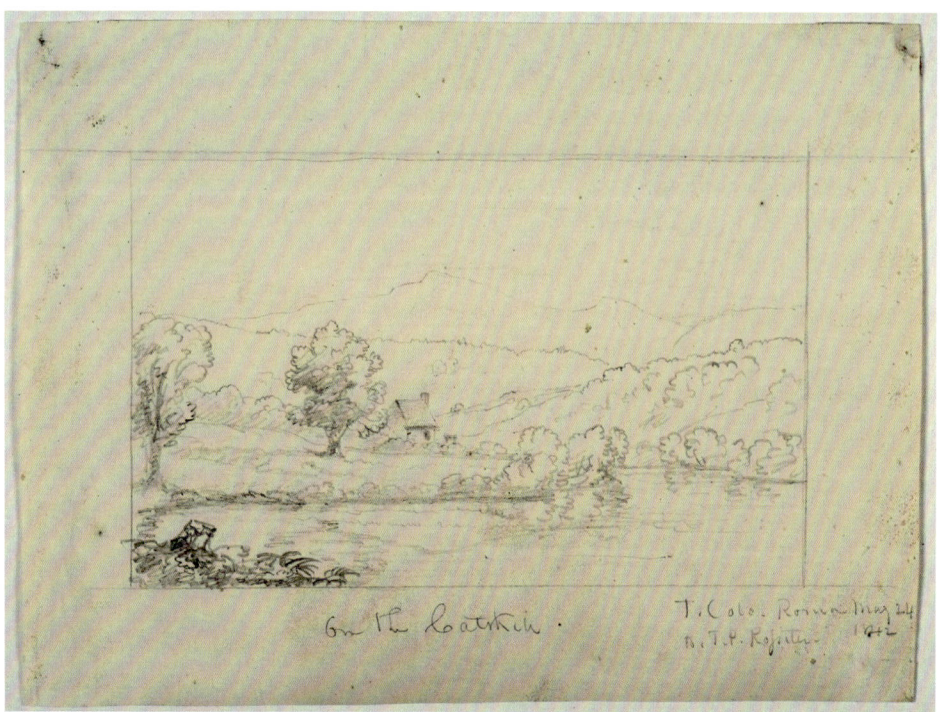

5.10 Thomas Cole, *On the Catskill, New York*, 1842. Graphite on paper, 4¾ x 7⅝ in. (12.1 x 19.4 cm). New-York Historical Society, gift of Mrs. William F. Bevan (1956.70).

116

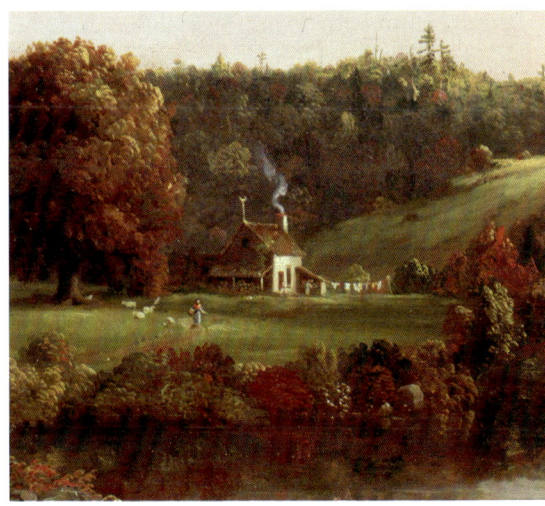

5.11 Detail of figure 5.9, *Settler's Home in the Catskills*, 1842

In painting his beloved Catskill Creek scene from memory, Cole reshaped its landscape features, but he also expanded his historical vision of it. The title's reference to a "settler's home" suggests possession by an original settler and implies that the scene represented here is located in the colonial era. (The woman's dress has such an aspect.) Living in the ancient city of Rome as Cole took up this project may have encouraged him to look deeper into the past of Catskill Creek. But the title is a pun, and it also conveys the idea of a homecoming, perhaps indirectly Cole's own anticipated return from Europe. As we shall see, during his relatively brief tour abroad he had greatly missed his family and his home landscape. *Settler's Home in the Catskills* appears to bring together the historical and the personal meanings that that landscape had for him.

The woman on the shore, with her expectant stance as she looks out over the water (fig. 5.11), reminds us of the lone figure in the deep background of Luman Reed's 1833 work, *Sunset, View on the Catskill* (fig. 4.12). In that painting, Cole recessed and miniaturized the colonial past, but in this work the settlers' time and place fill the canvas. Here the spatial relation of the rower and the woman, so distant in the 1833 work, is lateral rather than recessional; they exist in the same time zone and are fully aware of one another.

A Vision of the Past

Settler's Home in the Catskills is the only Catskill Creek painting fully committed to a vision of the past (there is no tannery smoke here), and Cole's framing of the scene shows how he has opened it to view. The sketch for this painting includes at its far left a short stump leaning rightward over the shoreline. In the completed work it has been replaced by a living tree (returned to life through its transport to the past) leaning diagonally leftward off the composition. Cole had experimented with this leaning form, which replaces the traditional tall, upright Claudian framing tree, in his early *View Near Catskill*. As he has used it here in *Settler's Home in the Catskills*, it suggests an unveiling, or the pulling open of a curtain.

With the past opened to view, its landscape dilated, we can see what the woman in Reed's painting was looking and hoping for. The arched back of the rower—a husband? a son?—shows us how much he wants this homecoming; he is pulling hard on his oars to close the space that separates him from her. The woman is holding a basket and is positioned near a large, rounded maple, with sheep grazing around it and burnished by autumnal color. To give centrality to the maple in the completed painting, Cole eliminated another tall tree to its left that he had drawn into the sketch (fig. 5.11).

Cole's reimagining the Catskill Creek landscape from memory in *Settler's Home in the Catskills* involved a significant reorientation to the scene. All the other works representing this landscape from a low vantage point focus on the northern shore, our view of which is sharply curtailed here, and position their figures (aside from the rower) on that northern shore. By placing the woman on the southern shore's broad pointbar, prominent in the artist's panoramic views (e.g., the scene of the young man chasing horses in *View on the Catskill—Early Autumn*), Cole has found a way to present this important part of the Catskill Creek landscape at much closer range. The (imagined) vantage point is at the level of the rower himself, who, now foregrounded, becomes central to the composition—located in the overlapping reflections of the trees and mountains—rather than a distant figure in a panorama.

This is the rower's homecoming, and Cole's reorganization of the Catskill Creek scene has aligned his objects of desire. In a rightward, recessional movement appear the woman with the nearby maple and sheep, then the farmhouse, and, through the graceful dipping curve of the clothesline, a clear-cut rising toward the hills and mountains beyond. This alignment served the purpose of conjoining these valued forms, which involved Cole's invisibly bridging Catskill Creek. Because of the way he has telescoped the position of the Van Vechten farmhouse, it appears to be on the pointbar, where the woman is standing, rather than just across the river.[17]

The sketch for this work is somewhat less illusionist in this regard; it shows shoreline foliage on the north shore, where the farmhouse is actually located, extending very close to this structure. Having brought the woman—intimately associated with the farmhouse through the painting's domestic imagery—across the river onto the pointbar, Cole needed to bring the farmhouse there too and, indeed, to reorient it to the surrounding landscape. Comparing the house's representation in the sketch with that of the completed painting, we see that in the latter the artist has tilted it toward the mountains and, reinforcing this new alignment, has added a porch with a slanted roof facing south that resembles the actual house's east extension.

In all these ways Cole has reconceived, from Italy, the Catskill Creek scene as a unified, integrated landscape, and because his art so often expresses separation and division, this reconception has symbolic as well as compositional significance. In composition, *Settler's Home in the Catskills* is, in fact, the most unified of the Catskill Creek paintings and in tone the most harmonious. What makes it also the most sentimental of these works is its subject matter and its nostalgia. But as we begin to see how Cole has stitched this scene together, how much synthesis has been involved in creating harmony, we may also sense its underlying tensions and fragility. It shares these qualities, as we have seen, with *Sunset in the Catskills*, completed a year earlier than *Settler's Home in the Catskills*. As the midstream crossings depicted in the 1833 and 1838 works remind us, the river the artist has eclipsed in this painting—in order to replant the settlers' home on the pointbar—is a division, a boundary, as well as a medium of continuity.

As I noted earlier, homecoming was on Cole's mind when he painted this picture in Rome. His second European tour had been rewarding and productive, but overall it was not so pivotal and transforming as his earlier one, and it was much shorter. In 1832 Cole had left Italy reluctantly after three and a half years abroad, to attend to the needs of his parents in New York. In 1842, missing Maria and his children after less than a year away from them, he was eager for a return. A few months following that return, he observed in his journal, "How much I . . . grieved during my absence from my family." From Rome the previous spring he had written to Maria, "You and the girls [Maria's sisters] must begin to think where we shall have my return pic-nic, for I am determined to take more recreation than I have for years past; so I intend to have a jollification on my return, and a pic-nic too, in the course of the season: so make every preparation. My spirits rise as the time approaches."[18] The basket held by the woman on the shore in *Settler's Home in the Catskills* may very well be a picnic basket, and it's difficult not to see the artist himself in the figure rowing strenuously in her direction.

The Trying Hour

The image of strenuous rowing found acute expression in a drawing Cole made, sometime in the months following his return from Europe, for the Artists' Sketching Club of New York. The club's membership included Asher B. Durand, John W. Casilear, and about a dozen other notable painters including Cole. Many years later the proceedings of the club's weekly meetings were chronicled by one of its members, Thomas Seir Cummings: "At the designated hour, the company sat down to work—everything was ready but the 'subject' which was to that moment unknown. 'It was then given.' The sketchers were allowed precisely one hour to make their drawing, and at the termination of that the bell rung [sic]." This challenge of spontaneity was taken seriously; its goal was the creation of particularly expressive images, produced under pressure and rendered quickly with pencil and sepia ink wash.[19]

When Cole took his turn at offering a subject, he proposed "The Trying Hour." Most responses were predictably solemn; Durand, for example, drew a woman mourning a dead or dying child in a darkened bedroom. Even though Cole, as the proposer, had obviously preconceived his sketch, it has far more energy than those of the other artists. It depicts a man rowing for his life, trying to pull clear from the violent currents drawing him toward a massive, strangely monolithic waterfall (fig. 5.12). Unlike the scene in *Manhood*, from the *Voyage of Life* series, where the voyager is (somehow) standing upright in prayer as his boat begins to descend the rapids, here there is only furious rowing. Nor is there an attending, hovering angel; this rower is on his own in his desperate attempt at survival.

No figure in the Catskill Creek paintings finds himself in such dire circumstances. But this drawing fills out our understanding of what, for Cole, it meant to be a rower. The arched back of the figure in *The Trying Hour* resembles that of the rower in *Settler's Home in the Catskills* and suggests an element of desperation in the settler's return—unsettling, we might say, this otherwise tranquil scene. This was not the only time that Cole arched his rower's back. A haunting oil study, *On Catskill Creek, Sunset*, executed in the mid-1840s, shows this figure in the same posture and, as in the other two works, rowing right to left (fig. 5.13).[20]

The strenuous rowing of these paintings may represent the artist's struggles, his own trying times, during the 1840s. But they also suggest a deeper, more persistent struggle within Cole. The space between the rower in *Settler's Home in the Catskills* and the woman on the shore, like the spaces dividing the isolated figures in *View on*

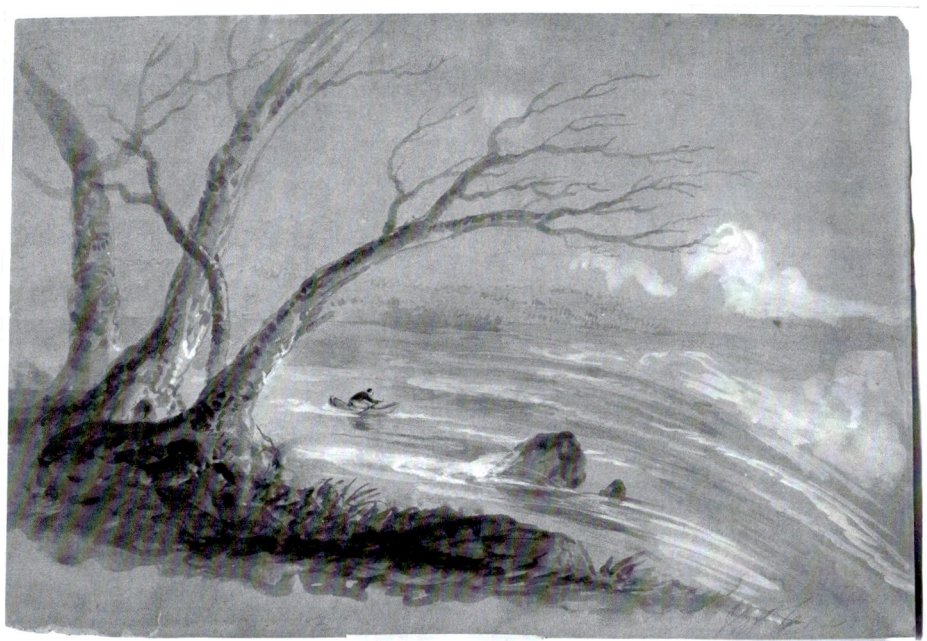

5.12 Thomas Cole, *The Trying Hour*, c. 1844–46. Brush and brown and white wash over graphite pencil on buff paper, sheet: 10⁵⁄₁₆ x 15¼ in. (26.2 x 38.7 cm). Karolik (1962) cat. 654, Museum of Fine Arts, Boston, gift of Maxim Karolik for the M. and M. Karolik Collection of American Watercolors and Drawings, 1800–1875 (57.277).

the Catskill—Early Autumn from one another, are spaces of desire. Rowing, like the running of the young man after the horses in that painting, works to close the gap, to fulfill the desire. Or, in the language of the works from 1833 and 1838, to reach the shore.

But these spaces are not unrelated to the one separating the rower in *The Trying Hour* from disaster, from a terrifying, undifferentiated mass of falling water. Cole has positioned him precisely at the point on the raging river where we can't be sure whether the current has captured him or might let him go. This threshold between doom and salvation is, of course, related to Cole's Puritanism.[21] But it is also related to the fundamental push and pull of his imagination, to his profound uncertainty about where the fulfillment of desire might lead.

River in the Catskills, 1843

As we have seen, Cole drew open a curtain on the past in *Settler's Home in the Catskills* by pulling his Claudian framing tree almost off the canvas. In his next Catskill Creek

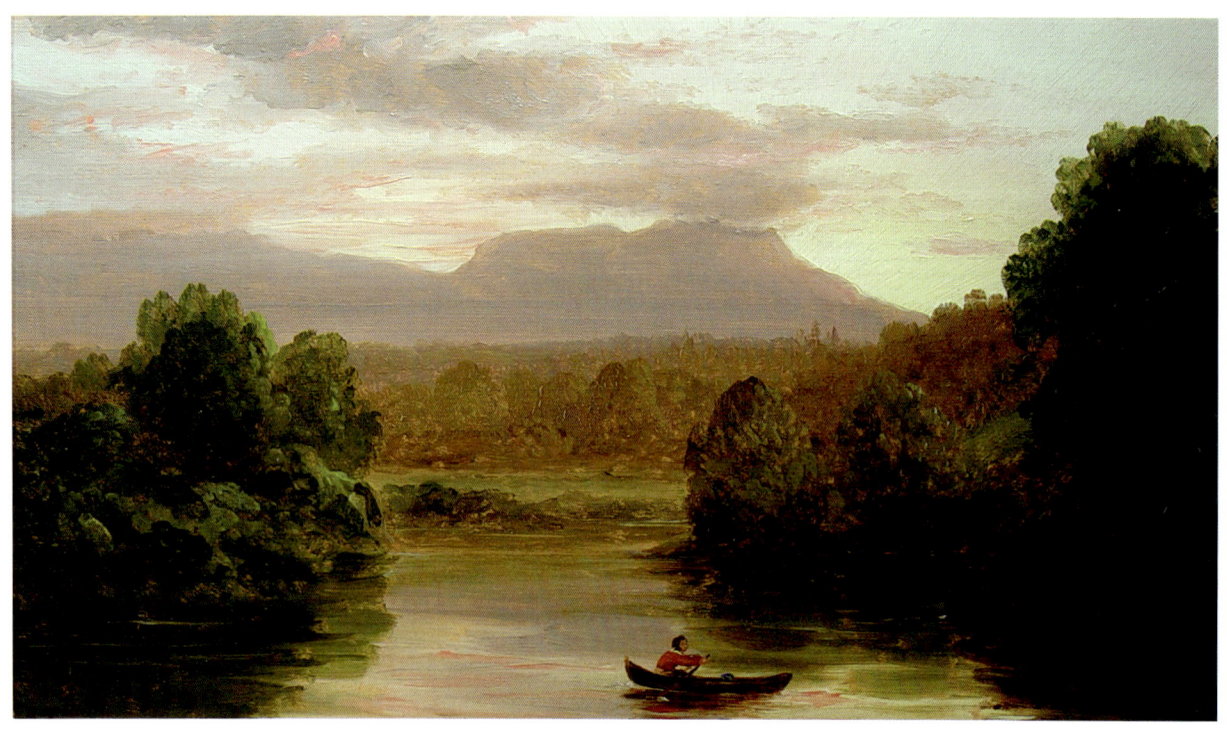

5.13 Thomas Cole, *On Catskill Creek, Sunset*, c. 1845–47.
Oil on wood panel, 9¼ x 14¾ in. (23.5 x 37.5 cm).
New-York Historical Society, bequest of Eileen
Newman (2015).

painting, *River in the Catskills*, he opened a view to the future by eliminating the framing tree altogether. Here a woodsman—ax at his side—has destroyed the tree, and its stump is a prominent feature of the painting's foreground (fig. 5.14).[22] Because of issues raised by its imagery of natural destruction, *River in the Catskills* is in our time the best known and most studied of the Catskill Creek paintings. At 27½ x 40⅜ inches, it is the second largest of these works after *View on the Catskills—Early Autumn*, and it resides in the Museum of Fine Arts, Boston. Cole completed this painting toward the end of 1843, more than a year after his return from his second European tour.

In *River in the Catskills*, both landforms and landmarks are exposed to a degree unique in the series. The scene opened to view includes a railroad train, which, according to Kenneth W. Maddox, makes this "the first important painting in the history of art" to do so.[23] As we know from our discussion of previous works in the Catskill Creek series, the line on which this train ran was the Canajoharie and Catskill, which operated from 1836 until mid-1842, when, because of accidents and operational difficulties, it was decommissioned by New York State.[24] Cole completed *River in the Catskills* about six months after trains stopped running on this line.

Maddox himself did not regard the train's presence in *River in the Catskills* as an expression of Cole's anger about the destructive effects of industrialism, but others have. In a brilliant reassessment of the painting, Alan Wallach understood it as a disguised "antipastoral"—"a deliberate attack on the conventions of pastoral landscape painting and consequently on a pervasive, if often contested, ideology that lauded improvement and material progress. " In arguing that *River in the Catskills* was a deliberate experiment, Wallach pointed out that Cole painted it without a commission.[25]

This understanding of *River in the Catskills* is not inconsistent with my analysis of Cole's encoding strategies in other Catskill Creek paintings, and, in fact, there are particular encoded elements, previously unobserved, in this work that strengthen Wallach's interpretation. One of the most striking of these elements is the thin stream of gray smoke issuing almost horizontally from the locomotive's engine. When we compare *River in the Catskills* with *View on the Catskill—Early Autumn*, allowing for their somewhat different perspectives from Jefferson Heights, we see that the smoke in the former work is in the same part of the composition where, in the latter, we glimpse the rapids. The rapids were important to Cole, perhaps as a symbol of wild nature in a predominantly agrarian environment; as we saw, they appeared in his very first Catskill Creek painting in 1827.[26] This flattened, wispy line of industrial smoke, which the artist has colored the same gray hue as he had colored the rapids in earlier works, has taken their

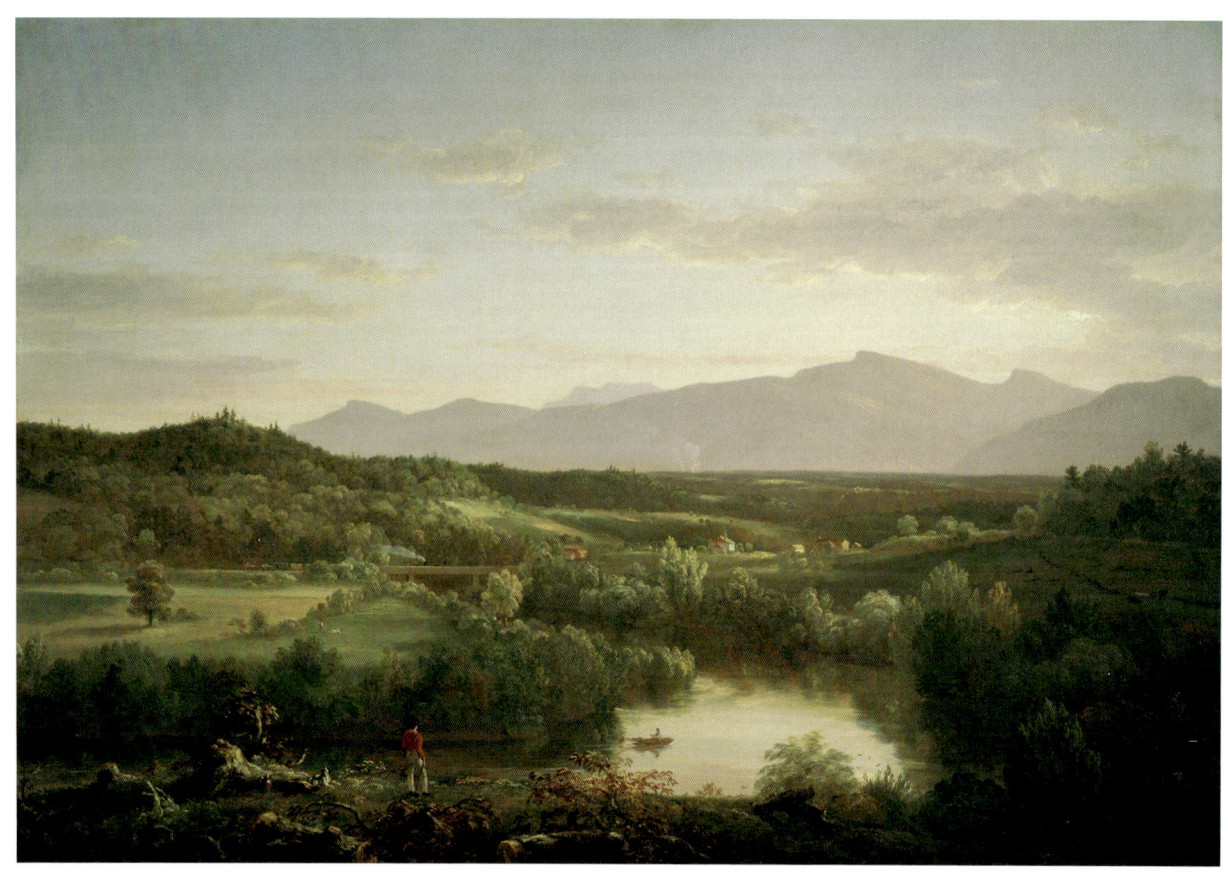

5.14 Thomas Cole, *River in the Catskills*, 1843. Oil on canvas, 27½ x 40⅜ in. (69.85 x 102.55 cm). Museum of Fine Arts, Boston, gift of Martha C. Karolik for the M. and M. Karolik Collection of American Paintings, 1815–1865 (47.1201).

place—a visual relationship that would not be discernible without knowledge of other Catskill Creek paintings and the template upon which they were collectively drawn.[27]

In fact, *River in the Catskills* has not very often been considered in relation to other works in the Catskill Creek series. Rather, it has usually been compared to paintings by other nineteenth-century American artists depicting railroad trains, such as George Inness's *The Lackawanna Valley* (c. 1856) and Jasper Francis Cropsey's *Starrucca Viaduct, Pennsylvania* (1865). These comparisons have greatly illuminated *River in the Catskills*, but they have also distanced it from its companion works in the series.[28] This painting, apparently so exceptional among Cole's landscapes, evolved from a template into which he had been painting for sixteen years. And, as we have seen, works in the series from the late 1830s and early 1840s anticipate its critique of industrialism and do so through strategies as subtle as its own.

One of these strategies is miniaturization, a process we have examined in several works preceding *River in the Catskills*. The train in this painting was viewed by some mid-twentieth-century scholars as a toy-like picturesque detail.[29] And it is indeed represented small and in the distance, where its locomotive is partially hidden behind a railroad bridge. Only the smokestack shows. Wallach's key, revisionary point is that by diminishing and partially masking the train, Cole did not intend to minimize its destructive effects, as American studies scholarship of the 1960s and 1970s had argued. Hardly an accommodation of industrialism, a reconciliation of the machine and the garden, this train expresses through indirection the artist's fury—which Wallach documents from his writings—in one of the only ways available to him as an antebellum artist.[30]

Cole consistently used miniaturization in earlier Catskill Creek paintings (and elsewhere) to convey meaning, and in this case the meaning is portentous. He paradoxically hides the train while broadly exposing the landscape it threatens—laying bare this landscape's erosions and warning of its continuing vulnerability. That there are vultures circling here too (along the ridgeline at the lower right of the composition) should come as no surprise.

A Rigid Geometry

But miniaturization and exposure are not the only strategies at work in *River in the Catskills*. We have seen how landforms (e.g., the oval pointbar) in earlier Catskill Creek

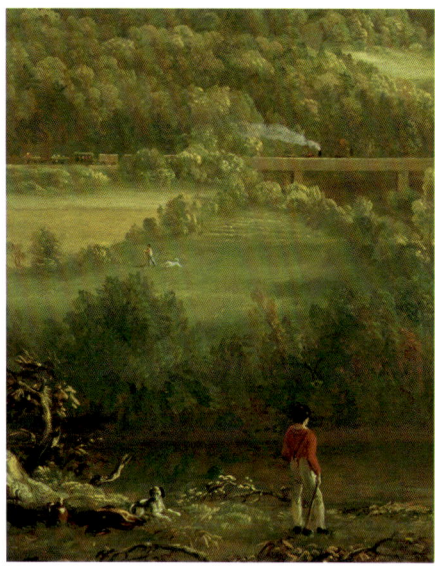

5.15 Detail of figure 5.14, *River in the Catskills*, 1843

paintings take on symbolic meaning because of the way Cole has delineated them and set them into relation with other parts of the landscape. The most distinctive aspect of Cole's representation of landscape in *River in the Catskills* is the painting's rigid geometry. From the elevated position of the woodsman in the foreground runs a relentlessly narrowing channel of space, a funnel or vortex, shaped by a green agricultural field hedged on both sides by bushes and low trees (fig. 5.15). This form works like a pointer, focusing our vision not on developments brought by industrialization but on the very agent of this process, the railroad.

One can get a vivid sense of how Cole shaped this vortex by examining what may have been his first, and certainly most formative, sketch for *River in the Catskills*. Dated by the artist September 9, 1842, soon after his return from Europe but more than year before he completed the painting, this sketch has strangely not been associated with it in scholarship from the last sixty years, despite the unmistakable lineage (fig. 5.16).[31] It has exactly the same orientation to the scene (including an identical mountain profile) as *River in the Catskills*, and it includes most of the same landmarks. Most notably, this may be the only sketch among Cole's many of the Catskill Creek scene that includes the railroad bridge. Regarding the vortex I have described, the sketch shows how the artist took the simple hedgerow on the left and the bushes and trees bordering the river on the right and tightened them into an intensely formal and symbolic shape in the completed painting.

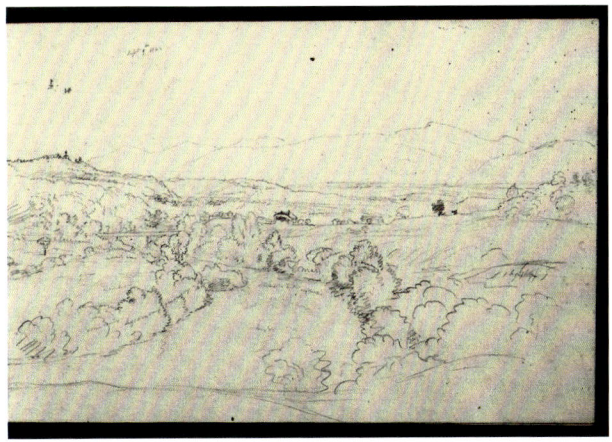

5.16 Thomas Cole, *River Landscape (Catskill Creek from Jefferson Heights)*, 1842. Graphite on cream wove paper, 11³/₁₆ x 16¹⁵/₁₆ in. (28.4 x 43 cm). Folio 6, recto, of sketchbook dated 1839–1844. Princeton University Art Museum, gift of Frank Jewett Mather Jr. (x1940-78.5v-6r). Courtesy Princeton University Art Museum/Art Resource, NY.

Sharply intersecting the funneled form in *River in the Catskills* is the horizontal vector of the railroad line; from left to right we view successively the cars trailing the locomotive, the bridge, and a ridgeline extending until it dissolves in a wooded area at the far right of the composition. (As map 2.1 shows, the line did not actually proceed along this ridgeline; after crossing the bridge the rails continued northwest toward another crossing of Catskill Creek about two miles to the north.) In the other direction, to the left of the bridge, Cole takes our view of the Catskill Front farther south than in any of the other works in the Catskill Creek series, as illustrated by map 5.2. (*View on the Catskill—Early Autumn* looks almost as far south, but its framing trees mask the breadth of its viewscape.) The artist thereby broadly extends the mountain profile and, as well, lengthens out the intermediate horizon line; even the river, before it makes its upstream turn around the point bar, has a horizontality unique among the series' panoramic views.

In these ways, Cole aligned the entire composition with the train's forward progress. The stark geometry of *River in the Catskills* is in keeping with the way the painting exposes the landscape, flooded, as Wallach points out, by "glaring noonday light."[32] Caught in the glare, on an unshaded part of the river, is our rower, who appears in a posture of greater toil than in other Catskill Creek paintings. And it is worth noting that, with the exception of the very first of these paintings (1827) with its auroral scene, *River in the Catskills* is the only work that does not depict a sunset. Finally, it is

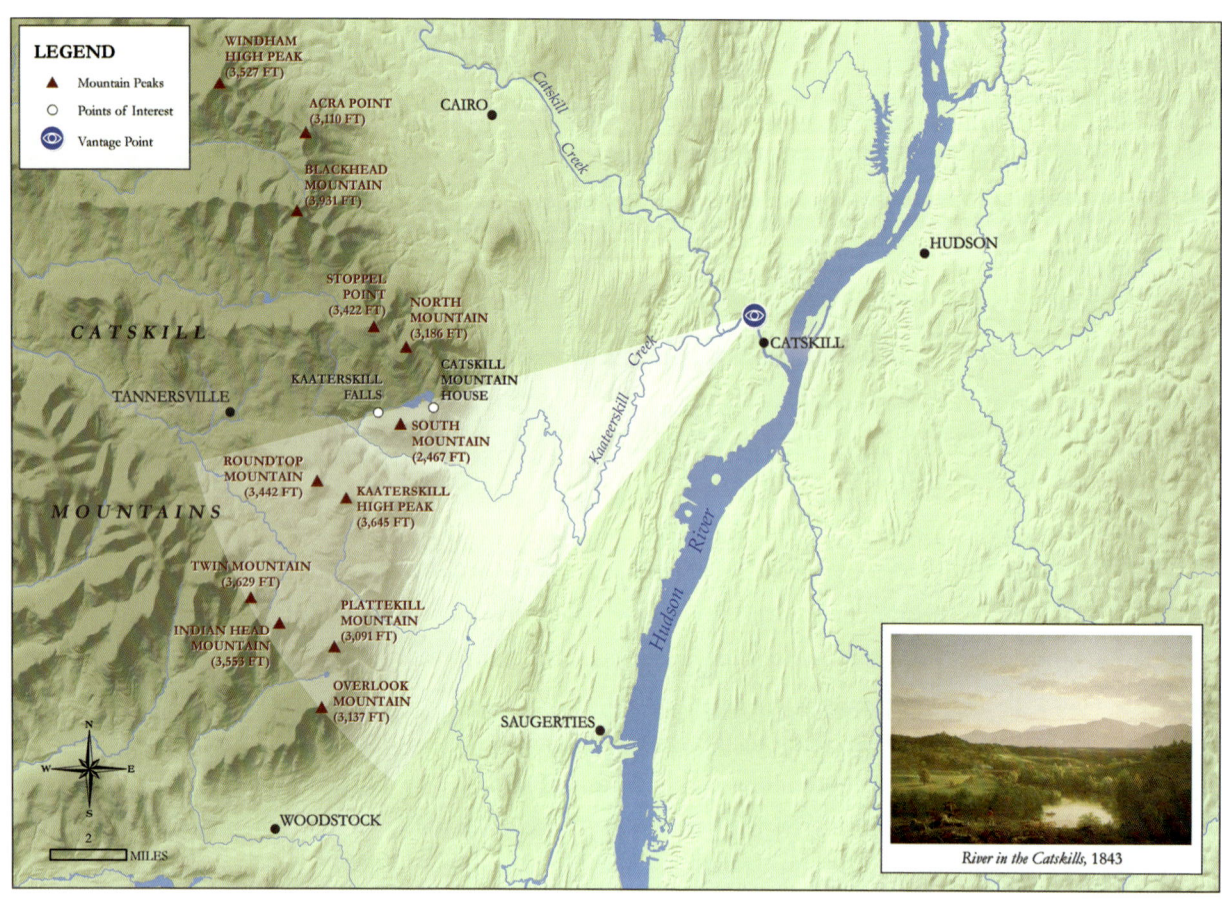

LEGEND

▲ Mountain Peaks
○ Points of Interest
◉ Vantage Point

WINDHAM HIGH PEAK (3,527 FT)

ACRA POINT (3,110 FT)

CAIRO

Catskill Creek

HUDSON

BLACKHEAD MOUNTAIN (3,931 FT)

STOPPEL POINT (3,422 FT)

CATSKILL

NORTH MOUNTAIN (3,186 FT)

C A T S K I L L

KAATERSKILL FALLS

CATSKILL MOUNTAIN HOUSE

Kaaterskill Creek

TANNERSVILLE

SOUTH MOUNTAIN (2,467 FT)

ROUNDTOP MOUNTAIN (3,442 FT)

KAATERSKILL HIGH PEAK (3,645 FT)

M O U N T A I N S

Hudson River

TWIN MOUNTAIN (3,629 FT)

PLATTEKILL MOUNTAIN (3,091 FT)

INDIAN HEAD MOUNTAIN (3,553 FT)

OVERLOOK MOUNTAIN (3,137 FT)

SAUGERTIES

N
W E
S

2 MILES

WOODSTOCK

River in the Catskills, 1843

Map 5.2 Viewscape of *River in the Catskills*, 1843. Map
by Neil Curri.

telling that of all the Catskill Creek paintings that Cole completed in the 1830s and 1840s, this is the only one in which reflections of the mountains—an image of spirituality for Cole—do not appear on the river's surface.[33]

Van Vechten Farmhouse Threatened

Cole's stretched-out, lateral composition in *River in the Catskills* has at its center the train crossing over the bridge. Earlier works in the series give meaning to the crossing of Catskill Creek as a signifier of passage from one state of being to another, as they also invite the viewer to find a temporal dimension in the composition of these works. The bridge, as I noted earlier, hides the locomotive, but there is further significance to Cole's positioning it on the bridge rather than approaching it or proceeding from it. In this position, midstream, the locomotive exists symbolically at the precise moment of transition between the past and the future and is set on a collision course with the Van Vechten house, the human structure across the river that for Cole embodied the values of an older rural order.

As construction of the Canajoharie and Catskill railroad actually played out in 1836, the line ran so close to this stone colonial structure, around its rear, southwest corner (see map 2.1), that it threatened to undermine the house's foundation—as illustrated by a photograph from the 1870s showing a subsequent line that followed the same path (fig. 5.17, with inset.) During the construction of that original line, the one Cole witnessed, the farmhouse's owner, John Van Vechten, was involved in a confrontation with the construction company's chief engineer. John's son Peter, many years later, provided a firsthand account. Different routings of the line were proposed, he wrote, one of them to run immediately "in front of the old stone house, between it and the barn." At a particularly explosive moment in this confrontation, according to Peter, "The engineer told my father he would run the road right through the house if he liked."[34] He almost did. The routing chosen, as we have seen, passed within feet of this old stone structure, and the massive berm that supported the tracks and led right to the house remains in place today. Incidents like the engineer's threat, to the degree that Cole knew about them, would have intensified his anger at the "copper-hearted barbarians," as he called the railroad builders in a well-known letter to Luman Reed.[35]

In *River in the Catskills* Cole does not show the railroad line bending around behind the Van Vechten house's southwest corner—the tracks seem to disappear from the north shore—and he has positioned the house considerably farther away (rightward)

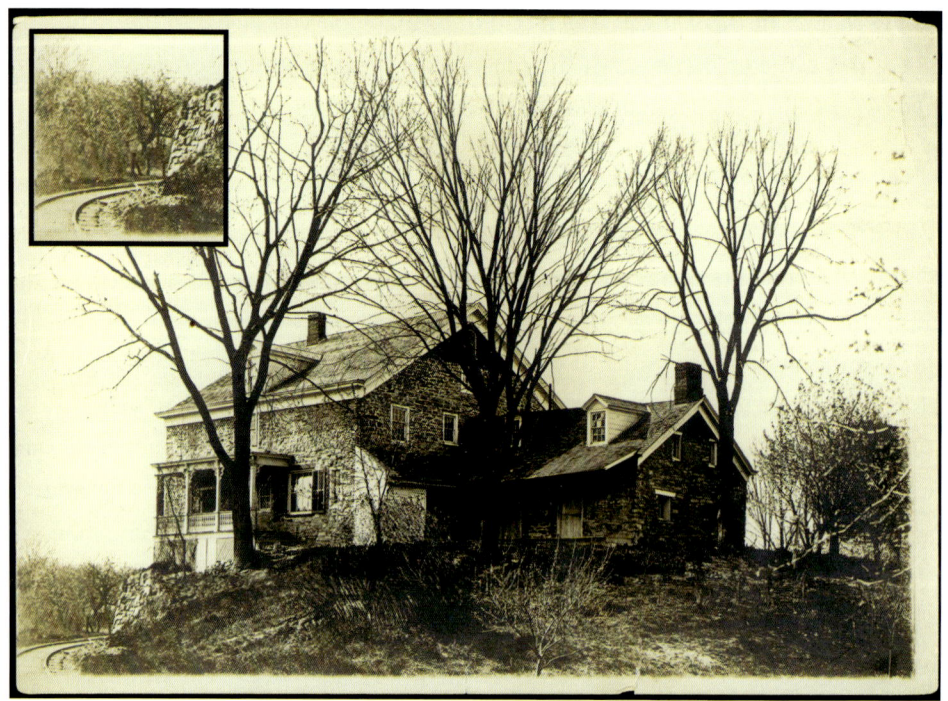

5.17 Van Vechten house, c. 1870, Leeds Photo File, Vedder Research Library

from the river and the bridge than it actually was. This repositioning of the house is consistent with the horizontality of the composition, part of its "stretching" of the landscape, and, as well, with Cole's exposure of this landscape. *River in the Catskills* is the only one of the Catskill Creek paintings in which the Van Vechten farmhouse is fully open to view (fig. 5.18). Even as the artist has created space around the house to mark its presence—and its importance to him—he has targeted it through the sheer geometry of the composition, that is, through an invisible but inexorable line of force.

To the left of the farmhouse and partially hidden by trees, as viewed in figure 5.18, is another important structure, the Van Vechten mill—identifiable by its location and by its rectangular shapes—the same mill, I have proposed, that the artist depicted from upriver in *Mill Dam on the Catskill Creek* (fig. 5.8). As we have seen, Cole seems not to have regarded American mills as a destructive force. He is even capable of portraying them as objects of sentiment and nostalgia, as he did in *The Mill, Sunset* (1844), possibly a highly abstracted (and intensely Claudian) rendering of the Catskill Creek scene, though its landscape features are not recognizable.[36] In other

130

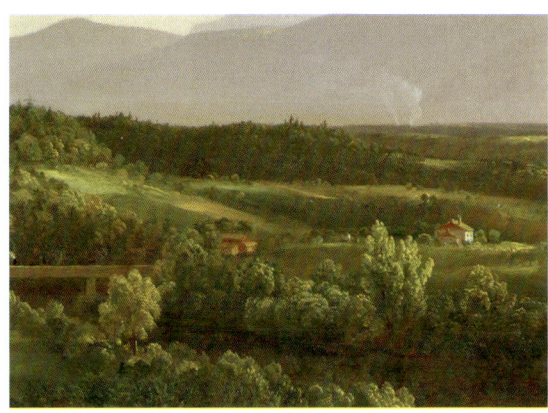

5.18 Detail of figure 5.14, *River in the Catskills*, 1843

words, a mill along a small American river was not for Cole a menacing technology like the railroad, perhaps in part, as we saw earlier, because he regarded it as a stable element in the local economy and landscape. The railroad, on the other hand, was a force relentlessly moving through—and indeed over—local landscapes as it traversed long distances with goods and passengers.

The contrast is vividly expressed in a speech Cole gave to his Catskill neighbors in April of 1841 in which he lamented the railroad's destruction of "that noble grove by Van Vechten's mill, through which wound what is called the Snake Road, and at the same time the ancient grove of cedar, that shadowed the Indian burying-ground."[37] The farmhouse and its mill, along with the two nearby groves, were for Cole a part of the same sacramental vision called up by his inclusion of the Indian burial ground. This whole world, he feared, was destined for a kind of burial. What the railroad threatened was not just a house or a mill or a grove but a way of life, one that the artist, like his literary contemporaries Cooper and Irving, associated with the Dutch colonial era.

Irving's stories "Rip Van Winkle" and "The Legend of Sleepy Hollow" are, of course, his most familiar expressions of his fondness for the Dutch. The latter work, through its characterization of Ichabod Crane as a greedy and self-interested Yankee, dramatizes Irving's resistance to what he perceived as his era's frantic and destructive go-aheadism, led by migrating New Englanders. Cooper shared these views (his land developer father had settled Cooperstown, New York, in part, with such migrating New Englanders) and looked back with historical nostalgia to the period of Dutch settlement.

Among his works, the novel *Satanstoe* (1845) most fully expresses this nostalgia. Along with two companion novels in the so-called Littlepage Trilogy, *Satanstoe* was written partly in response to the antirent war, a revolt of tenant farmers in the Hudson Valley. This revolt began in 1839 upon the death of Stephen Van Rensselaer III—who had descended from Kiliaen Van Rensselaer, the first patroon of the Manor of Rensselaerswyck—when his heirs attempted to collect overdue rents from the farmers. In the resulting conflict, which lasted for a decade, Cooper sided with the landholders.[38]

As noted earlier, Stephen Van Rensselaer III was one of Cole's most important early patrons, and the artist can be linked indirectly with Cooper (and Irving) in their idealization of the Dutch settlement era—especially through his representations of the colonial Van Vechten house. The miniaturized red and white human figures along the shoreline in the deep background of Cole's 1838 Catskill Creek painting belong to that era, as does, of course, the entire landscape of *Settler's Home in the Catskills*—the work in the series immediately preceding *River in the Catskills*.

The Lament of the Forest

While the Van Vechten farmhouse and its mill survived the railroad line's construction, the groves did not, and Cole gave open expression to his sorrow about their destruction in poems such as "The Lament of the Forest" (1838).[39] In *River in the Catskills*, he expresses his sorrow more indirectly. From Jefferson Heights, Cole's vantage point for this painting, the groves would have appeared distantly in the valley, directly along the path of advancing railroad construction. In *River in the Catskills* remnants of the destroyed groves do not appear in that distant part of the landscape. But the painting's degraded, disordered foreground, where the woodsman is standing, suggests Cole's strategy. He seems to have brought images of the destroyed groves forward in the composition—foregrounding them, which is to say, bringing them to our attention. A large stump to the woodsman's left appears to represent them metonymically.[40] The two groves, with all their many trees, are condensed into a single, disturbing image—or what at first appears to be a single image.

When we widen our view of the foreground somewhat, however, we find a second large stump. The doubling of forms often has significance in Cole's work, and, as others have noted, trees in many of his drawings have anthropomorphic features.[41] These two stumps, tilted leftward away from the woodsman, may suggest twinned postures of fear and withdrawal (fig. 5.19). Centered between and in front of these deadened forms is a cluster of mullein, leaning (straining?) leftward in seeming concert with the

132

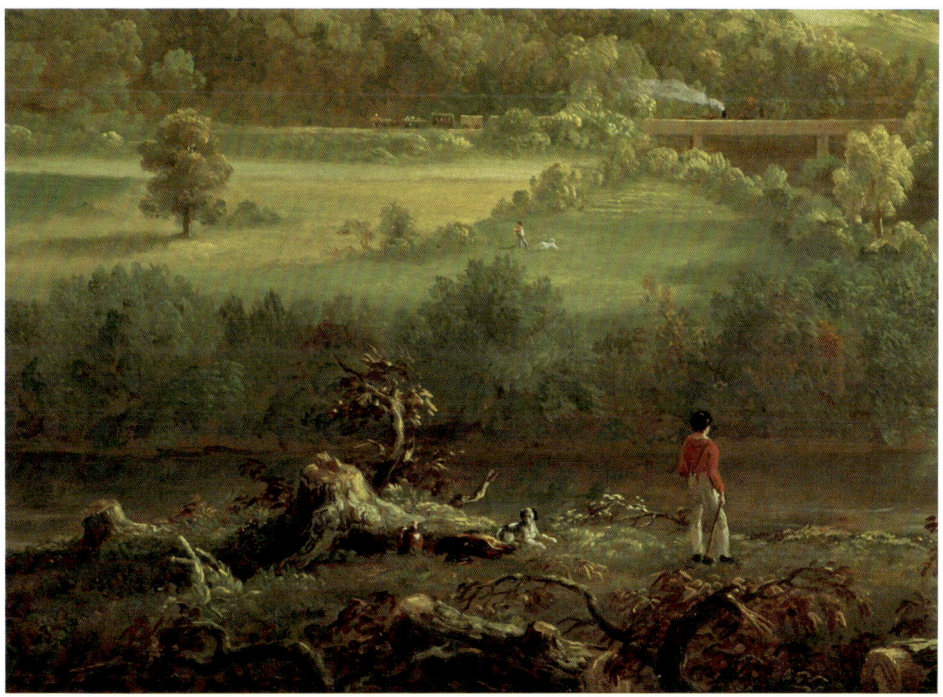

5.19 Detail of figure 5.14, *River in the Catskills*, 1843

stumps. The mullein appears here in a form much diminished and attenuated from its representation in some of the other Catskill Creek paintings, but it is nevertheless alive and is somehow still the "Great Mullen"—to call up the title of William Carlos Williams's poem about this vigorous, enduring plant.[42] By doubling the stumps, Cole has intensified the imagery of natural destruction in *River in the Catskills*, but with the mullein he has planted between them an image of possible regrowth and continuance.

There is another, important form of doubling at work in *River in the Catskills* that we have seen in other Catskill Creek paintings, a recessional form in which a figure in the foreground has a symbolic relation to one in the deep background. The 1833 and 1838 Catskill Creek paintings make this relation between their rowers and colonial figures in the distance. Of greater pertinence because its composition is so similar to *River in the Catskills* is the earlier *View on the Catskill—Early Autumn*.

Between the largest stump and the woodsman, in *River in the Catskills*, is a spaniel whose position aligns it recessionally with another dog, following a boy, on the pointbar far below (fig. 5.19).[43] This is the same part of the landscape, in *View on the Catskill—Early Autumn*, where a young man chases horses. The implicit relationship we examined earlier between the young man and the hunter in that work invites us to link the boy and the woodsman in *River in the Catskills*—both of them with their dogs as well as their matching red shirts and black caps. Each is holding an instrument, the man an ax and the boy what appears to be a walking stick—instruments that suggest different orientations to the world.

Like the figures in *View on the Catskill—Early Autumn*, the woodsman and the boy in *River in the Catskills* are situated at completely different elevations of the terrain; in the latter work they are also turned in opposite directions. On the foreground plateau both the woodsman and his spaniel, in relaxed stationary positions, are oriented to the right, in the direction the painting establishes as the future. In the valley below the boy and his dog are afoot, and moving leftward. Cole has placed them inside the vortex that points toward the railroad train but has located them on the margin of this form. They are about to cross its boundary into a different spatial zone—in the direction that the escaped horses in *View on the Catskill—Early Autumn* are galloping, and away from the direction of the train's progress in *River in the Catskills*.

The horses' representation of freedom and escape in the former work prepares this part of the Catskill Creek landscape for the dramatic action of the latter one. Now, in *River in the Catskills*, the always important pointbar becomes a stage on which the boy and his dog are stepping away, removing themselves, from what would seem to be an inevitable line of force. And the space into which they are about to step contains one of the Catskill Creek series' most familiar, and indeed felicitous, images—that of a fully rounded maple or oak standing by itself on open ground. In *View on the Catskill—Early Autumn* it had appeared on the plateau near the woman and infant. Here Cole has moved it down into the valley to play a role in a different kind of drama. Unlike the trees whose stumps appear in the foreground, it has survived.

River in the Catskills differs greatly in its mode of representation from *View on the Catskill—Early Autumn*. Both works are, in part, responses to troubling change and both speak to loss—but in very different ways. Wallach understood *View on the Catskill—Early Autumn* as an expression of an Arcadian, or retrospective, landscape tradition, and convincingly recognized *River in the Catskills* as a variation on the prospect view—a conventional view overlooking a landscape that shows future developments enabled by the clearing of land.[44]

In Cole's representation of an operating railroad line, with direct visual references to the harm its construction had caused, he had in *River in the Catskills* shown a "future" development that already existed for him. The resulting clash

134

between the convention of a future-gazing prospect view and Cole's living reality of the present is what charges the painting with irony. The irony is subtly though powerfully expressed through the figure of the woodsman. His sauntering stance suggests his satisfaction with what he has done, but what he has done is appalling to Cole and, the artist must have hoped, unsettling to viewers sensitive enough to have grasped the irony.

But the woodsman himself, we can surmise, has merely carried out the orders of the "copper-hearted barbarians" who ordered the destruction. His role is like that of Cooper's Billy Kirby in *The Pioneers* (1823)—a possible prototype for Cole's woodsman. Good-natured and simple-minded Billy, so proud of his capacity to level forests, is characterized in the novel as a thoughtless agent of destructive land development.[45] Cole, like Cooper, had his eye on larger processes that—if unchecked—could ruin not just a particular landscape but the whole of American scenery. Perhaps this is why the artist gave such a generic title to *River in the Catskills*, naming a regional rather than a local setting. What had happened to Catskill Creek is what could happen to any river in the Catskills and, indeed, to any river, or any environment, in a new industrial age.

But what gave power and energy to Cole's critique of this destructive process in *River in the Catskills* was precisely his focus on a local scene to which he was deeply attached. This was, after all, not just any American landscape into which the artist drove a railroad train but one charged with meaning for him, both as a real place and as a deeply layered imaginative construction. Cole's earlier versions of the Catskill Creek scene became for him a template on which he could respond, in *River in the Catskills*, to troubling developments of industrial intrusion, and, indeed, express his anger about them. But those earlier versions of the scene contained their own disturbances and dislocations—often encoded and sometimes almost hidden. In this way and many others, earlier paintings in the Catskill Creek series anticipate and illuminate *River in the Catskills*, which in turn retrospectively illuminates them.

Catskill Creek, N.Y., 1845

As we have seen, Cole's title for *River in the Catskills* gives the work regional meaning while veiling the local sources that energized its creation. The title of his next Catskill Creek painting does the opposite. In *Catskill Creek, N.Y.,* despite the localized focus of

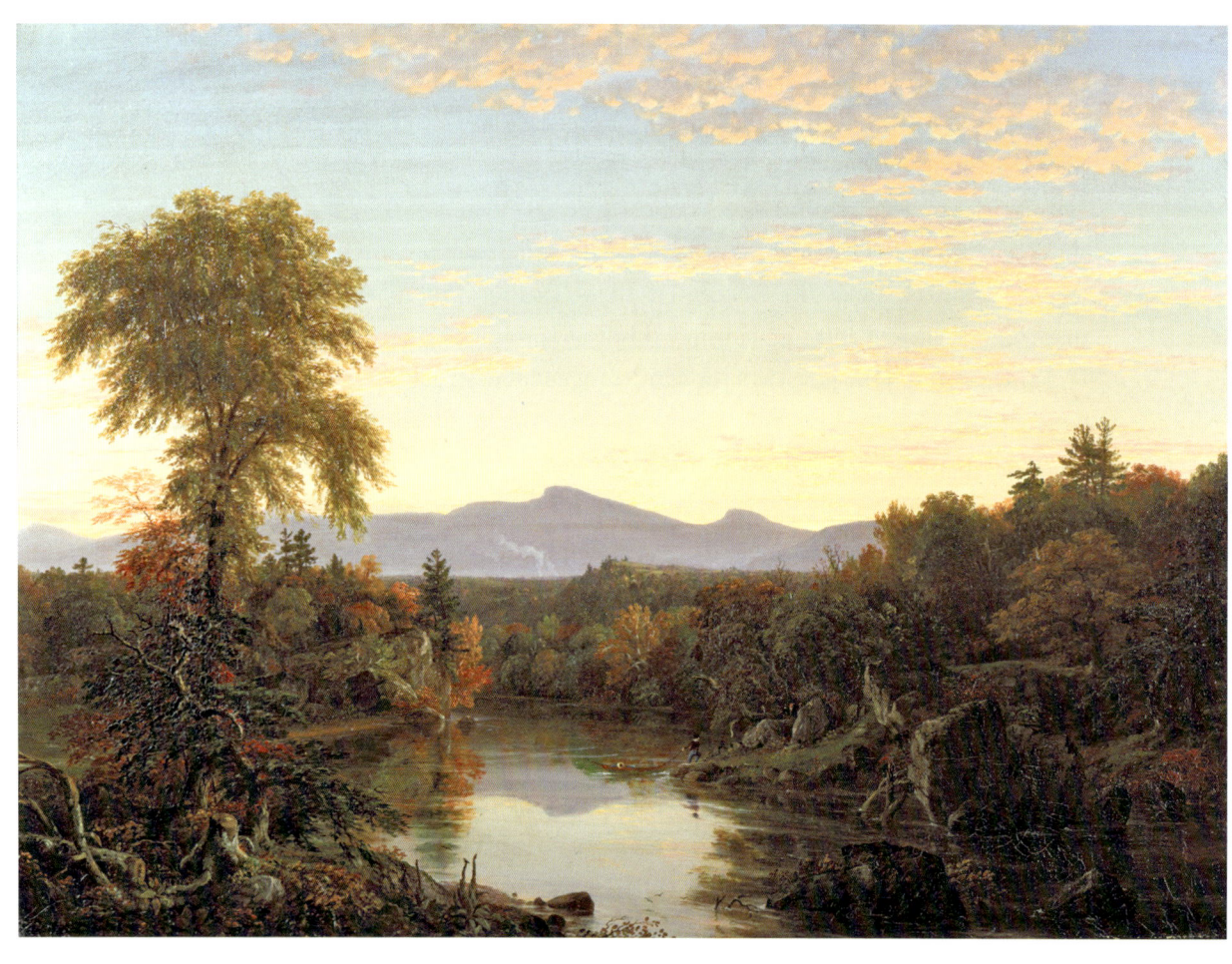

5.20 Thomas Cole, *Catskill Creek, N.Y.,* 1845. Oil
on canvas, 26½ x 36 in. (67.3 x 91.4 cm). New-York
Historical Society, The Robert L. Stuart Collection,
gift of his widow Mrs. Mary Stuart. Digital image
created by Oppenheimer Editions (S-157).

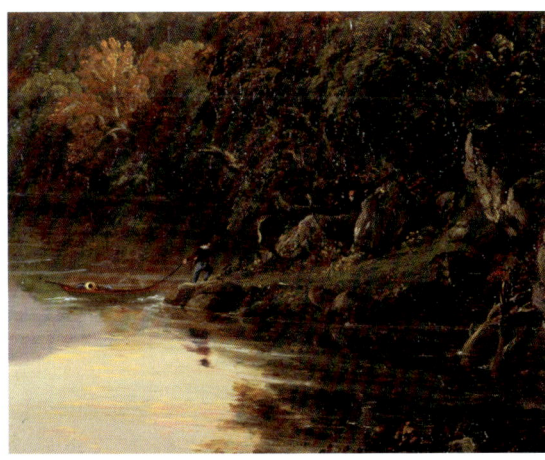

5.21 Detail of figure 5.20, *Catskill Creek, N.Y.*, 1845

its title, Cole explored issues no less broad than those of the other works in the series (fig. 5.20). He executed this painting in 1845, three years before his death, and it is, so far as we know, his last completed oil painting in the series.[46] This is the period in which Cole was working on his unfinished allegorical series *The Cross and the World*, and the miniaturized cross shaped by trees at the far left of the intermediate horizon line is a possible reference to the conception of this series.

It's tempting to believe that Cole himself understood this work as the last, because in it the rower finally completes his crossing. Pulling his boat ashore, he appears with a companion, to his right, who seems to have come over the river with him (fig. 5.21). Both figures are painted very small and are easy to miss.

The scene contrasts with the 1838 Catskill Creek painting, in which the relation between the rower, at midstream, and a horseman on shore is one of separation. Here we have an image of close connection between the work's two figures and, indeed, of their common purpose. The one on the right is pointing vigorously at something on the rise above him, as if to say, "Here it is!" In one of the few commentaries that exist about this painting, it is said that the figure is "gestur[ing] toward the still-wild, primeval woods."[47] But he is pointing, not gesturing, which is to say toward some specific object or site rather than a generalized wilderness. And, in any case, the area immediately upriver from the village of Catskill, when Cole lived there, had not been wilderness for a very long time. Trails of smoke from tanneries appear in the distance in *Catskill Creek, N.Y.,* as they do as well in earlier works in the series.

In fact, the specific site along Catskill Creek depicted in this painting included one of the oldest Dutch settlement farmhouses in the region, a structure we have seen repeatedly in the series, the 1690 Van Vechten house. *Catskill Creek, N.Y.* has roughly the same upriver vantage point as an earlier work in the series, *Sunset in the Catskills* (1841)—from which the artist had a river-level, channeled view of Kaaterskill High Peak and Roundtop Mountain (fig. 5.2 and map 5.1). The two paintings' shared depiction of this mountain profile confirms their common setting, as do the two works' matching shoreline configurations and the positions and species of trees.[48] And while neither the Van Vechten farmhouse nor its mill is visible in *Catskill Creek, N.Y.*—there is not even a glimpse of them as there was in *Sunset in the Catskills*—Cole provides clues to their presence that we will examine later in this discussion.

For all these reasons, *Catskill Creek, N.Y.* and *Sunset in the Catskills*, painted four years apart, can be considered companions. They establish their relationship not only through their similarities but also through contrasting treatments of the same scene. *Sunset in the Catskills* portrays a single figure reclining in a drifting boat, and *Catskill Creek, N.Y.* dramatizes vigorous activity with two animated figures coming ashore.

Atmospheric effects in the two works are also dramatically different from one another. The azure sky in *Sunset in the Catskills*, reminiscent of the very first (1827) Catskill Creek painting and highlighted by the work's arched frame, contrasts with the layered, salmon-colored clouds in *Catskill Creek, N.Y.* These clouds may remind us of those in Cole's 1838 Catskill Creek painting, but their luminosity is more pronounced. As Franklin Kelly has observed to me, the artist's treatment of clouds in *Catskill Creek, N.Y.* anticipates the skies of Frederic Church, who was Cole's student during the period when *Catskill Creek, N.Y.* was painted. An oil study for this work in the National Gallery of Art is even more suggestive in this regard (fig. 5.22).

Another interesting contrast between *Sunset in the Catskills* and *Catskill Creek, N.Y.* is the way the latter work opens up and widens the mountain view in a composition less formally organized by framing trees than the earlier one. The fact that Cole has imaginatively elevated his vantage point somewhat in *Catskill Creek, N.Y.*, as if he were even higher than he was on the railroad bridge in *Sunset in the Catskills*, gains for this riverside painting some of the aspects of panoramic works in the Catskill Creek series. (The composite illustrated by figures 2.6–2.9 shows it in relation to such works.) Among the six paintings in the series that assume a low perspective, *Catskill Creek, N.Y.* has the

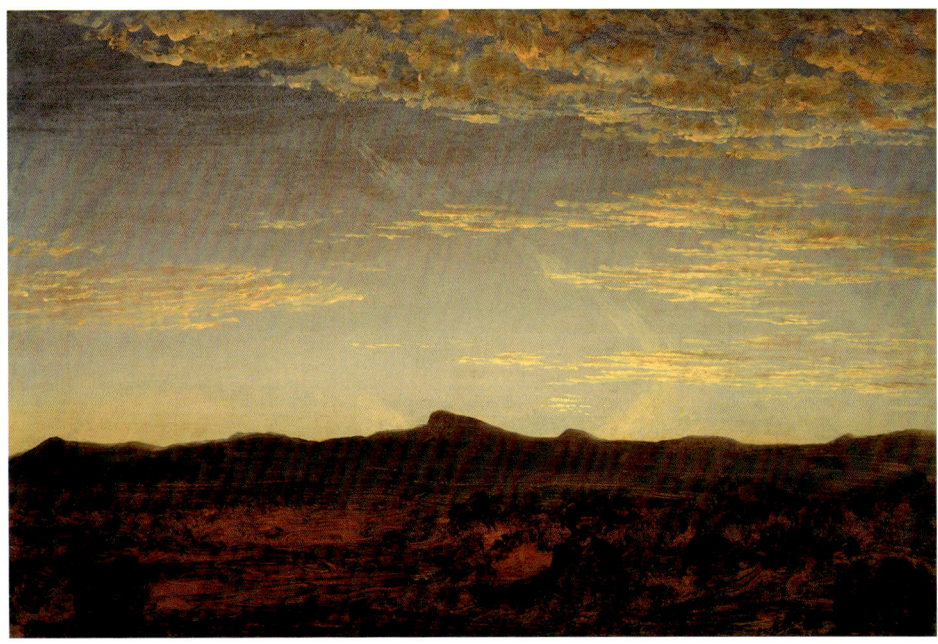

5.22 Thomas Cole, *Study for "Catskill Creek,"* c. 1844–45. Oil on wood, 12 x 18 in. (30.5 x 45.7 cm). National Gallery of Art, Avalon Fund (1998.67.1).

highest (imagined) vantage point. It presents a view of the Catskill Creek landscape that is both grounded and elevated, intimate and distanced.

Even as Cole opens up our view of the mountains in *Catskill Creek, N.Y.* he obscures our vision of particular landscape features closer at hand. The rapids, clearly represented in *Sunset in the Catskills*, are merely gestured toward in *Catskill Creek, N.Y.*—by ripples around a rock at the far left of the stream. Gone too is the dam, though the smoke from tanneries that appeared in *Sunset in the Catskills*, as I mentioned earlier, is present here too.

The Railroad and the Gigantic

One of the most striking contrasts between *Sunset in the Catskills* and *Catskill Creek, N.Y.* concerns their respective allusions to the railroad, both extremely subtle. In the former work, a conifer's gnarled root protruding from the riverbank near the position where the bridge had its southern shore anchor may symbolically mark the railroad's presence. In the latter painting, we find instead—in the same part of the composition—a recently hewn and downed tree aligned with the railroad's oncoming path, an explicit reference to the process that prepared for its construction.

We know from Cole himself that this construction damaged the Catskill Creek landscape. Just how violently it shook that landscape is vividly described by Peter Van Vechten in the same account we examined earlier. He remembered that during a phase of the project's "rock work," "the air [was] filled with debris of all sizes." Describing a scene along the shoreline right behind the Van Vechten farmhouse, he recalled "a succession of blasts" from explosives "that hurled large rocks into the creek and over it."[49] This account gives literal meaning to Cole's description, in his February 1837 letter to Sturges, of *View on the Catskill—Early Autumn*: "My picture may for years to come—tell what the Valley of the Catskill was before what is called 'improvement' blasted the scene."[50]

Most of the "large rocks" described by Van Vechten probably were removed from the river before Cole painted *Catskill Creek, N.Y.,* but in this work he has restored them and, indeed, greatly enlarged them.[51] They appear as five great boulders running in a broad semicircle beginning in the middle of the stream—bridging it—and continuing along the north shoreline, following roughly the course that the tracks actually took in their approach toward the Van Vechten farmhouse. The pointing figure in the painting stands behind the two smallest of these boulders.

Where Cole had erased the railroad in *Sunset in the Catskills*, here he has turned it to stone. The boulders depicted in *Catskill Creek, N.Y.* are glacial erratics, which the artist could have seen in other parts of the Hudson Valley and which he definitely saw in New England. As Rebecca Bedell has shown, he was intensely interested in erratics and found dramatic use for them in wilderness paintings like his two 1827 versions of *Scene from "The Last of the Mohicans."*[52] Here is an unusual case in which he imported them imaginatively into a pastoral landscape.

Alongside and closely related to Cole's interest in geology was his fascination with the gigantic, reflected in his paintings of ancient ruins like the Colosseum and the temples of Paestum. His representation of Stonehenge in *The Pastoral State* of the *Course of Empire* series is another example. Like other polarities characteristic of Cole's vision, gigantism and miniaturization coexisted, on equal terms, in his imagination. For example, he combined them fancifully in *The Titan's Goblet* (1833)—with whole tiny civilizations set within the towering goblet.[53] If huge ancient ruins lay at one end of the historical spectrum for Cole, another form of the gigantic belonged to his own time: the rise of industrial capitalism, with the specter of machines and other structures, including social and economic ones, that could overwhelm the human scale.[54] Perhaps his miniaturization of the railroad train in *River in the Catskills* can be understood partly as a response to such forces, that is, as a willed diminishment of their power.

In whatever form the gigantic took for Cole he associated it with the sublime, and sublime emotions may be at work in *Catskill Creek, N.Y.*, its prosaic title notwithstanding.[55] In replacing the railroad, which had ceased operations three years before Cole painted this work, these huge boulders can also be seen as its tombstone, a ruin in precisely this sense. They may express both vengeance and wish fulfillment.

With its tiny human figures and enormous boulders, *Catskill Creek, N.Y.*—like *The Titan's Goblet* but much more subtly—combines the miniature and the gigantic and in doing so runs our perceptions in and out. At first we squint to make out the figures, whom we may not even see at first. Then, as we find them and reset our focus, we suddenly realize that they are environed by huge natural forms, themselves miniaturized by the scale of the painting. It takes two or three adjustments of the eye to come to terms with this work, which, like other paintings in the Catskill Creek series, challenges the viewer to look very closely.

The great stones in *Catskill Creek, N.Y.* can also be understood as a barrier. In the larger Catskill Creek series, Cole consistently represents certain natural and humanly constructed forms as boundaries—a river to be crossed, fences, hedgerows—and the semicircle of boulders in *Catskill Creek, N.Y.* presents itself as a wall, the crude outer perimeter of a fortressed space. From one point of view, as we have seen, the boulders in *Catskill Creek, N.Y.* symbolize the railroad and the destructive forces it represents. From another perspective, they may paradoxically represent Cole's barrier against these forces.

But there is another way of understanding the boulders as a barrier. The pointing figure in *Catskill Creek, N.Y.* is not only eclipsed by one of them; he is impeded by it. His companion and he may have completed their crossing at last, but they have by no means reached their destination. In this painting Cole depicts not an arrival so much as a threshold moment, and the work illustrates how the dramatic actions of the Catskill Creek paintings characteristically remain incomplete. The figures in these works never quite bridge the spaces that separate them from their objects of desire, and repetition in these paintings can be understood, from one point of view, as their unending attempts to do so.

The destinations of figures in the Catskill Creek paintings are represented by a number of symbolic forms, including a Dutch colonial farmhouse. It's difficult to tell, from the vantage point of *Catskill Creek, N.Y.* whether it might be one of these forms that the figure behind the boulder is pointing to. No structure peeks through the foliage, as it did in *Sunset in the Catskills*. But Cole gives us another pointer. The arrow-shaped upper facet of the largest boulder, this one the size of a two-story building, is aimed directly at a meadow above. This meadow appears as a horizontal stripe of green and shows itself in but a glimpse, just as the rapids do in other Catskill Creek paintings.

At the center of the meadow is a large tree in full autumnal color. It is a white oak, and most important an open-grown oak, with long, low horizontal limbs and a broad canopy —a tree that could have matured alone only on pastureland rather than in the forest. Here is another of Cole's valued forms, one that is continuous with the Van Vechten farmhouse and its mill. These forms belong to the same vision of a settled space, like that of the aptly titled *Settler's Home in the Catskills*. In that work Cole had opened his fantasy of an uninterrupted pastoral landscape fully to view. Here, in *Catskill Creek, N.Y.,* he has characteristically hidden most of it, and hiddenness, as we saw in earlier Catskill Creek paintings, served the purposes of protection for Cole. The glimpse, a distinctive and important visual form for him in these works, confers meaning on valued structures and forms by both concealing and revealing them.

A Leaf Painter After All

The white oak in the meadow has significance beyond its reiteration of an important motif. The fact that we are able to recognize and identify this tree, in the deep background of a relatively small painting—it measures 26½ x 36 inches—owes to Cole's careful representation of it. He was not, he said emphatically, a leaf painter, but he was exceedingly interested in the particularity of natural forms, as we can see from his often copious annotation of landscape sketches, where he identified species of trees and plants. An example can be seen in the sketch illustrated in figure 5.4, where Cole wrote "Buttonwood" on the crown of the largest tree at the right. Such annotations were a way of remembering and being faithful to the particular elements of the scenes he had sketched.

When Cole claimed he was not a leaf painter, he meant to distinguish himself from artists he believed were merely transcribing nature rather than attributing deep human meaning to it. But there is another way in which he was not a leaf painter. While some of Cole's allegorical works, like *The Garden of Eden* (1828), include minutely detailed leaves and flowers specifically related to the themes of these works, Cole's horticultural and arboreal representations in the Catskill Creek paintings are more generalized.[56]

The white oak in *Catskill Creek, N.Y.* is a good example; its color and overall shape, not its distant leaves, give it away. We recognize the locust in the early *View Near the*

Village of Catskill partly by its leaves but more definitively by its growth form. The red maples in *View Near Catskill* identify themselves with their brilliant autumnal color, and the Lombardy poplars in this same work are recognizable because of their distinctive shape. The willows in the works from 1833 and 1838 Catskill Creek paintings are identifiable by their location along the riverbank and by the breadth and depth of their canopies. But the fact that we do recognize all these trees tells us that distinguishing their species was important to Cole. Like the annotation on his sketches, it was part and parcel of his ranging observation, of his concern to really see, even as the trees and plants he saw often had rich symbolic importance for him.

Of special significance to Cole were the mullein, and he made them central to the composition of *Catskill Creek, N.Y.* (fig. 5.23). Foregrounded and silhouetted against the water, as they were in the very first Catskill Creek painting from eighteen years earlier, they bring to the scene the same values of generativity and endurance that they brought to other works in the series. As in a panel that Cole created for Luman Reed's home in 1836 (fig. 5.24), these mullein have birds perched on top of them, and perhaps

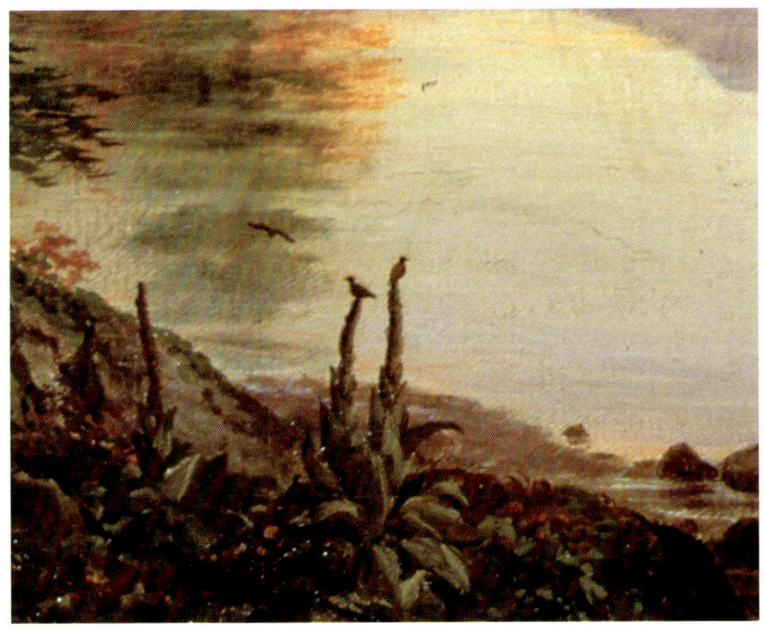

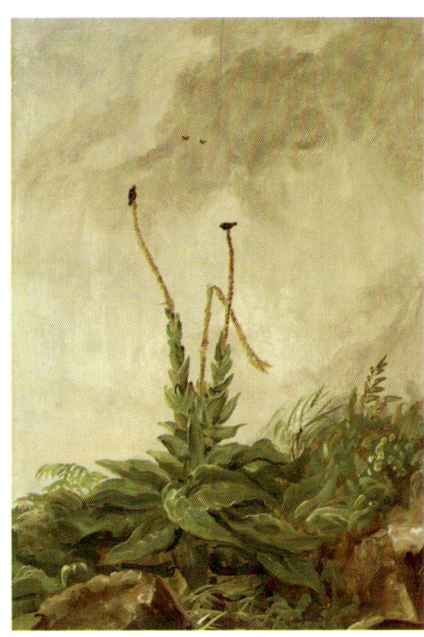

5.23 Detail of figure 5.20, *Catskill Creek, N.Y.*, 1845

5.24 Thomas Cole, *The Mullein Stalk*, 1836. Oil on wood, 18 9/16 x 12 3/8 in. (47.1 x 31.4 cm). Wadsworth Atheneum Museum of Art, Hartford, CT, gift of Mr. and Mrs. Frederick Sturges, III (1979.171).

the artist meant in this painting to evoke his patron's pleasure in observing the Catskill Creek landscape with him—their "mutual delight"—that he had described in his February 1837 letter to Sturges.[57] In this letter he had identified his sadness about Reed's death with his mournful feelings about the degradation of the Catskill Creek landscape.

In *Catskill Creek, N.Y.*, the birds perched on the mullein stalks are looking off in opposite directions, their views sweeping the scene—from one shoreline to the other and from the distant mountains to the reflections of these mountains in the water. The reflections are enhanced by Cole's foreshortening of the river, giving it the appearance of a pond or lake—an effect he had created in the first two paintings in the Catskill Creek series. With the perched birds overlooking this stilled and highly reflective body of water, the artist has embedded within the work itself a figure for comprehensively envisioning the Catskill Creek landscape. But it is Cole, of course, who has the broadest view of this landscape—an overview literally heightened by his invented vantage point—and all that it meant to him. While it is very unlikely that he understood *Catskill Creek, N.Y.* as a final summarizing vision of the Catskill Creek series, this apparently simple landscape painting gives complex expression to the series' deepest issues.

EPILOGUE

THE REFRAIN OF CATSKILL CREEK

We will never know exactly why the Catskill Creek landscape so compelled Thomas Cole. Remembering his singularly aesthetic responses to the scenery of the Hudson River Valley, as recorded in his 1825 list of drawings, we could surmise that he found in this landscape particular atmospheric effects and spatial forms that he recognized from his reading and earlier visual experience. Perhaps in the river's broad meander and the oval pointbar carved by it he saw the serpentine line of beauty that William Hogarth had identified, in his *Analysis of Beauty* (1753), as a fundamental aesthetic form.[1]

This form, inspired by Hogarth or not, is the central feature of two large canvases Cole completed during 1836–37, *View on the Catskill—Early Autumn* and *The Oxbow*. A pointbar is an oxbow in the making; someday Catskill Creek will double back upon itself in the same way as did the Connecticut River at Mt. Holyoke. In the Catskill Creek series, the pointbar first appeared distinctly in Cole's early *View Near Catskill* (1828–29), and it became fully articulated in *View on the Catskill—Early Autumn*. His decade-long acquaintance with the Catskill Creek meander, before painting *The Oxbow*, may have prepared him to create another agricultural and pastoral landscape islanded by a river.

Whatever inspired Cole to paint Catskill Creek for the very first time in 1827 and then to paint it again the following year, the scene's primary elements appear to have organized themselves quickly into a stable composition. Even at the outset, before his first European tour, he may have envisioned the Catskill Creek land-scape, as some have suggested, through a Claudian template, that is, through a vision inspired by the seventeenth-century European artist Claude Lorrain.[2] But this landscape soon became its own template—a distinctive assemblage of forms and motifs that Cole would re-create intermittently during the course of almost two decades. The Catskill Creek series might be called a refrain, but a refrain measured irregularly.

These are occasional works, each one called to an occasion—a commission, the hope to inspire a commission, an artistic experiment, or simply, on a given day, the impulse to paint again a beloved scene. The beginning of the series may have been fortuitous, but once it was under way it sustained itself through its intense fidelity to a signature landscape whose perspective was anchored along a particular short stretch of Catskill Creek.[3] That stretch of river, both along its shores and from nearby Jefferson Heights, was in Cole's backyard. For him this was a landscape of home, literally the walk of a mile or two from Cedar Grove, and his attachment to it—expressed in his repeated renderings—is a deep source of the series' coherence. This is a very different kind of coherence from that of Cole's allegorical works such as *The Voyage of Life*, which are driven and shaped by narrative.

Yet the Catskill Creek paintings are not without important narrative elements. In the end Cole could not keep narrative out of this landscape, nor did he want to. But as we have seen, he obscured the meanings of his figures and motifs through miniaturization and other strategies; they belonged to a private and guarded network of association. In one sense, these figures and motifs were his variables, the elements at play within the template of Catskill Creek. The stability of the template allowed for this play and for the introduction of modes of experience—anger and desire, even the sublime—that a familiar agrarian and pastoral landscape appeared to exclude.

But a motif is, by definition, a repeated image. Cole's key images, appearing in painting after painting, create their own form of consistency: the rower, the woman by the shore or in a meadow, the meadow itself with its isolated oak or maple, the baskets in their various forms, the rapids, the mullein, the reflections, the colonial stone farmhouse, domestic animals, and, yes, circling vultures. Repetition reinforces the landscape template of the Catskill Creek paintings and, at the same time, brings continuity to their diverse, particular images. In this way, repetition gives these works their integrity as a series, holding it together.

Perhaps it held Cole together too, in something of the way a refrain structures its song. In their noted essay on this form, Gilles Deleuze and Felix Guattari define a refrain as an "answer to chaos," a rhythmical attempt "to fix a fragile point as a center." This fragile center "exist[s] by virtue of a periodic repetition . . . of components," components that are themselves coded to mark its boundaries. An imaginative space brought into being by a refrain is thus a "territorial assemblage" that possesses a certain measure of "consistency"—"the 'holding together' of heterogeneous elements."[4]

Thinking about Cole's Catskill Creek as a fragile center returns us to where we started, the artist's guarded but very real sense of place. As I wrote earlier, these works are place-centered in their nature simply because—unlike Cole's allegorical series—they

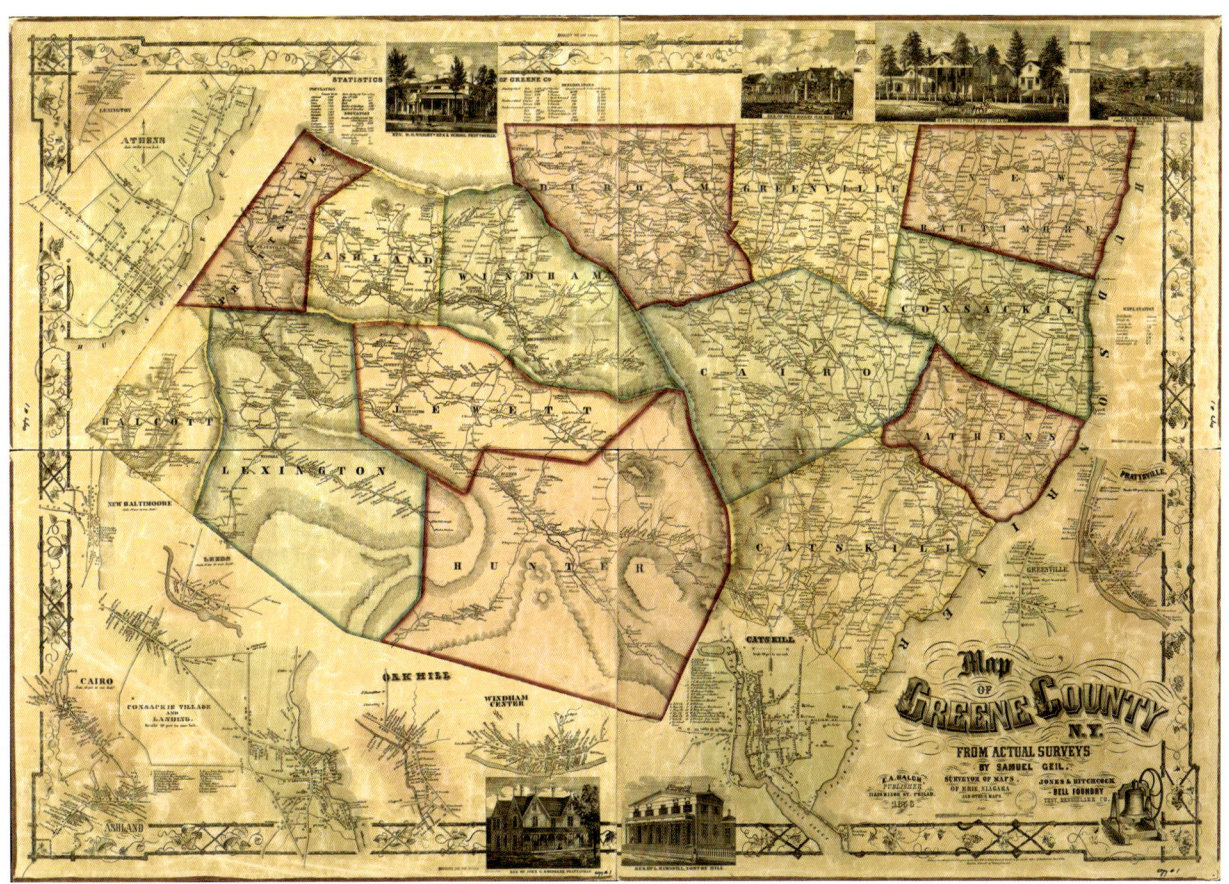

E.1 Samuel Giel, E. A. Balch, Robert Pearsall Smith, and Jones & Hitchcock, *Map of Greene County, N.Y.* From actual surveys, 1 map on 4 sheets, color, 35 x 52¼ in (89 x 134 cm), sheets: 18⅞ x 27½ in. (48 x 70 cm). Library of Congress, Geography and Map Division, G3803.G7 1856.G4.

depict a highly specified, local landscape that he knew firsthand. Furthermore, the Catskill Mountains represented in the background of these paintings, with their own recognizable features, place this scene regionally; here is a "river in the Catskills"—to call up the title of one of the works—and not a river in some other place. But the Catskill Creek paintings, for me at least, never seem merely local or regional. Like certain places evoked by Romantic writers of Cole's era—Thoreau's Walden Pond or the landscape above Wordsworth's Tintern Abbey—Catskill Creek is a specific place charged with meanings that transcend the local.

Wordsworth, with his deep and complex sense of place, was one of Cole's two favorite poets. The other one was Byron. His forcefully narrative verse, as we saw earlier in this discussion, spoke to Cole's restless nature. Byron represented for the artist the heroic side of restlessness, dramatized in works like *Manfred* (from which Cole painted a scene), and while its heroism was dark, it was also self-possessed.[5] But the other side of restlessness, for Cole, was a profound sense of dislocation, of being forever ungrounded (rest-less), that shows up in a number of his own poems. He wrote one of these poems when he may literally have been at sea, in June of 1829 during his passage on a ship called the *Columbia* from New York to England. Untitled and written in a sketchbook, it describes an unmoored soul "whose wanderings are alike unmark'd—unknown / By Mother, Sister, Wife, by any loving one," and continues,

> He is a torn weed on a desolate sea
> Toss'd by the waves and beaten by the winds
> And driven by currents unresistingly
> From deep to deep, and never finds
> A peaceful haven when the tide will fling
> It gently round some mossy rock to cling.[6]

The Catskill Creek of Cole's imagination became for him that "peaceful haven." That he had begun to paint the scene before his first voyage to Europe made its template available to him when he returned to the United States late in 1832, and his moving permanently from New York to Catskill in 1836 reflected its power over him. Cole's departure from New York and its art market—not to mention essential supplies and materials—was potentially a risky move for him. It must have been powerfully motivated by his aversion to urban life and his attraction to the Catskill countryside. And even though he saw it coming, the construction of a railroad line running through that countryside—in the very year he moved to Catskill—must have been painful for him.

But, with some significant exceptions, Cole's public expressions do not register the pain. They do not open a window on the inner life of this intensely private artist, who is known to have revised and edited some of his personal writings to protect himself from the intrusions of future readers.[7] Nineteenth-century biographers who knew and interviewed Cole about his life gave idealized or melodramatic accounts, and the artist largely cooperated with them in their mythmaking.[8] While his allegorical paintings express his deepest moral concerns and religious beliefs, their universal themes—and universalized settings—also reflect the most public dimension of Cole's personality, his ambition for fame and widespread approbation.

The Catskill Creek paintings, on the other hand, have about them an apparent modesty of conception. They depict a familiar landscape, a landscape of home, though at their deepest levels they reflect the complicated process through which Cole made himself at home. His representations of Catskill Creek are mysteriously encoded and their meanings protected. But the glimpses of valued sites and structures in these works do, in their repetition, give us a glimpse of Cole himself. This may be all he wanted us to have, but his pointers in a number of these works suggest that some part of him wanted us to know more. Perhaps it was the part that asked viewers to look more closely, to really see.

Jane Hirshfield, in her essay on the hidden, refers to "certain writers' minute meaning-clues and interweavings: they are set down with full awareness that only the most alert readers will ever make them conscious, yet in hope that a followable trail has been laid."[9] To follow the trail laid down in the Catskill Creek paintings is not to follow the thread of a conventional narrative or the predetermined course of a journey. Rather, it is to recognize within these works certain key, emblematic images whose reverberating presence brings their meanings into focus and makes of them a series.

ACKNOWLEDGMENTS

The Andrew W. Mellon Foundation generously awarded me a two-year emeritus fellowship for research that led to this book. The publication of *Thomas Cole's Refrain* was supported by the Vassar College Research Committee, through the Susan Turner Fund, and by the Thomas Cole National Historic Site, with assistance from the Wyeth Foundation for American Art.

Special thanks are due to Elizabeth Jacks, executive director of the Cole Historic Site, which is hosting the exhibition associated with my book. As guest curator of this exhibition, I am indebted to permanent curator Kate Menconeri for her guidance, leadership, and dedication to the project. Annette Blaugrund played an important role in planning for the exhibition. My thanks go, as well, to Masha Turchinsky and Laura Vookles, respectively director and curator of the Hudson River Museum, where the exhibition is continuing as part of the museum's 100th anniversary celebration.

This book was conceived several years ago when I delivered a paper about Cole's serial paintings at a Princeton University symposium honoring John Wilmerding. Later, Professor Wilmerding became an advisor to the project and a key reader of my manuscript; he has thus been a guiding spirit from beginning to end. Another guiding, indeed sustaining, spirit was Patricia Wallace, who read my developing manuscript in all its many versions, offering astute commentary at every stage.

Others who read the full manuscript with care and insight are Karen Lucic, Sharyn Udall, and David Barnes. Mr. Barnes was a steady source of support and encouragement, and he was instrumental in bringing my project to the Cole Historic Site for the exhibition. Wayne Franklin kindly read the book's introductory sections and provided important information about New York State history and geography. Franklin Kelly generously shared with me significant findings from his archival research.

Without extraordinary research assistants this book could not have been written. Kaitlin Manning joined the project at the very beginning and helped me formulate it. After our collaboration resumed at a later stage, she made invaluable contributions, including her discovery of pivotal sketches by Cole and key passages in his writings. Most important were her remarkable interpretive insights.

Adam Grimes, an immensely capable young scholar whose help was generously provided by the Cole Historic Site, played an indispensable role. He made an important sketch discovery of his own and participated, with great discernment, in every aspect of the project's developments. These include his preparation of the book's illustrations for Cornell University Press, key assistance in planning for the exhibition, and unfailing good judgment in matters both editorial and artistic. At other stages research assistants Evander Price, Vincent Hiscock, and Peter Fedoryk made significant contributions.

Because knowledge about areas beyond my training was needed to write this book, I have depended on experts in these areas. For the identification of trees and plants in Cole's paintings I am indebted to botanist Margaret Ronsheim, and to ecologists Lynn Christenson and Keri Van Camp. Geologists Robert Titus and Jeffrey Walker taught me about pointbars and other landforms that appear in the artist's works. Holly Hummell instructed me in early American period dress for my discussion of human figures in the paintings, and Susan Kuretsky enlightened me about the significance of detail in landscape art. Peter Stillman and Michael Hanagan talked with me about the effects of industrialization in Europe and the United States during the nineteenth century, and Elisabeth Arlyck illuminated for me the cinematic aspects of Cole's serial works. Painter Tom Berg helped me understand Cole from the perspective of a contemporary artist.

I am indebted to Greene County historian David Dorpfeld and Village of Catskill historian Richard Philp for sharing their extensive knowledge of the Catskill region. Jonathan Palmer, head archivist at the Vedder Research Library, located for me a key nineteenth-century photograph and information regarding it. Linda Hunt, also with the Vedder Library, guided me through the library's rich resources. Several residents of Catskill gave me access to their properties for photography and GIS measurements, and others provided important background about the village. This group includes Kiki Smith and Zoran Skoko, Ann Gibbons Markou and Peter Markou, as well as Lisa Fox-Martin and Daniel Arshack.

Technical assistance is an inadequate term for what the following people contributed to the project. The maps that appear throughout the book, created by Neil Curri, speak for themselves and to Mr. Curri's imagination and skill. He was a collaborator as well as an illustrator. Meg Stewart helped with cartography in the initial stages. During Baynard Bailey's long history with the project he created for me a valuable inventory of working images, while Thomas Hill and Victoria Manning assisted with photography. Alon Koppel is responsible for the beautiful drone photography illustrating the vantage points of the paintings. Curators and their staffs at the museums whose archives I consulted treated me with the greatest kindness and consideration.

Every author needs moral support during a project's "trying hours," to paraphrase Cole's title of a drawing I consider in this study, and several of the people named earlier in these acknowledgments gave me such support. I would also like to thank, indeed give special thanks to, my Vassar College colleagues Lizabeth Paravisini-Gebert, Mark Amodio, Joann Potter, and Dean of the Faculty Jonathan Chenette.

Exhibition Checklist

Thomas Cole's Refrain: The Paintings of Catskill Creek
Thomas Cole National Historic Site, May 4–November 3, 2019
Hudson River Museum, November 21, 2019–February 28, 2020
Curated by H. Daniel Peck

THOMAS COLE
Crossing the Stream, 1827
Oil on wood panel, 24½ x 35 in.
Jamee and Marshall Field Collection

THOMAS COLE
Autumn Landscape (View of Mount Chocorua), 1827–28
Oil on canvas, 38⅝ x 48½ in.
The Jack Warner Foundation,
Tuscaloosa, Alabama

THOMAS COLE
View Near Catskill, 1828–29
Oil on wood panel, 24¼ x 33¾ in.
Private collection*

THOMAS COLE
Sunset, View on the Catskill, 1833
Oil on wood panel, 16½ x 24½ in.
New-York Historical Society, Gift of
The New-York Gallery of
the Fine Arts, 1858.44

THOMAS COLE
View of Catskill Creek (formerly
Distant View of Roundtop), c. 1833
Oil on composition board, 17 x 25 in.
Albany Institute of History and Art
Purchase, Evelyn Newman Fund, 1964.70

THOMAS COLE
On Catskill Creek, 1836
Oil on wood pulp paper board, 19½ x 15 in.
Drs. Matthew and Maria Brown

THOMAS COLE
North Mountain and Catskill Creek, 1838
Oil on canvas, 26⁷⁄₁₆ x 36⁷⁄₁₆ in.
Yale University Art Gallery, Gift of
Anne Osborn Prentice, 1981.56

THOMAS COLE
Mill Dam on the Catskill Creek, 1841
Oil on canvas, 22¼ x 30¼ in.
Currier Museum of Art, Manchester, NH,
Bequest of Henry Melville Fuller, 2002.20.19

THOMAS COLE
Settler's Home in the Catskills, 1842
Oil on canvas, 22^{15}/$_{16}$ x 28½ in.
Private collection*

THOMAS COLE
Study for "Catskill Creek," c. 1844–45
Oil on wood, 12 x 18 in.
National Gallery of Art, Washington D.C.,
Avalon Fund, 1998.67.1

THOMAS COLE
Catskill Creek, N.Y., 1845
Oil on canvas, 26½ x 36 in.
New-York Historical Society,
The Robert L. Stuart Collection,
Gift of his widow Mrs. Mary Stuart, S-157

THOMAS COLE
On Catskill Creek, Sunset, c. 1845–47
Oil on panel, 8^{13}/$_{16}$ x 14½ x ⅜ in.
New-York Historical Society,
Collection of Arthur and
Eileen Newman, Bequest of
Eileen Newman, 2015.33.8

ASHER B. DURAND
Catskill Mountains, 1830
Oil on canvas, 13¾ x 18 in.
Albany Institute of History and Art,
Gift of Miss Jane E. Rosell, 1987.20.2

FREDERIC EDWIN CHURCH
The Catskill Creek, 1845
Oil on panel, 11⅞ x 16 in.
Olana State Historic Site, Hudson,
N.Y., New York State Office of Parks and
Recreation and Historic Preservation,
1980.1873

CHARLES HERBERT MOORE
The Catskills in Spring, 1861
Oil on canvas, 12¼ x 20^{5}/$_{16}$ in.
Frances Lehman Loeb Art Center,
Vassar College, Gift of Matthew
Vassar, 1864.1.58

On view at the first venue only.

Notes

Prologue

1 The passages from Cole's journal entry quoted in this and the next paragraph appear in *Thomas Cole: The Collected Essays and Prose Sketches*, ed. Marshall Tymn (St. Paul: John Colet Press, 1980), p. 141. The passages from *Walden* are found in "The Ponds" chapter.

2 "Essay on American Scenery," in Tymn, *Thomas Cole*, p. 17. This essay was first presented by Cole as a lecture at the New York Lyceum on May 16, 1835, and was published in *American Monthly Magazine*'s January 1836 issue (n.s., volume 1), pages 1–12.

3 "Essay on American Scenery," pp. 3, 8–9.

4 "Essay on American Scenery," p. 8.

5 "Essay on American Scenery," p. 9.

6 "Essay on American Scenery," p. 10.

7 "Essay on American Scenery," pp. 11–12.

8 "Essay on American Scenery," pp. 12–13.

9 "Essay on American Scenery," pp. 13, 16.

10 "Essay on American Scenery," pp. 13, 14, 5.

11 "Essay on American Scenery," p. 5.

12 "Essay on American Scenery," p. 15.

13 "Essay on American Scenery," p. 15.

14 "Essay on American Scenery," p. 17.

1. The Discovery of Thomas Cole

1 Cole's friend and first biographer Louis Legrand Noble reported Durand's making this (undated) remark in his book *The Life and Works of Thomas Cole*, first published in 1853; reprint edited by Elliott S. Vesell (Cambridge, MA: Belknap Press of Harvard University Press, 1964), p. 36.

2 The list, contained in a larger notebook archived at the Detroit Institute of Arts, is three pages long and was titled by Cole "List and explanation of the Sketches." The most thorough study of Cole's list is Tracie Felker, "Thomas Cole's Drawings of His 1825 Trip up the Hudson River," *American Art Journal* 24, no. 1–2 (1992): 60–93. See also Rita Carr, "Catskill Calling: Thomas Cole's 1825 Hudson River Journey," Archive of the Thomas Cole National Historic Site, 2014.

3 Cole had originally placed five paintings in Colman's bookstore, and by the time Trumbull came by two of them, both scenes of Cold Spring (unlocated) had been purchased by other parties. The three that remained are the ones bought, respectively, by Trumbull, Dunlap, and Durand. Dunlap's article appeared in the November 22, 1825, issue of the *New-York Evening Post*.

4 The most notable of such future patrons, in relation to the development of Cole's career, was a dry goods merchant, Luman Reed, who commissioned Cole's allegorical series *The Course of Empire* (1833–36).

5 See Noble, *Life and Works*, pp. 3–5, for a brief account of Cole's early life in England.

6 Tim Barringer, "The Englishness of Thomas Cole," in *The Cultured Canvas: New Perspectives on American Landscape Painting*, ed. Nancy Siegel (Lebanon: University of New Hampshire Press, 2011), pp. 6–7, 4–5. See also Barringer's "Thomas Cole's Atlantic Crossings," in Elizabeth Mankin Kornhauser and Tim Barringer, with Dorothy Mahon, Christopher Riopelle, and Shannon Vittoria, *Thomas Cole's Journey: Atlantic Crossings* (New York: The Metropolitan Museum of Art, 2018), pp. 19–61.

7 See especially Angela Miller, *The Empire of the Eye: Landscape Representation and American Cultural Politics, 1825–1875* (Ithaca: Cornell University Press, 1993), pp. 21–39.

8 In 1824, the year before the Erie Canal's grand opening in New York, Horatio Gates Spafford called it "the masterwork of the age" in his compendium *A Gazetteer of the State of New-York: Embracing an Ample Survey and Description of Its Counties, Towns, Cities, Villages, Canals, Mountains, Lakes, Rivers, Creeks, and Natural Topography* (Albany, NY: B.D. Packard, 1824), p. 164. An especially useful study of the Erie Canal is Carol Sheriff, *The Artificial River: The Erie Canal and the Paradox of Progress, 1817–1862* (New York: Hill and Wang, 1996).

9 After turning due west at Cohoes, New York, on the south side of the Mohawk River, the Erie Canal crossed the Mohawk twice by aqueducts before continuing on the river's south bank toward Rome, New York—the westward termination of the canal's eastern segment.

10 See Alan Wallach, "Thomas Cole's *River in the Catskills* as Antipastoral," *Art Bulletin* 84, no. 2 (June 2002): 334–50.

11 The formulation is that of Leo Marx in his influential book *The Machine in the Garden: Technology and the Pastoral Ideal in America* (London: Oxford University Press, 1964).

12 Felker, "Thomas Cole's Drawings," meticulously tracks aesthetic influences on Cole in his early career, as they are expressed in various of his works including the drawings from his 1825 expedition into the Hudson River Valley.

13 For a close examination of works such as *The Hudson River Portfolio* in relation to American landscape traditions, and specifically in relation to Cole's early paintings, see Edward J. Nygren, *Views and*

Visions: American Landscapes before 1830 (Washington, DC: Corcoran Gallery of Art, 1986), pp. 41ff., 63–64. For a direct, extended comparison of Cole's work to that of Wall, including commentary on their personal relationship, see Sophie Lynford, "Thomas Cole, William Guy Wall, and the Hudson River," in Tim Barringer, Gillian Forrester, Sophie Lynford, Jennifer Raab, and Nicholas Robbins, *Picturesque and Sublime: Thomas Cole's Trans-Atlantic Inheritance* (New Haven, CT: Thomas Cole National Historic Site in association with Yale University Press, 2018), pp. 67–81.

14 Burke's *A Philosophical Enquiry into the Origins of Our Ideas of the Sublime and the Beautiful* was first published in 1757. For Cole's absorption of European landscape aesthetics from print sources such as engravings, and the importance of the artist's own early works on paper to his development, see Tim Barringer and Jennifer Raab, "An Inheritance in Print: Thomas Cole and the Aesthetics of Landscape," in Barringer et al., *Picturesque and Sublime*, pp. 1–49.

15 For Gilpin's influence on Cole see Felker, "Thomas Cole's Drawings," p. 81.

16 "Essay on American Scenery," in *Thomas Cole: The Collected Essays and Prose Sketches*, ed. Marshall Tymn (St. Paul: John Colet Press, 1980), p. 16.

17 A pioneering work linking tourism in the Catskills to painting and literature is Kenneth John Myers's *The Catskills: Painters, Writers, and Tourists in the Mountains, 1820–1895* (Yonkers, NY: Hudson River Museum of Westchester, 1988); see pp. 40–49 for a section specifically treating Cole. Also see Myers's "Thomas Cole and the Popularization of Landscape Experience in the United States: 1825–1829," in *America! Storie Di Pittura Dal Nuovo Mondo*, ed. Marco Goldin (Treviso: Linea d'ombra Libra, 2007), English text version, pp. 50–61. For Cole's relation to the regional culture of the Hudson River Valley, see David Schuyler, *Sanctified Landscape: Writers, Artists, and the Hudson River Valley, 1820–1909* (Ithaca: Cornell University Press, 2012), chap. 2.

18 "Essay on American Scenery," p. 8.

19 "Essay on American Scenery," p. 3.

2. A Different Kind of Series

1 Cole's letter to Wadsworth regarding Trumbull's Kaaterskill Falls painting is collected as letter no. 2 in *The Correspondence of Thomas Cole and Daniel Wadsworth*, ed. J. Bard McNulty (Hartford, CT: Connecticut Historical Society, 1983), p. 4. The artist's letter to Wadsworth concerning the copy of *The Last of the Mohicans,* "*Cora Kneeling at the feet of Tamenund*" that he made for Gilmor appears as letter no. 9 in the same volume, pp. 20–21. For context, see Ellwood C. Parry III, *The Art of Thomas Cole: Ambition and Imagination* (Newark: University of Delaware Press, 1988), pp. 51, 59–60.

2 Tymn identifies "The Storm" as "an early prose sketch preserved in manuscript among Cole's papers in the New York State Library, Albany." Thomas Cole, *The Collected Essays and Prose Sketches*, ed. Marshall Tymn (St. Paul: John Colet Press, 1980), p. 96. It is paraphrased in Louis Legrand Noble, *The Life and Works of Thomas Cole*, first published in 1853; reprint edited by Elliott S. Vesell (Cambridge, MA: Belknap Press of Harvard University Press, 1964), pp. 43–45.

3 On Cole's ambition, see Ellwood C. Parry III, "Thomas Cole's Early Career: 1818–1829," in *Views and Visions: American Landscapes before 1830,* ed. Edward J. Nygren (Washington, DC: Corcoran Gallery of Art, 1986), p. 184. In a journal entry of May 19, 1838, Cole wrote, "I do feel that I am not a mere

leaf painter, that I have loftier conceptions than any mere combinations of inanimate & uninformed Nature." *Collected Essays and Prose Sketches*, p. 156. The phrase "a higher style" appears in a letter from Cole to Gilmor dated May 21, 1828, in which the artist told this patron that his 1828 paintings *The Garden of Eden* and *Expulsion from the Garden of Eden* were "attempts at a higher style of landscape than I have hitherto tried." Appendix I: Correspondence between Thomas Cole and Robert Gilmor Jr., comp. Howard S. Merritt, in *The Baltimore Museum of Art Annual II: Studies on Thomas Cole, An American Romanticist* (Baltimore: Baltimore Museum of Art, 1967), p. 58.

4 Franklin Kelly writes about how Cole's inspiration toward serial landscapes may have derived, in part, from seventeenth- and eighteenth-century European paired paintings, in which the artist found "a way of breaking the constraints on meaning imposed by depicting a single scene." "American Landscape Pairs of the 1850s," *Antiques*, November 1994, p. 652. For the cinematic aspects of Cole's *Course of Empire* series, see Parry, *Art of Thomas Cole*, p. 186; for such effects in *The Voyage of Life* see Scott MacDonald, *The Garden in the Machine: A Field Guide to Independent Films about Place* (Berkeley: University of California Press, 2001), pp. 25, 28–29.

5 The waterfall passage derives from *Cole Journal*, March 1843, New York State Library at Albany. Cole's poem "The Vision of Life" (1825) appears in *Thomas Cole's Poetry: The Collected Poems of America's Foremost Painter of the Hudson River School Reflecting His Feelings for Nature and the Romantic Spirit of the Nineteenth Century*, comp. and ed. Marshall B. Tymn (York, PA: Liberty Cap Books, 1972), poem no. 3, pp. 34–35. For "The Bewilderment," see *Collected Essays and Prose Sketches*, where the quoted passage appears on pp. 98–99; cf. Noble, *Life and Works*, pp. 46–51. Alan Wallach writes that Cole's "deepest concerns as an artist revolved around a sense of the world in a state of unremitting crisis." "Thomas Cole: Landscape and the Course of American Empire," in *Thomas Cole: Landscape into History*, ed. William H. Truettner and Alan Wallach (New Haven: Yale University Press, 1994), p. 82. Sarah Burns writes, "To the end of his days, Cole both nurtured and resisted a strong attraction toward darkness: the plunge into the abyss, the headlong rush down black rapids underground, the desolate contemplation of nothingness." *Painting the Dark Side: Art and the Gothic Imagination in Nineteenth-Century America* (Berkeley: University of California Press, 2006), p. 43.

6 For these changes, see esp. Wallach, "Landscape and the Course of American Empire." For Cole's religious background in the Dissenting tradition of England, and the ways in which this tradition influenced him, see Alan Peter Wallach, "The Ideal American Artist and the Dissenting Tradition: A Study of Thomas Cole's Popular Reputation" (PhD diss., Columbia University, 1973).

7 Bryan Jay Wolf links Cole's inner life, in psychoanalytic terms, to the sublime. *Romantic Re-Vision: Culture and Consciousness in Nineteenth-Century American Painting and Literature* (Chicago: University of Chicago Press, 1982); see esp. chapter 5, "Thomas Cole and the Creation of a Romantic Sublime," pp. 177–236.

8 Cole painted *The Voyage of Life* twice, the first set in 1839–40 and the second in 1842 while he was in Rome. He created the second set because he worried that the first set would be broken up on resale; see Parry's account of the circumstances in *Art of Thomas Cole*, pp. 262–63. The set represented in figures 2.1–2.4 is the second, now in the National Gallery of Art. The ingenuity of *The Course of Empire*—for example, its vantage point shifting with the temporal progression it dramatizes—has often been remarked on in our time, that of *The Voyage of Life* less so. Joy S. Kasson finds originality in the way it brings together "the concept of pilgrimage and the theme of the stages of human life." "*The Voyage of Life*: Thomas Cole and Romantic Disillusionment," *American Quarterly* 27, no. 1 (March 1975): 44–45.

9 Parry believed that "theatrical devices, such as the moving panorama or Daguerre's Diorama, in which movement through time and space became part of the visual experience" influenced Cole's development of *The Course of Empire* series. *Art of Thomas Cole*, p. 147; see also pp. 169, 174, 180, 124–25. Alan Wallach provides a succinct description and history of the panorama, a development of the late eighteenth century, and links it to a mode of visualizing landscape he calls "the panoptic sublime," which confers power and control to the viewer. "Making a Picture of the View from Mount Holyoke," in *American Iconology: New Approaches to Nineteenth-Century Art and Literature*, ed. David C. Miller (New Haven: Yale University Press, 1993), pp. 81–91.

10 For the influence of Martin's illustrations, including an accusation in the American press that Cole, in his *Garden of Eden* series (1828), had plagiarized from them, see Parry, *Art of Thomas Cole*, pp. 68–76, 87–89.

11 Susan Stewart, *On Longing: Narratives of the Miniature, the Gigantic, the Souvenir, the Collection* (Durham, NC: Duke University Press, 1993), p. 3.

12 For specific ways in which Cole's religious background influenced his allegories, see pt. 2, "Cole and the Dissenting Tradition," of Wallach's "The Ideal American Artist."

13 *The Voyage of Life* presents a case in which Cole anticipated the series in prose descriptions, dating back more than a dozen years before it was completed (see next note). Regarding the order in which the artist created the individual works in his series, the first two *Course of Empire* paintings (*The Savage State* and *The Pastoral State*) were completed in 1834 and the last three in 1836. With *The Voyage of Life* (first set), he began the series by working on *Childhood*, which he completed in 1839, and then turned to *Youth*; he completed *Youth*, along with *Manhood* and *Old Age*, in 1840. See Paul D. Schweizer, *Thomas Cole's Voyage of Life* (Utica, NY: Munson-Williams-Proctor Institute, 2014), p. 15.

14 Cole titled his list "Subjects for Pictures" and inscribed the sketchbook in which it appears "Thomas Cole, N York, 1827," now in the New York State Library at Albany. In extracting the list, Howard S. Merritt annotated and numbered it and published it in "Appendix II: Thomas Cole's List 'Subjects for Pictures,'" in *Baltimore Museum of Art Annual II*, pp. 82–101. Items 23 and 73 anticipate *The Course of Empire*, and items 83 and 91 render a remarkably full description of *The Voyage of Life* series, painted more than a decade later.

15 Alan Wallach, in an endnote to a groundbreaking article about one of the Catskill Creek paintings, *River in the Catskills* (1843), published a list of these works and thereby established a basis for their further study. "Thomas Cole's *River in the Catskills* as Antipastoral," *Art Bulletin* 84, no. 2 (June 2002): 348n2. He lists ten works, the same number that I examine, but his ten are different in some particulars from mine. Missing from his list are the 1828–29 *View Near Catskill* and the 1842 *Settler's Home in the Catskills*, both in private collections. He includes a work from 1834 that actually depicts a New England scene, owing probably to the fact that a 1982 museum catalog had mistitled it *View on Catskill Creek*, whereas it is now known as *Summer Twilight, A Recollection of a Scene in New England*. Richard J. Koke, *American Landscape and Genre Paintings in the New-York Historical Society*, vol. 1 (New York: New-York Historical Society, 1982), pp. 203–4. The work Wallach titles *Catskill Scene*, now known as *On Catskill Creek, Sunset*, is not a completed painting but instead an oil study of uncertain date. I discuss this painting but do not include it in my basic ten. Finally, *Sunset in the Catskills* appears on both our lists, but Wallach dates it to 1831, whereas it actually was completed in 1841, according to provenance information at the Museum of Fine Arts, Boston. Cole painted other works depicting scenes along Catskill Creek, but the ten I have grouped together share a westward view toward the Catskill Front,

or escarpment, with viewpoints immediately above or along the distinctive large meander of Catskill Creek just outside Catskill, New York.

16 Cole painted *Settler's Home in the Catskills* (1842) in Rome; see my discussion of this work in chapter 5.

17 Regarding Cole's claim for freedom of the imagination, see his often-quoted letter to Gilmor in which the artist states, "If the imagination is shackled, and nothing is described but what we see, seldom will anything truly great be produced in either Painting or Poetry." "Correspondence between Cole and Gilmor," letter number 4, December 25, 1826, p. 47.

18 Tanneries began to appear in Greene County, where Catskill is located, in 1817, when the New York State legislature passed a law allowing the incorporation of the well-funded New York Tannery. The industry was drawn to this region because the Hudson River provided easy transport of hides and because the bark of eastern hemlocks, abundant in the Catskills until their depletion by midcentury, provided a source of tanning acid. See Alf Evers, *The Catskills: From Wilderness to Woodstock*, revised and updated (Woodstock, NY: Overlook Press, 1982), pp. 329–31, 332–40; Tom Lewis, *The Hudson: A History* (New Haven: Yale University Press, 2005), pp. 216–20; and David Stradling, *Making Mountains: New York City and the Catskills* (Seattle: University of Washington Press, 2007), pp. 28–36.

19 Kenneth J. LaBudde observes that after returning to the United States from his first European tour in 1832, Cole painted very few rural landscapes, and that prior to this tour most of such landscapes were done on commission to paint specific scenes, such as the estate of George William Featherstonhaugh. "The Rural Earth: Sylvan Bliss," *American Quarterly* 10, no. 2, pt. 1 (Summer 1958): 144–49.

20 Among the works I am calling middle-sized, two of them—*Sunset in the Catskills* (1841) and *Settler's Home in the Catskills* (1842)—measure somewhat less than two by three feet, and another, *River in the Catskills* (1843), somewhat more. But the largest difference in scale is between the Metropolitan Museum's large *View on the Catskill—Early Autumn* and all the other Catskill Creek paintings. The two smallest works are *Sunset, View on the Catskill* (1833) and a replica that Cole made of this work, discussed in chapter 4. It is David Steinberg who proposes the idea that because of their oval frames these paintings were understood by Cole as ornamentation for domestic settings, in "Thomas Cole's *North Mountain and Catskill Creek*," *Yale University Art Gallery Bulletin* 39 (Winter 1986): 28. Cole's interest in such ornamentation has recently been brought to attention by the discovery, in 2014, of friezes he painted in two parlors of his Catskill home, Cedar Grove.

21 For the circumstances of Cole's sale of *Sunset, View on the Catskill* (1833) to Reed, see Timothy Anglin Burgard's catalog entry for this painting, in Ella M. Foshay, *Mr. Luman Reed's Picture Gallery: A Pioneer Collection of American Art* (New York: Harry N. Abrams, in association with the New-York Historical Society, 1990), p. 124. For Sturges's commission of *View on the Catskill—Early Autumn* (1836–37), see my discussion in chapter 4.

22 Considering *View Near Catskill* (1828–29), the second of the Catskill Creek paintings and discussed in the next chapter, Parry observes that "for Cole, attractive views of real scenery kept the pot boiling by bringing in the money he needed to live on." "Thomas Cole's Early Career," p. 184.

23 Parry describes the circumstances of the Cooper commission in *Art of Thomas Cole*, pp. 83–85.

24 *Thomas Cole's Poetry*, no. 86, p. 180.

25 For Cole's sense of displacement following his emigration to the United States, see esp. Alan Wallach, "Thomas Cole and Transatlantic Romanticism," in *Transatlantic Romanticism: British and American Art and Literature, 1790–1860*, ed. Andrew Hemingway and Alan Wallach (Amherst: University of Massachusetts Press, 2015), p. 208.

3. Discovering Catskill Creek

1 I am indebted to Adam Grimes, research assistant at the Thomas Cole National Historic Site, for locating this important drawing in the archive of the Detroit Institute of Arts and, through his careful study, confirming its relationship to the completed painting.

2 For an account of the 1827 exhibition of *View Near the Village of Catskill,* see Ellwood C. Parry III, *The Art of Thomas Cole: Ambition and Imagination* (Newark: University of Delaware Press, 1988), p. 51. The work surfaced in 1962 in a private collection and, after changing hands, was exhibited in 1969 under the title *Near Catskill Village* (on a loan from Kennedy Galleries, New York), at the Memorial Art Gallery of the University of Rochester. See Howard S. Merritt, *Thomas Cole: 1801–1848* (catalog for an exhibition at the Memorial Art Gallery of the University of Rochester, Rochester, New York, February 14–March 23, 1969), p. 64. It was Mr. and Mrs. John D. Rockefeller 3rd who donated the work in 1993 to the Fine Arts Museums of San Francisco (M. H. de Young Memorial Museum).

3 Cole would have known Kaaterskill High Peak as Roundtop and vice versa. In the 1870s a noted geographer, Arnold Henry Guyot, surveyed the Catskills and reversed the names of these mountains. Alf Evers, *The Catskills: From Wilderness to Woodstock*, revised and updated (Woodstock, NY: Overlook Press, 1982), pp. 491–95. Indian Head Mountain has sometimes been misidentified in Cole scholarship as Sleeping Giant (Hunter Mountain); see, e.g., Parry, *Art of Thomas Cole*, p. 289.

4 In observing that "this mountain profile would become a signature image for Cole and a virtual icon of the region for fellow artists," Linda S. Ferber shows how Christopher Pearse Cranch's *View on the Catskill River* (1846) "echoes Cole's views." *The Hudson River School: Nature and the American Vision* (New York: New-York Historical Society, 2009), p. 83. For Frederic Church's renderings of the Catskill Creek scene in relation to Cole's mentorship of Church, see John Wilmerding, *Master, Mentor, Master: Thomas Cole and Frederic Church* (catalog for an exhibition at the Thomas Cole National Historic Site, Catskill, New York, April 30–November 2, 2014). In the next generation, Charles Herbert Moore painted the scene, most notably in *The Catskills in Spring* (1861), Frances Lehman Loeb Art Center, Vassar College.

5 "Essay on American Scenery," in *Thomas Cole: The Collected Essays and Prose Sketches*, ed. Marshall Tymn (St. Paul: John Colet Press, 1980), p. 9.

6 That the large tree in *View Near the Village of Catskill* is a black locust rather than another species is confirmed by its lack of a thorny base. For this identification and all subsequent plant and tree identifications in this book I am indebted to the botanist Margaret Ronsheim.

7 Some indirect evidence exists supporting the idea that the mullein was one of Cole's earliest perceived images of a "wild" American nature. Nancy Siegel quotes from a journal kept by Cole's father, James Cole, as he, with his wife and daughters, made his way through the rugged Allegheny Mountains of Pennsylvania on the way from Philadelphia to Ohio in 1818: "Traveled up the Alegany [sic] Mountain with great stalks of mullein, the most memorable place that I ever saw and would imagine." Siegel speculates that Thomas, who a year later probably followed the same route, "was equally impressed with the scenery." *Along the Juniata: Thomas Cole and the Dissemination of American Landscape Imagery* (Huntington, PA: Juniata College Museum of Art, in assoc. with University of Washington Press, 2003), pp. 22–23. See also Franklin Kelly's commentary on a set of panels (which I discuss in chapter 5) that the artist painted for Luman Reed's home in 1836;

one of them depicts a cluster of mullein stalks, which Kelly associates "with the New World" and "nature's untamed force." But Kelly also points out that mullein appear in Cole's wilderness paintings, including *Sunrise in the Catskills* (1826) (fig. 3.1): "By visually linking the vibrant plant stalks with the dead and dying tree forms, Cole may have been alluding to the inevitable passing of the old order of things—an order largely determined by nature's actions and causes—to a new one influenced and ultimately dominated by a transplanted European civilization." *American Paintings of the Nineteenth Century, Part 1*, The Collections of the National Gallery of Art Systematic Catalogue (Washington, DC: National Gallery of Art, 1996), pp. 81, 78. Certainly, Cole could have entertained both meanings of the mullein.

8 Timothy Anglin Burgard has pointed out the relationship between this painting and Cole's observation in "Essay on American Scenery," "American Arcadia," in *Masterworks of American Painting at the De Young*, ed. Timothy Anglin Burgard (San Francisco: Fine Arts Museums of San Francisco, 2005), pp. 68–69. For the passage, see *Collected Essays and Prose Sketches*, p. 12.

9 For background on the Van Vechten family and its estate, see Alan Wallach, "Thomas Cole's *River in the Catskills* as Antipastoral," *Art Bulletin* 84, no. 2 (June 2002): 334–50..

10 Trails of smoke from tanneries appear in this same portion of the landscape in others of the Catskill Creek paintings, though with effects different from those here in *View Near the Village of Catskill;* see chapter 5 for discussion of those works.

11 The blasted tree is a familiar motif in Cole's work and that of other nineteenth-century American painters; summarizing the extensive commentary on this motif, Franklin Kelly describes it as "an emblem of the forces of untamed nature." "American Landscape Pairs of the 1850s," *Antiques*, November 1994, p. 654.

12 Regarding Snake Road, Cole made a significant reference to it in an 1841 speech he gave to his Catskill neighbors; he described its winding form connecting sites that had been destroyed or threatened by the construction of the Canajoharie and Catskill railroad. See my discussion of Cole's later Catskill Creek painting *River in the Catskills* (1843) in chapter 5.

13 In the small amount of commentary that exists about this painting, the presence of the couple has rarely been noted, and when it has been, their determined stride has been missed. Margaretta Lovell, for example, sees them instead as "pausing in conversation," a posture in keeping with her understanding of the landscape as one in which "man is integrated into this harmonious scene." Margaretta M. Lovell, *American Painting 1730–1960: A Selection from the Collection of Mr. and Mrs. John D. Rockefeller 3rd* (exhibition organized by the National Museum of Western Art, Japan Society, and the Fine Arts Museums of San Francisco, 1982), p. 19.

14 A more literal translation of *Et in Arcadia ego* would be "Even in Arcadia there am I [death]." Alan Wallach discusses this classical motif in relation to a later Catskill Creek painting, *View on the Catskill—Early Autumn* in "Thomas Cole: Landscape and the Course of American Empire," in *Thomas Cole: Landscape into History*, ed. William H. Truettner and Alan Wallach (New Haven: Yale University Press, 1994), p. 73. Aaron Sachs places Cole in relation to a specifically nineteenth-century American version of the melancholic, Arcadian tradition, linking some of his paintings to other antebellum cultural forms including the rural cemetery. *Arcadian America: The Death of an Environmental Tradition* (New Haven: Yale University Press, 2013), pp. 120–36. The most influential study of Arcadian themes in American culture is Leo Marx, *The Machine in the Garden: Technology and the Pastoral Ideal in America* (London: Oxford University Press, 1964).

15 The immediate environment of Catskill Village had not seen wilderness for at least a century when Cole began to paint it. Dutch settlement agriculture in the area went back to the early seventeenth century and was itself long predated by large Iroquois farming settlements, or "forts." See Shirley W. Dunn, *The Mohicans and Their Land 1609–1730* (Fleischmanns, NY: Purple Mountain Press, 1994). Cf. Kenneth John Myers's discussion of Native American tribes in the Hudson River Valley during the colonial and precolonial periods. *The Catskills: Painters, Writers, and Tourists in the Mountains, 1820–1895* (Yonkers, NY: Hudson River Museum of Westchester, 1988, pp. 22–23).

16 The right-hand sector of Cole's later Catskill Creek painting, *View on the Catskill—Early Autumn*, is rendered by him as a darkened space with tropical aspects; see my discussion of this work in chapter 4.

17 Regarding the significance of Cole's representation, in *View on the Catskill—Early Autumn*, of a child not yet conceived by him and Maria, see my discussion in chapter 4.

18 Parry describes the circumstances of Cole's remaining in Catskill beyond the summer in 1828. *Art of Thomas Cole*, p. 40. For a brief, general discussion of *View Near Catskill* see Ellwood C. Parry III, "Thomas Cole's Early Career: 1818–1829," in *Views and Visions: American Landscapes before 1830*, ed. Edward J. Nygren (Washington, DC: Corcoran Gallery of Art, 1986), p. 183.

19 See Parry on Cole's completing *View Near Catskill* just before the 1829 spring exhibition of the National Academy of Design. *Art of Thomas Cole*, p. 93. Franklin Kelly has generously shared with me his archival research, at the Albany Institute of History and Art, showing that Cole painted *View Near Catskill* for the Van Rensselaer family as a pendant to their *View on Lake Winnipesaukee*. The letter commissioning the pendant, in the Cole Papers at the New York State Library at Albany, is dated July 8, 1828.

20 Cole titled the drawing "Scene in the Alleghany Mountains." Siegel has written the fullest account of Cole's traversing the rugged Alleghenies, in 1819 and again in 1823, and the effects of this experience on him. On the basis of her examination of the journal kept by Cole's father referred to in note 7, she speculates that the scene depicted in the drawing is "a famous bridge crossing [over the Juniata River] in Bedford County [Pennsylvania] a few miles off the Pennsylvania Road and a likely stopping point for the artist." *Along the Juniata*, p. 24. For a brief summary of the period between Cole's arrival in the United States in 1818 and his move to New York in 1825, see Parry, "Cole's Early Career," pp. 163–67. Parry calls *Crossing the Stream* "a memory image of [Cole's] earlier wanderings in western Pennsylvania." *Art of Thomas Cole*, p. 58.

21 See Franklin Kelly's discussion and illustration of these two drawings, both titled *The Bridge of Fear* (1827–28), which may, he writes, have been part of Cole's developing vision for the composition of *Expulsion from the Garden of Eden*. *Thomas Cole's Paintings of Eden* (Fort Worth: Amon Carter Museum, 1994), pp. 32ff. Siegel writes, "The bridge [i.e., as a structural form] appears in later paintings by Cole such as the similarly themed *Crossing the Stream* (1827, Private Collection), which [like the drawing] also utilizes a fallen timber bridge." *Along the Juniata*, p. 16. Cf. Parry, *Art of Thomas Cole*, pp. 57–58.

22 This entry is number 88 on Cole's list. One of his favorite poems was James Thomson's "The Seasons" (1726, 1730). On Cole's list, see also number 93, "Two pastoral landscapes. A morning & evening." Even before 1827 Cole appears to have begun thinking in such terms. Tracie Felker observes that a group of drawings from nature made in Pennsylvania by Cole in 1823 (now in the Albany Institute of History and Art) have inscriptions noting "date, locale and even the time of day of their execution." "Thomas Cole's Drawings of His 1825 Trip up the Hudson River," *American Art Journal* 24, no. 1–2 (1992): 67. A decade later Cole produced a remarkable work, *The Four Times of Day in Italy* (1833–36, Albany Institute of History and Art), in which he painted four continuous landscapes, each shading into the next left to right, on a long, narrow wood panel (4 x 49 inches).

4. Taking a Different View

1 The poem's title had several variations in the various nineteenth-century editions of Bryant's works where it appeared. It was first published in the 1830 volume of *The Talisman*, a journal with which Cole also was associated.

2 Ellwood C. Parry III quotes from Cole's report to Dunlap. *The Art of Thomas Cole: Ambition and Imagination* (Newark: University of Delaware Press, 1988), p. 126.

3 Alan Wallach studies the shift from Cole's "aristocratic patronage" in the early years of his career to his "bourgeois patronage" in the 1830s and 1840s. "Thomas Cole: Landscape and the Course of American Empire," in *Thomas Cole: Landscape into History*, ed. William H. Truettner and Alan Wallach (New Haven: Yale University Press, 1994), pp. 33–47.

4 The works remaining in Cole's studio at his death were exhibited at the Kennedy Galleries in New York in 1962, and a catalog produced for this exhibition illustrated the replica under the title *Distant View of Roundtop, Catskill* (*An Exhibition of Paintings by Thomas Cole N.A. from the Artist's Studio, Catskill, New York* (New York: Kennedy Galleries, 1964), p. 5; see my discussion of the work's mistitling later in this chapter.

5 Another possibility is that Cole copied *Sunset, View on the Catskill* for a client who expressed interest in it but ultimately didn't buy it. Less likely is the possibility that the Albany work was not painted during the same period as the original but was created later based upon the same sketch or sketches; common sketches would not have provided the basis for so exact a copy.

6 David Steinberg, "Thomas Cole's *North Mountain and Catskill Creek*," *Yale University Art Gallery Bulletin* 39 (Winter 1986): 28. Cf. Timothy Anglin Burgard, who believes that the replica alone "served as the point of departure for" the Yale painting. Catalog entry for *Sunset, View in the Catskills,* in Ella M. Foshay, *Mr. Luman Reed's Picture Gallery: A Pioneer Collection of American Art* (New York: Harry N. Abrams, in association with the New-York Historical Society, 1990), pp. 124–25. I concur, because Cole may have retained the replica to have at hand specifically for a future composition.

7 The geologist Robert Titus first alerted me, in 2015, that the central mountain in this work could not be North Mountain, and in 2016 the GIS analyst Neil Curri identified it as Blackhead; see its location in map 4.1. Windham High Peak, extending to the north and west beyond Blackhead, has a similar, distinctive downward cleft at its southern end, but Windham would not have appeared in this shape from Cole's vantage point in the 1833 and 1838 Catskill Creek paintings. To see Windham in this shape, Cole would have had to assume a vantage point considerably to the north of these works' riverside location. In a videotaped lecture at the Yale University Art Gallery, John Walsh recognized that the mountain in Yale's Catskill Creek painting is not North Mountain and that the work is mistitled. "American Views, Viewpoints, and Manipulations: Thomas Cole's Catskills," October 27, 2017.

8 Powell, *Thomas Cole* (New York: Harry N. Abrams: 1990), pp. 22–23. See also Powell's article "Thomas Cole and the American Landscape Tradition: The Picturesque," *Arts Magazine*, March 1978, pp. 110–17; and Tracie Felker, "Thomas Cole's Drawings of His 1825 Trip up the Hudson River," *American Art Journal* 24, no. 1–2 (1992): 81, 92.

9 In recent years, the Albany painting has been retitled *View of Catskill Creek*, though the object file for this work suggests that this new title is merely descriptive of the scene and not derived from provenance information. In the period immediately after the Yale University Art Gallery acquired its Catskill Creek

painting (1981–82), correspondence archived at the Gallery attributed two different titles to the work, *View of Esopus Creek with Cupcake Mountain* and *Sunset in the Catskills*. It appears to have taken its current title, *North Mountain and Catskill Creek*, in 1984, on the recommendation of the Cole scholar Ellwood C. Parry III, who is reported, in a memorandum by Barbara Heins of February 6, 1984, to have said "he believes the work is the one included as number 18 in the 1848 exhibition bearing the title 'North Mountain and Catskill Creek' which belonged to Mr. Abraham M. Cozzens and was dated 1838." The memorandum continues, "He [Parry] urged us to re-title the work as 'North Mountain and Catskill Creek' or as 'Sunset in the Catskills' after the poem [found in the backing; see later in this chapter] and similar painting." The titling of the work thus appears to be a judgment call by Parry and is based on provenance information going back only as far as 1848. A letter of August 20, 1981, from the Yale University Art Gallery's Helen Cooper to the donor Anne Osborn Prentice, requesting further provenance information, apparently went unanswered (confirmed by my 2014 interview with Ms. Cooper).

10   *Correspondence of Thomas Cole and Daniel Wadsworth*, ed. J. Bard McNulty (Hartford, CT: Connecticut Historical Society, 1983), letter number 17 (April 23, 1828), p. 38. I am grateful to David P. Barnes for bringing this letter to my attention.

11   Today the gazebo of a restaurant is positioned atop this outcrop, near the intersection of Main Street and Maple Avenue (U.S Route 9W) in Catskill. Burgard writes that an (unnamed) oil sketch in a private collection reveals that Cole "introduced a pastoral note by adding the wooden structure on the hill at the right." Catalog entry for *Sunset, View on the Catskill*, in Foshay, *Mr. Luman Reed's Picture Gallery*, p. 124. But a shed appears in the pencil sketch illustrated in figure 4.6, and, as noted, to its left Cole has written the phrase "broken house," suggesting the possibility that some kind of structure was present in the scene that he observed.

12   Because rushes are pure grasses, they do not have woody structures or extensions. Wallach refers to the rower in a later Catskill Creek painting, *View on the Catskill—Early Autumn* as "a rush gatherer tak[ing] up the oars of his boat" and prominently illustrates the 1838 (Yale) Catskill Creek painting—which he does not discuss—on the page where he makes this observation. "Thomas Cole: Landscape and the Course of American Empire," p. 72. But the boat depicted (distantly) in *View on the Catskill—Early Autumn* has no visible cargo, and Wallach's discussion thus appears indirectly to identify the rower in the Yale painting—and by extension in all the Catskill Creek paintings where he appears—primarily as a "rush gatherer." Setting the plant species aside, I argue that the figure should be identified not so much by his cargo (the Yale painting is the only work in the series that unmistakably shows plants in the boat) as by his activity as a rower, a role whose meanings shift from one work to the next; see my analyses in later chapters.

13   Thoreau's parable appears in the opening chapter, "Economy," of *Walden* (1854). A regional mythology that Cole may have known about concerns a mysterious and reclusive group of basket makers called "The Bushwhackers" who supposedly lived for generations across the Hudson River from Catskill, New York. See a Smithsonian American Art Museum Collections web page of June 2012, http://americanart.si.edu/collections/search/artwork/researchNotes/1976.114.pdf.

14   See my discussion of *River in the Catskills* in chapter 5.

15   That Cole sometimes put his figures into period dress for thematic purposes is confirmed by Elise Effmann Clifford, who points out that in Cole's early painting *View of Fort Putnam* (1826) (fig. 1.9)

the figure in the foreground viewing the famous Revolutionary War ruin "is dressed in the fashion of the late eighteenth century, adding a touch of nostalgia to the picture." "Thomas Cole's *View of Fort Putnam*," *Antiques*, November 2004, p. 157. Cf. Wallach's observation that "many of Cole's landscapes embodied parts or fragments of a narrative tracing America's past and future—a mythic history in large measure spelled out through the use of pictorial devices." "Thomas Cole: Landscape and the Course of American Empire," p. 74.

16 Shirley W. Dunn describes patterns of Iroquois settlement: "To accommodate their agricultural network, Mohicans lived in scattered small communities spread across their territory. Present Greene County offered a good example. There was a reported village and fort at the confluence of the Kaaterskill and the Catskill." *The Mohicans and Their Land 1609–1730* (Fleischmanns, NY: Purple Mountain Press, 1994), p. 231. In May of 2018, the Greene Land Trust established on this site the Mawignack Preserve. According to the Trust, the preserve "is named after a Native American word meaning 'the place where two rivers meet' and was the name of an Algonquian village on the flats along Catskill Creek in the 17th century" (https://www.scenichudson.org/parks/mawignack).

17 As Parry noted, Cole drew his initials ("T C") directly under the boy, on the large stone bridge on which he is drawing, thus associating himself with the origins of art. *Art of Thomas Cole*, p. 162.

18 Susan D. Kuretsky explains how a seemingly unimportant reclining cat in the shadows of Rembrandt's *The Holy Family with a Curtain* (1646) is meant to call up a whole set of characteristics associated with this animal—quickness, devotion to home, and acute night vision—that make it "an ideal guardian of the Holy Family." "Rembrandt's Cat," in *Aemulatio: Imitation, Emulation and Invention in Nether-landish Art from 1500–1800, Essays in Honor of Eric Jan Sluijter*, ed. A. W. A. Boschloo et al. (Zwolle, Switz.: Waanders Publishers, 2011), p. 270.

19 Close photographic examination of these works might reveal underpainting related to the faint images appearing in the barns' darkened doorways.

20 Reviews and brief notices of Cole's *Sunset, View on the Catskill* (1833), published in the period following its appearance in the National Academy of Design annual exhibition, show no specific interest in the human figures. For example, the reference to this painting in a review in the *Knickerbocker* from its May 1834 issue reads in full: "Mark the light from the descended sun, through the breaks in the foliage of the tree on the right of the picture—the placid water—and the dank mists gathering about the summit of the mountain in the distance" (p. 400). The May 1834 issue of the *American Monthly Magazine* characterized *Sunset, View on the Catskill* as a "pleasing picture," with no other descriptive commentary (p. 27).

21 Hirshfield, *Ten Windows: How Great Poems Transform the World* (New York: Knopf, 2015), pp. 94, 106.

22 Matthew Baigell and Allen Kaufman contended that the forms read right side up are the Hebraic letters for "NOAH" and upside down "SHADDAI," or the "Almighty." "Thomas Cole's 'The Oxbow': A Critique of American Civilization," *Arts Magazine*, January 1981, pp. 136–39. For an interesting elaboration of this idea, see David Bjelajac, "Thomas Cole's *Oxbow* and the American Zion Divided," *American Art* 20, no. 1 (Spring 2006): 70–71.

23 Cole's early interest in Irving's story is made clear by an 1825 sketch he titled *Ninepins—A Scene from Rip Van Winkle*. This drawing is illustrated in Ellwood C. Parry III, "Thomas Cole's Early Drawings: In Search of a Signature Style," *Bulletin of the Detroit Institute of Arts* 66, no. 1 (1990): 8. Other drawings by Cole depicting scenes in "Rip Van Winkle" are in the collection of the Albany Institute of History and Art; one of them is illustrated in Kenneth John Myers, *The Catskills: Painters,*

Writers, and Tourists in the Mountains, 1820–1895 (Yonkers, NY: Hudson River Museum of Westchester, 1988), p. 34, as plate 8.

24 The fullest consideration of the gothic in Cole's imagination is chapter 1, "Doom and Gloom," of Sarah Burns's *Painting the Dark Side: Art and the Gothic Imagination in Nineteenth-Century America* (Berkeley: University of California Press, 2006), where she interestingly compares this element in his work with that of writers Charles Brockden Brown, Cooper, and Edgar Allan Poe (pp. 1–43).

25 Freud's famous essay "The Uncanny" (1919) inevitably comes to mind here, for the way in which it describes the uncanny as a process of the familiar returning as strange. Schor uses the term "eccentric detail" to describe the bias against details in Joshua Reynolds's enormously influential *Discourses on Art*, published toward the end of the eighteenth century and part of Cole's aesthetic legacy. Schor, *Reading in Detail: Aesthetics and the Feminine* (New York: Routledge, Taylor and Francis Group, 2007), pp. 10–11. In her interesting study of "detail" in the work of Frederic Church, Jennifer Rabb allies Cole with Reynolds and thereby makes him a foil to Church. For Cole, in this view, "details should remain 'comparatively unobserved' [a phrase from Cole's 'Notes on Art'] as if silenced by the grandeur of a scene and the import of its moral message," whereas "Church's details work to a singular *effect*." But, as we have seen, Cole's use of detail—though different from that of Church—is complex and decisive. Raab, *Frederick Church: The Art and Science of Detail* (New Haven: Yale University Press, 2015, p. 30.

26 The birds represented in this work are turkey vultures (*Cathartes aura*), identifiable by the distinctly dihedral shape of their wings. They are scavengers, not predators, and characteristically they circle in tight columns around carrion, in the manner Cole has depicted in this painting.

27 Blackhead Mountain does appear in an oil study, *On Catskill Creek, Sunset* (c. 1845–47), and it may be the mountain profile that appears in Cole's *Catskill Scenery* (c. 1833)—not previously identified as a Catskill Creek scene—whose vantage point is significantly upriver from works in the Catskill Creek series, at the confluence with Kaaterskill Creek.

28 As transcribed by Steinberg, "Thomas Cole's *North Mountain and Catskill Creek*," p. 26. As he points out, removal of the painting's backing also revealed that Cole signed the work in two places. I am grateful to the curatorial staff of the Yale University Art Gallery for showing me the poem during a visit to the gallery in 2014.

29 Steinberg, "Thomas Cole's *North Mountain and Catskill Creek*," p. 26, believed this was Cole's own poem, and subsequent commentators have agreed. I am grateful to Kenneth John Myers for discovering the actual author. The poem appeared on p. 139 of the relevant issue.

30 As Cole wrote in his journal in the spring of 1837, "In the winter I painted four pictures[:] A View on the Catskill for Mr. Sturges; An Autumnal Scene for a friend of Mr. Inman's[;] a small landscape for Mr. Cooke[;] & a View of Florence." Louis Legrand Noble, *The Life and Works of Thomas Cole*, first published in 1853; reprint edited by Elliott S. Vesell (Cambridge, MA: Belknap Press of Harvard University Press, 1964), p. 176, and *Thomas Cole: The Collected Essays and Prose Sketches*, ed. Marshall Tymn (St. Paul: John Colet Press, 1980), pp. 142–43. In contextualizing this journal entry, Parry discusses contemporary critics' understanding of the comparison between American and European settings in *View on the Catskill—Early Autumn* and *View of Florence from San Miniato*, quoting reviews in the *New-York Mirror* from its issues of May 13 and May 20, 1837. *Art of Thomas Cole*, pp. 190–91; see also pp. 192, 203. Franklin Kelly considers the two works in relation to the larger subject of nineteenth-century American paired paintings. "American Landscape Pairs of the 1850s," *Antiques*, November 1994, p. 652.

31 Oswaldo Rodriguez Roque, catalog entry for "View on the Catskill—Early Autumn, 1837," in *American Paradise: The World of the Hudson River School* (New York: Metropolitan Museum of Art, 1987), p. 129. The 1832 sketch that Rodriguez Roque identified as the basis for *View on the Catskill—Early Autumn* appears on pages 44 and 45 of Cole's 1832 sketchbook, Cole Archive, Detroit Institute of Arts. The railroad constructed in 1836, the Canajoharie and Catskill line, had been chartered in 1830. See map 2.1 for its course in and beyond the village of Catskill, and see my account of its significance for Cole in chapter 4 and in chapter 5.

32 Rodriguez Roque, catalog entry for "View on the Catskill—Early Autumn, 1837," p. 129.

33 This previously unlocated letter from Cole to Sturges, in a private collection, is quoted in Christine I. Oaklander, "Jonathan Sturges, W. H. Osborn, and William Church Osborn: A Chapter in American Art Patronage," *Metropolitan Museum Journal* 43 (2008): 175–76. Reed died on June 7, 1836.

34 Rodriguez Roque, catalog entry for "View on the Catskill—Early Autumn, 1837," p. 129. He was supporting an earlier and highly impressionistic interpretation of *View on the Catskill—Early Autumn* by E. P. Richardson, whose 1956 publication he quotes approvingly: "a picture which he [Cole] never surpassed in imaginative realism or lyric sentiment. . . . The brushstroke is minute in detail, but the details fall into place in a luminous and spacious whole." *Painting in America: From 1502 to the Present* (New York: Thomas Y. Crowell, 1956), p. 166. Cf. Kenneth Maddox, who also quotes from Richardson, regarding the work's "sense of well-being": "Pastoral figures flit through the landscape like nymphs in a sylvan glade." "Thomas Cole and the Railroad: Gentle Maledictions," *Archives of American Art Journal* 26, no. 1 (1986): 7). William H. Truettner points out that for Richardson Cole's "Italian landscapes ('rich in the deep cello tones of reverie') were singled out as his most successful efforts." "Nature and the Native Tradition: The Problem of Two Thomas Coles," in Truettner and Wallach, *Landscape into History*, p. 149.

35 Wallach makes this observation; he understands the painting as a "Claudian pastorale" which, on one level, it undoubtedly is. "Thomas Cole: Landscape and the Course of American Empire," pp. 72, 73.

36 Cole letter to Sturges of February 24, 1837, in Oaklander, "Jonathan Sturges."

37 In his landscapes Cole often added his figures after creating the larger composition, but several sketches for works in the Catskill Creek series include human figures whose presence continues into the completed paintings. For example, the important and central place of the rower in *Sunset in the Catskills* is anticipated by his presence in a sketch for this work (fig. 5.4); see my discussion in chapter 5.

38 In making this distinction, I want to carefully define my use of the term "emblematic" because it has application to Cole's work in another important, and not unrelated, way. As Alan Peter Wallach has shown in his definitive study of Cole's religious background in the Dissenting tradition of English Puritanism, that tradition involved moral instruction from emblem books—especially Francis Quarles's *Emblems, Divine and Moral* (1635) and Bunyan's *Book for Boys and Girls* (1686)—and, along with this instruction, a distinctive emblematic habit of mind in which Cole was deeply implicated. Wallach's study is far too ranging and complex to summarize in this short space, but in relation to my discussion the main point relates to terminology. In Wallach's analysis "emblem" and "symbol" are more or less interchangeable, or, put another way, emblems have symbolic force of a particular, that is, allegorical, kind. Wallach, "The Ideal American Artist and the Dissenting Tradition: A Study of Thomas Cole's Popular Reputation" (PhD diss., Columbia University, 1973); see esp. part 2, chap. 5, "Divine Emblems," pp. 158–86. What I mean by "symbolic," on the other hand, is a directly referential relationship between image and meaning, which makes it applicable to the didactic character of *The Voyage of Life* and others of Cole's allegorical works. In turn, for the purposes of my discussion, "emblematic" means an indirect and even deliberately obscure relationship between image and import.

39 Stewart, *On Longing: Narratives of the Miniature, the Gigantic, the Souvenir, the Collection* (Durham, NC: Duke University Press, 1993), p. 66.

40 Cole's compositional zones in *View in the Catskill—Early Autumn*, and in several of his other landscapes, are markedly distinct from one another; while they meet, they do not quite adjoin. In terms of compositional strategies, he may have learned to work in distinct zones of a composition from a book he read in 1825, at the beginning of his mature career, William Oram's *Precepts and Observations on the Art of Colouring in Landscape Painting*, ed. Charles Clarke (London, 1810). As Wallach explains, "Oram . . . advised dividing the composition into zones parallel to the picture plane so that the limits of the lights and darks for each zone . . . could be given." "The Ideal American Artist," p. 188. Cf. Parry, *Art of Thomas Cole*, p. 23.

41 The phrase is that of Kenneth W. Maddox, referring to the "hunter with gun over his shoulder returning to his family." "Thomas Cole and the Railroad," p. 7. Parry calls *The Hunter's Return* "a strictly American semiwilderness scene intended to please the many." *Art of Thomas Cole*, p. 310. Around these issues, see my discussion of Cole's 1842 painting *Settler's Home in the Catskills* in chapter 5.

42 See John Conron, *American Picturesque* (University Park, PA: Pennsylvania State University Press, 2000), p. 122. Conron identifies the scene as a "prosperous farm," and says that "the figures [are] all enjoying (except for the running man) a moment of late afternoon leisure" (p. 122).

43 Thoreau's parable appears in the "Economy" chapter of *Walden* (1854): "I long ago lost a hound, a bay horse, and a turtle dove, and am still on their trail. Many are the travellers I have spoken to concerning them, describing their tracks and what calls they answered to. I have met one or two who had heard the hound, and the tramp of the horse, and even seen the dove disappear behind a cloud, and they seemed as anxious to recover them as if they had lost them themselves."

44 In *River in the Catskills*, discussed in chapter 5, the rower's course is somewhat ambiguous; it is uncertain whether he is crossing the river or is starting to turn upstream. But when we compare this work with *View on the Catskill—Early Autumn*, which it closely resembles in overall composition, clear differences emerge between their rowers. The one in *River in the Catskills* appears in the middle distance, on the near side (for the viewer) of the pointbar, whereas the rower in *View on the Catskill—Early Autumn* is pictured distantly, at the far end of the pointbar and soon to go out of sight around the river's bend. Correspondingly, the rower in *River in the Catskills* is, like his counterparts in the 1833 and 1838 Catskill Creek paintings, involved in a traditional rural activity—in this case fishing, as indicated by the hoop dangling off the stern—and has at his feet some form of cargo. The rower in *View on the Catskill—Early* Autumn has no cargo but himself; he is singularly involved in rowing himself upstream.

45 See my discussion in chapter 5 of Cole's *Settler's Home in the Catskills* (1842).

46 Conron, *American Picturesque,* p. 121. Conron uses this term in his characterization of what he regards as a distinctively American version of the picturesque tradition.

47 Paul D. Schweizer, quoting from Cole's own 1839 account to Samuel Ward, says that the artist "solidified his ideas about the [*Voyage of Life*] series during the last three months of 1836 when he exhibited *The Course of Empire* in New York." *Thomas Cole's Voyage of Life* (Utica, NY: Munson-Williams-Proctor Institute, 2014), pp. 8, 64n18.

48 These suspended narratives are related to the emblematic character of figural images in *View on the Catskill—Early Autumn*. See Angus Fletcher on "the remnants of an action" in certain emblematic poems that he distinguishes from allegories. *Allegory: The Theory of a Symbolic Mode* (Ithaca: Cornell University Press, 1962), p. 26.

49 It may have been Parry who first drew attention to the fact that Thomas and Maria's firstborn, Theodore, was not born until January 1, 1838, making it impossible for the child to have been conceived by the time the artist had completed *View on the Catskill—Early Autumn. Art of Thomas Cole*, p. 192.

50 Wallach writes, "The mother's fecundity seems an extension of the natural fecundity surrounding her." "Thomas Cole: Landscape and the Course of American Empire," p. 72.

51 Examples of tropical landscapes showing vine-encircled trees by Heade and Church are *Brazilian Forest* (1864) by the former and *Morning in the Tropics* (1877) by the latter.

52 Such associations were popularized in the United States during the mid-nineteenth century, in part by travel literature. A notable example is Herman Melville's first novel, *Typee: A Peep at Polynesian Life* (1846), based partly on the writer's experiences in 1842 in the South Pacific Marquesas Islands.

53 Whitman's evocation of the mullein appears in the most overtly erotic part of the poem; in later editions it would be numbered section 5, which concludes with his celebration of "elder / and mullen and pokeweed." *Leaves of Grass: The First* (*1855*) *Edition*, ed. Malcolm Cowley (New York: Viking, 1959), p. 29.

54 As Kelly points out, Thoreau, a contemporary of Whitman, described in his book *A Week on the Concord and Merrimack Rivers* (1849) the energy of the mullein in a very different way, that is, as an invasive species that had crowded out Native American plants. *American Paintings of the Nineteenth Century, Part 1*, The Collections of the National Gallery of Art Systematic Catalogue (Washington, DC: National Gallery of Art, 1996), p. 78.

55 Scholarship in this field took its impetus, in part, from the work of Annette Kolodny, especially her books *The Lay of the Land: Metaphor as Experience and History in American Life and Letters* (Chapel Hill: University of North Carolina Press, 1975), and *The Land before Her: Fantasy and Experience of the American Frontiers, 1630–1860* (Chapel Hill: University of North Carolina Press, 1984).

56 Parry, *Art of Thomas Cole*, p. 192. Cf. Maddox, who says that the hunter "might be a surrogate image for Cole, as he wears the tall wide-brimmed hat that Cole conspicuously wears in *The Oxbow*." "Thomas Cole and the Railroad," p. 7.

57 For example, in a journal entry of March 15, 1852, Thoreau wrote, "May I gird myself to be a hunter of the beautiful that naught escape me." *Journal 4: 1851–1852*, ed. Leonard N. Neufeldt and Nancy Craig Simmons (Princeton: Princeton University Press, 1992, p. 390).

58 For an example of cultural commentary about *The Oxbow*, see the catalog entry by Oswaldo Rodriguez Roque, "View from Mount Holyoke, Northampton, Massachusetts, after a Thunderstorm (The Oxbow)," in *American Paradise*, pp. 125–27. For Cole's idea of measured progress in "Essay on American Scenery," in *Essays and Prose Sketches*, see esp. p. 17.

5. Living through Trying Times

1 See Ellwood C. Parry's description of the circumstances surrounding Cole's departure. *The Art of Thomas Cole: Ambition and Imagination* (Newark: University of Delaware Press, 1988), p. 263. The poem appears in *Thomas Cole: The Collected Essays and Prose Sketches*, ed. Marshall Tymn (St. Paul: John Colet Press, 1980), p. 167, and is also collected by Tymn as no. 60 in *Thomas Cole's Poetry: The Collected Poems of America's Foremost Painter of the Hudson River School Reflecting His Feelings for Nature*

and the Romantic Spirit of the Nineteenth Century, comp. and ed. Marshall B. Tymn (York, PA: Liberty Cap Books, 1972), p. 130. Cole's journal passage lamenting his career was later transcribed by his friend and biographer Louis Legrand Noble, in *The Life and Works of Thomas Cole*, first published in 1853; reprint edited by Elliott S. Vesell (Cambridge, MA: Belknap Press of Harvard University Press, 1964), p. 220, for the transcribed passage; Parry quotes a fuller version of it in *Art of Thomas Cole*, p. 262, and comments on Cole's worries about *The Voyage of Life*. Against these worries Cole re-created the series in Rome in 1842.

2   For a ranging discussion of Cole in relation to the economic, political, and cultural forces of his time, see Christine Stansell and Sean Wilentz, "Cole's America: An Introduction," in *Thomas Cole: Landscape into History*, ed. William H. Truettner and Alan Wallach (New Haven, CT: Yale University Press, 1994), pp. 3–21. A work treating Cole's response to his turbulent era is chapter 1 of Ross Barrett, *Rendering Violence: Riots, Strikes, and Upheaval in Nineteenth-Century American Art* (Berkeley: University of California Press, 2014), where the author focuses on *The Destruction of Empire* in *The Course of Empire* series.

3   The donor of the Yale painting, Anne Osborn Prentice, was the great-granddaughter of William Henry Osborn, who in turn was the son-in-law of Jonathan Sturges.

4   Considering the 1838 (Yale) Catskill Creek painting in relation to other works that Cole formatted for oval and arched frames (including ones not in the Catskill Creek series), David Steinberg observes that "these pictures almost all represent views of land at sunset," which, he says, "further strengthens their identity as a unit among Cole's productions." "Thomas Cole's *North Mountain and Catskill Creek*," *Yale University Art Gallery Bulletin* 39 (Winter 1986): 28. See Cole's description of the "glowing landscape" of autumn in "Essay on American Scenery," in *Collected Essays and Prose Sketches*), p. 15.

5   The GIS analyst Neil Curri discovered at this site depressions in the landscape, which he has represented with broken lines in map 2.1. The inlet that appears prominently, in the same map, on the north shore to the west of the Van Vechten house and mill may have been connected in Cole's time to the further reach of the river to the north.

6   I am indebted to Kaitlin Manning for drawing my attention to this important sketch.

7   Here too I am indebted to Kaitlin Manning, for recognizing the glimpse of the mill in the completed painting, and for the idea that Cole may, through such imagery, have been asking viewers to look more closely and deeply into his paintings.

8   Wendy N. E. Ikemoto shows how Cole complicates the perspectives and optics of *The Departure* and *The Return. Antebellum American Pendant Paintings: New Ways of Looking* (New York: Routledge, 2018), pp. 76–117.

9   Franklin Kelly's "American Landscape Pairs of the 1850s," *Antiques*, November 1994, pp. 550–57, is pertinent to this discussion. See also Kelly's "The Legacy of Thomas Cole's Imaginative Creations," in Annette Blaugrund, *Thomas Cole: The Artist as Architect* (New York: Monacelli Press, 2016), pp. 83, 90.

10 Of course Cole was interested in before-and-after imagery in a context broader than that of American scenery, as can be seen in his two-part 1838 series, *The Present* and *The Past*.

11 *Mill Dam on the Catskill Creek* also depicts a high hill in the right middle ground, which could possibly be an exaggerated and somewhat displaced rendering of Jefferson Heights. Cole's importation of Mount Chocorua into his scenes from *The Last of the Mohicans* has often been observed; see, e.g., Parry, *Art of Thomas Cole*, pp. 65–66.

12 *Collected Essays and Prose Sketches*, p. 5. Steinberg quotes this passage in his characterization of a sunset motif in several works by Cole with oval and arched frames. "Thomas Cole's *North Mountain*," p. 28.

13 Of course, sunsets in Cole's work (and in that of many artists) can be glorious, melancholy, and tragic all at once. Many have observed that *Desolation* is the most beautiful of the paintings in the *Course of Empire* series. And, given Cole's belief in the cyclical nature of time and history, the scene depicted in *Desolation* would not be the absolute end of things but rather the ground for beginning a new cycle.

14 Cole's signature on the rock reads "T. Cole / 1842."

15 This small sketch is in the collection of the New-York Historical Society. Rossiter was a prominent figure in his own right; he was elected to the National Academy in 1849. May 24 may not be the date on which Cole completed the sketch but the date he gave the work to Rossiter.

16 Parry found the topography of *Settler's Home in the Catskills* "exaggerated" and speculated that it might have been produced from memory in Rome—a well-informed guess. He refers to George Washington Greene's 1860 biographical sketch of Cole in which Greene reported having seen in the artist's Rome studio "a small landscape, an Autumn scene, from some spot, if we remember right, near Catskill." Parry, *Art of Thomas Cole*, pp. 287–89; Greene, "Cole," in *Biographical Sketches* (New York, 1860), p. 104.

17 For a clearer example of Cole's telescoping this view, see his later sketch of the scene—from a different, more elevated vantage point-—in a sketchbook dated 1839–44, prints and drawings collection of the Princeton University Art Museum. The relevant sketch is folio 6, verso, and is dated by Cole August 5, 1844.

18 The quoted phrase, from a journal entry of November 27, 1842, appears in *Collected Essays and Prose Sketches*, p. 170, and, in abbreviated form, in Noble, *Life and Works*, p. 250; see Parry's discussion of the journal entry in *Art of Thomas Cole*, p. 273. The letter to Maria, dated April 2, 1842, is archived at the Museum of Fine Arts, Boston, and is excerpted in Noble, *Life and Works*, p. 241; see Parry for its context. *Art of Thomas Cole*, p. 268. In relation to this letter, Cole's 1846 painting *A Pic-Nic Party* (formerly, *The Pic-Nic*, the Brooklyn Museum), set on a riverside with a large hooped picnic basket in the foreground, comes to mind. Parry saw in its human figures portraits of Cole and his family, *Art of Thomas Cole*, p. 318, though another commentary by Teresa A. Carbone identifies the central male figure (playing a guitar) as Cole's friend, Cornelius Ver Bryck, an accomplished artist and guitarist who had died in 1844. Carbone, *American Paintings in the Brooklyn Museum: Artists Born by 1876*, vol. 1 (Brooklyn: Brooklyn Museum, 2006), pp. 388–91. However, there are several elements in the landscape of this large work that suggest features of the Catskill Creek scene, and it is possible to understand its figures as having more than one meaning for the artist.

19 Fourteen of the drawings by club members, including Cole's *The Trying Hour*, are archived in the M. and M. Karolik Collection of American Water Colors and Drawings in the Museum of Fine Arts, Boston. They are accompanied by a detailed museum note, from which my account and its quotation are derived, describing and documenting the club's proceedings, by Anne Blake Smith, whose research became the basis for a much shorter account: "the bell rang in one hour," *American Heritage: Collections, Travel, and Great Writing on History*, vol. 16, no. 4, June 1965, pp. 74–79.

20 The mountain profile in this oil study, like that of the 1833 and 1838 completed Catskill Creek paintings, is Blackhead Mountain, not the "classic" background of High Peak, Roundtop, and South Mountain.

21 This aspect of Cole's religious background, and its influence on him, is described by Alan Peter Wallach: "The tendency to divide everything in two—to contrast faith with sin, hope with despair,

other-worldliness with worldliness—constituted a fundamental puritan 'habit of mind' [which is encountered] everywhere in the literature of Dissent." "The Ideal American Artist and the Dissenting Tradition: A Study of Thomas Cole's Popular Reputation" (PhD diss., Columbia University, 1973), p. 124.

22 Parry recognized the compositional similarity between *Settler's Home in the Catskills* and *River in the Catskills*, regarding both works as aesthetic experiments in "dispens[ing] with any trees to frame the view." *Art of Thomas Cole*, p. 289. Wallach refers to a scholarly consensus dating *River in the Catskills* to the late fall of 1843. "Thomas Cole's *River in the Catskills* as Antipastoral," *Art Bulletin* 84, no. 2 (June 2002): 348n3.

23 Maddox, "Thomas Cole and the Railroad: Gentle Maledictions," *Archives of American Art Journal* 26, no. 1 (1986): 3. See also Maddox, "The Railroad in the Eastern Landscape: 1850–1900," in *The Railroad in the American Landscape, 1850–1950*, ed. Susan Danly Walther (Wellesley, MA: Wellesley College Museum, 1981), pp. 19ff. (exhibition catalog).

24 The railroad historian William F. Helmer recounts these developments: "On May 20, 1842, the Canajoharie & Catskill was sold by the State of New York to Amos Cornwall and associates for $11,600. The rails were torn up and the equipment dispersed." *Rip Van Winkle Railroads* (Berkeley, CA: Howell-North Books, 1970), p. 35.

25 Wallach, "*River in the Catskills* as Antipastoral," p. 339. His evidence for Cole's painting *River in the Catskills* without a commission is a letter the artist wrote to a lawyer from New Haven named Aaron Nicholas Skinner, to whom he tried unsuccessfully to sell the work (p. 342). In his 2002 article Wallach was taking direct issue with Maddox's 1986 article, "Thomas Cole and the Railroad."

26 As we saw earlier, Cole depicted the rapids head-on, from a low vantage point but distantly, in the 1841 *Sunset in the Catskills*.

27 The smoke from the wood-burning engine of a train on the Canajoharie and Catskill line would have been gray, a fact that perhaps inspired Cole toward this visual analogy—which, in turn, may have led him to flatten out the trail of smoke into a horizontal form resembling his glimpse of the rapids.

28 The one Catskill Creek painting that has been studied in close relation to *River in the Catskills* is *View on the Catskill—Early Autumn*. For example, see my summary of Wallach's comparison later in this chapter.

29 So far as I know, the first specific reference to a "toy train" in *River in the Catskills* is in a 1956 article by Louis Hawes regarding an important Cole sketchbook, which I discuss later in this chapter. "A Sketchbook by Thomas Cole," *Record of the Art Museum, Princeton University*, vol. 15, no. 1 (Princeton: Princeton University Art Museum, 1956), pp. 7, 19–20. Many years later Leo Marx referred to the train in *River in the Catskills* as a "gentle, small, unobtrusive feature." *The Machine in the Garden: Technology and the Pastoral Ideal in America* (London: Oxford University Press, 1964), pp. 98–99.

30 In describing the artistic options available to Cole toward such expression, Wallach writes about "the limitations of style and circumstance" in his era. "*River in the Catskills* as Antipastoral," p. 343. Cf. Susan Danly, who discusses Cole's "early attempt [in *River in the Catskills*] to integrate the image of the railroad into a view of his most private retreat in the Catskills." Introduction to *The Railroad in American Art: Representations of Technological Change*, ed. Susan Danly and Leo Marx (Cambridge, MA: MIT Press, 1988), p. 1.

31 This sketch appears as folio 6, recto, in an important but largely unstudied Cole sketchbook from 1839–44 that came into the Princeton University museum's prints and drawing collection in the 1940s. I am indebted to Prof. John Wilmerding for leading me to this sketchbook. It was described in a Princeton

museum publication in 1956 by Hawes, who decisively and unequivocally linked the relevant sketch to *River in the Catskills* and provided a number of useful comparisons between individual features of the two works. But he made no mention of the railroad bridge that appears in both the painting and its sketch. "Sketchbook by Thomas Cole," pp. 7, 19–20.

32 Wallach, "*River in the Catskills* as Antipastoral," p. 344.

33 The mountains' reflections are prominent in all but one of these works from the 1830s and 1840s. In *View on the Catskill—Early Autumn*, they are more minimal but do appear just to the left of and below the rower. In the one Catskill Creek painting that follows *River in the Catskills*, that is, *Catskill Creek, N.Y.* (1845), the mountains' reflections are central motifs (see my discussion of this work later in this chapter).

34 Peter Van Vechten Jr., "Anecdotes of Time When Catskill & Canajoharie R.R. Was Built," *Catskill Creek Weekly Examiner*, September 12, 1908, p. 8. The author of this article, John Van Vechten's son, had been raised for a time by his uncle Peter Van Vechten and later in life informally added "Jr." to his name. I am indebted to Greene County, New York, historian David Dorpfeld for locating this article for me during my research at the Vedder Research Library, Coxsackie, New York.

35 Cole used this phrase in a letter to Reed dated March 6, 1836. In a subsequent letter to his patron he appears to retract this harsh characterization of the railroad builders; Wallach believes that Cole's second letter to Reed is a carefully crafted, and inauthentic, retreat from his earlier expression of anger. "*River in the Catskills* as Antipastoral," pp. 340–41.

36 Parry speculated that two foreground figures in *The Mill, Sunset* represent Cole's children, Theddy and Mary. *Art of Thomas Cole*, p. 297.

37 This lecture to Cole's Catskill neighbors reprised his 1836 "Essay on American Scenery" with added material about the railroad's construction and was the following month published in a local newspaper as "Lecture on American Scenery: Delivered before the Catskill Lyceum, April 1, 1841," *The Northern Light*, May 1841, pp. 25–26. It is reprinted in *Essays and Prose Sketches*, where the relevant passage appears on p. 211.

38 The full title of Cooper's novel is *Satanstoe, or the Littlepage Manuscripts: A Tale of the Colony*. See Wayne Franklin's cogent account of the antirent war in his *James Fenimore Cooper: The Later Years* (New Haven: Yale University Press, 2017), pp. 361–66. See also H. Daniel Peck's chapter, "*Satanstoe*: The Case for Permanence," in his book *A World by Itself: The Pastoral Moment in Cooper's Fiction* (New Haven: Yale University Press, 1977), pp. 163–78. For the Van Vechten homestead as "an emblem of the stolid, uncomplicated virtues of an old-fashioned rural society," see Wallach, "*River in the Catskills* as Antipastoral," p. 340.

39 Cole's "The Lament of the Forest" was published in *The Knickerbocker* 17 (May 1841), and appears in *Thomas Cole's Poetry*, as poem no. 47, pp. 107–12. Tymn dates Cole's writing of the poem to 1838.

40 Scholarship around the role of axmen and the stumps they left behind, as portrayed in American art, derives largely from an article by Nicolai Cikovsky Jr., "The Ravages of the Axe': The Meaning of the Tree Stump in Nineteenth-Century American Art," *Art Bulletin* 61, no. 4 (December 1979): 611–26. Cikovsky includes discussion of several of Cole's works.

41 See illustrations of Cole's tree drawings in *Thomas Cole: Drawn to Nature* (Albany, NY: Albany Institute of History and Art, 1993), based on an exhibition of the same name; and in Parry, "Thomas Cole's Early Drawings: In Search of a Signature Style," *Bulletin of the Detroit Institute of Arts* 66, no. 1 (1990): 11–13.

42 *The Collected Poems of William Carlos Williams*, vol. 1, *1909–1939*, ed. A. Walton Litz and Christopher MacGowan (New York: New Directions, 1986), p. 162. "Great Mullen" was first published in Williams's collection *Sour Grapes* in 1921.

43 Because the figure in the valley is represented so small and because figure drawing wasn't Cole's strength, it may not be self-evident that he is a boy rather than a man. Maddox identifies him as a boy, "Thomas Cole and the Railroad," p. 7, and Hawes is decisive about the matter, seeing him as "a young boy." "Sketchbook by Thomas Cole," p. 19. I am arguing that the larger symbolism of the painting supports the view that the figure in the valley is a boy—that he may embody for Cole the idea of choice and possibility that Wordsworth claimed for childhood in his "Immortality Ode" (1807), a poem Cole must have known.

44 Wallach refers to an early work by Cole that "epitomizes the prospect convention," *View of L'Esperance on the Schoharie River* (1826–27), where a woodsman—closely resembling the figure in *River in the Catskills* in dress, posture, orientation to the scene, and the position of his ax—overlooks a landscape showing future developments. "*River in the Catskills* as Antipastoral," pp. 343–44. Angela Miller, in her 1993 study *The Empire of the Eye: Landscape Representation and American Cultural Politics, 1825–1875* (Ithaca: Cornell University Press, 1993), had earlier explored the cultural meanings of panoramic views in the work of American nineteenth-century painters, including Cole, as had Albert Boime in a 1991 study, *Manifest Destiny and the Magisterial Gaze in Nineteenth-Century American Painting* (Washington, DC: Smithsonian Institution Press, 1991).

45 There are other possible models for Cole's woodsman, but Billy Kirby is a possibility because of the timing. Cooper's *The Pioneers*, a best seller, was published in 1823, and Cole's *View of L'Esperance on the Schoharie River*, with a woodsman virtually identical to the one in *River in the Catskills*, was painted three or so years later, during 1826–27.

46 The present home of *Catskill Creek, N.Y.*, is the New-York Historical Society; its nineteenth-century provenance is uncertain.

47 This observation appears in the New-York Historical Society gallery label for *Catskill Creek, N.Y.* (object number 1867.314). See also Maddox, who writes that the painting "lyrically expresses the quietude of the American wilderness," "Thomas Cole and the Railroad," p. 7, and Cikovsky, who says that it "shows the prelude to settlement" and "American nature on the eve of civilization's arrival." "Ravages of the Ax," p. 623.

48 The large framing tree on the left in both works is an elm, and in the middle distance both paintings portray on the right shore a sycamore—identifiable by its white trunk. Cole obscured and diminished the rapids in *Catskill, N.Y.* perhaps because his focus in this painting is its dramatic and symbolic action on the northern shore, whereas in *Sunset in the Catskills* the reclining rower is taking in a more comprehensive view.

49 Account by Peter Van Vechten Jr., "Anecdotes of Time."

50 Letter from a private collection, quoted in Christine I. Oaklander, "Jonathan Sturges, W. H. Osborn, and William Church Osborn: A Chapter in American Art Patronage," *Metropolitan Museum Journal* 43 (2008): 175–76.

51 In Van Vechten's account, he describes the removal of the blasting debris from Catskill Creek in the period following the railroad's construction.

52 Bedell studies the importance of the new geological discoveries of the early nineteenth century for American artists, including Cole, and discusses his specific representations of glacial erratics. As she points out, when such erratics were found balanced on top of other rock formations, they were known in Cole's time as "rocking stones"—such as appear in the artist's two 1827 paintings from the Cooper novel. *The Anatomy of Nature: Geology and American Landscape Painting, 1825–1875* (Princeton: Princeton University Press, 2001), pp. 29–33. On this point, see also Parry, *Art of Thomas Cole*, pp. 64–65.

53 Cole's paintings of ancient ruins referenced here are *Interior of the Colosseum, Rome* (1832) and *Ruins of the Temples at Paestum* (1832–33).

54 As Susan Stewart writes, "Within the rise of industrial capitalism the gigantic becomes located within the abstraction of an exchange economy." *On Longing: Narratives of the Miniature, the Gigantic, the Souvenir, the Collection* (Durham, NC: Duke University Press, 1993), p. 80.

55 Among the key characteristics of the sublime in Edmund Burke's highly influential essay "A Philosophical Enquiry into the Origin of Our Ideas of the Sublime and the Beautiful" (1757) is "vastness."

56 Another such allegorical work is Cole's *Childhood* in the *Voyage of Life* series (1839–40), whose depictions of leaves and flowers (near a cave from which the infant voyager emerges) are minutely detailed; here too these horticultural details support specific aspects of the painting's narrative meanings.

57 See Cole's letter to Sturges of February 24, 1837, in Oaklander, "Jonathan Sturges," 175–76. The mullein panel, as well as three others depicting, respectively, a ruined castle, an ascending balloon, and a waterspout, were painted in 1836. A catalog entry for a 2005 exhibition of these works relates them usefully to the themes of rising and falling in Cole's *Course of Empire*, completed that year. Here is how the entry describes the panel titled *The Mullein Stalk*: "Birds fly and then return to earth; stalks grow and then collapse. In its own subtle way, the painting depicts a simple cycle in the natural world." Kevin Sharp, *For Spacious Skies: Hudson River School Paintings from the Henry and Sharon Martin Collection* (New Britain, CT: New Britain Museum of American Art, 2005), pp. 27–28. Cf. Franklin Kelly's commentary on the panels, in *American Paintings of the Nineteenth Century, Part 1*, The Collections of the National Gallery of Art Systematic Catalogue (Washington, DC: National Gallery of Art, 1996), p. 81.

Epilogue

1 Franklin Kelly suggested to me a possible Hogarthian inspiration for Cole's Catskill Creek paintings.

2 Alan Wallach refers to "the Claudian template he [Cole] had so frequently applied to the [Catskill Creek] scene." "Thomas Cole's *River in the Catskills* as Antipastoral," *Art Bulletin* 84, no. 2 (June 2002): 342. Elsewhere he describes Cole's adoption, early in the artist's career, of "a basic Claudian formula" for rendering American rural landscapes, and he understands the Catskill Creek paintings as "homages to Claude." "Thomas Cole: Landscape and the Course of American Empire," in *Thomas Cole: Landscape into History*, ed. William H. Truettner and Alan Wallach (New Haven, CT: Yale University Press, 1994), p. 70.

3 Of course there were other American artists of the antebellum period who returned intermittently to their favorite landscapes and painted them many times. An example is Jasper Francis Cropsey and Greenwood Lake in New Jersey, which he first visited in 1843. Cropsey's paintings of Greenwood Lake, like Cole's of Catskill Creek, have a tonal consistency, but his orientation toward the scene is more varied than Cole's.

4 Deleuze and Guattari, "1837: Of the Refrain," chapter 11 of *A Thousand Plateaus: Capitalism and Schizophrenia*, translation and foreword by Brian Massumi (Minneapolis: University of Minnesota Press, 1987), pp. 312–14, 322–23. Originally published as *Mille Plateaux*, vol. 2 of *Capitalisme et Schizophrenic* (Paris: Les Editions de Minuit, 1980).

5 Cole's painting *Scene from Byron's "Manfred"* (1833) is in the Yale University Art Gallery.

6   Dated 1829, this poem is collected as no. 11 in *Thomas Cole's Poetry: The Collected Poems of America's Foremost Painter of the Hudson River School Reflecting His Feelings for Nature and the Romantic Spirit of the Nineteenth Century*, comp. and ed. Marshall B. Tymn (York, PA: Liberty Cap Books, 1972), p. 52. The parts of the poem quoted here are the last two lines of stanza one and all of stanza two. The possibility that Cole wrote it during his June 1829 passage to England is proposed by Brett Dorfman, who examined the poem in an 1829 Cole sketchbook in the New York State Library archive. "The Autobiographical Nature of Thomas Cole's Biblical Landscapes" (senior thesis, Middlebury College, 2002), pp. 27–29ff. David P. Barnes alerted me to Cole's poem and Dorfman's study.

7   Christine T. Robinson makes this point about Cole: "Because he knew he was a public figure, he carefully wrote and sometimes extensively edited his own journal and those essays intended for an audience. Through these efforts, Cole showed his perception of the division between the public and the private life and used masks for his writing and his art." "Thomas Cole: Drawn to Nature," in *Thomas Cole: Drawn to Nature* (Albany, NY: Albany Institute of History and Art, 1993), p. 70. Qualifying Robinson's observation is recent work by researchers at the Thomas Cole National Historic Site; in carefully examining the artist's 1834–48 journal, they have found a surprisingly large number of intensely emotional passages.

8   See Tim Barringer, "The Englishness of Thomas Cole," in *The Cultured Canvas: New Perspectives on American Landscape Painting*, ed. Nancy Siegel (Lebanon: University of New Hampshire Press, 2011), pp. 15–17. See also Barringer's "Thomas Cole's Atlantic Crossings," in Elizabeth Mankin Kornhauser and Tim Barringer, with Dorothy Mahon, Christopher Riopelle, and Shannon Vittoria, *Thomas Cole's Journey: Atlantic Crossings* (New York: The Metropolitan Museum of Art, 2018), pp. 19–61.

9   Hirshfield, *Ten Windows: How Great Poems Transform the World* (New York: Knopf, 2015), pp. 112–13.

Index

The letter *f* following a page number denotes a figure; the letter *m* denotes a map.